THE FORMATION OF EUROPEAN POLICY
IN POST-FRANCO SPAIN

For my parents, Lynn and Mickey Marks

The Formation of European Policy in Post-Franco Spain

The Role of Ideas, Interests and Knowledge

MICHAEL P. MARKS
Department of Politics
Williamette University

Avebury

Aldershot · Brookfield USA · Hong Kong · Singapore · Sydney

Published by
Avebury
Ashgate Publishing Ltd
Gower House
Croft Road
Aldershot
Hants GU11 3HR
England

Ashgate Publishing Company
Old Post Road
Brookfield
Vermont 05036
USA

British Library Cataloguing in Publication Data
Marks, Michael P.
    The formation of European policy in post-Franco Spain : the
    role of ideas, interests and knowledge
    1.Spain - Foreign relations - Europe - 1975- 2.Europe -
    Economic integration
    I.Title
    327.4'6'04

    ISBN 1 85972 377 2

Library of Congress Catalog Card Number: 96-086696

Printed in Great Britain by Antony Rowe Ltd, Chippenham, Wiltshire

Contents

Preface

This book examines changes in Spanish foreign policy towards the rest of Europe in the first half of the 1980s. Two issue areas are examined: The Socialist government's reversal on NATO membership, and its re-thinking of economic priorities during the process of Spain's accession to the European Community. The main questions are: why did the Socialist government reverse its long-standing opposition to NATO? why did it also alter its economic interests when negotiating EC entry? finally, how were Spanish security and economic interests reconciled with ideas about European integration?

The Spanish case serves as a good test for the validity of current theorizing on the role of ideas and knowledge in politics. Research on Spain indicates that ideas and knowledge are analytically distinct categories that operate separately in the political process. The book argues that Spanish officials' favorable ideas about European integration predisposed them to consider new knowledge concerning the creation of foreign policy in Europe. Understanding of the realities of European integration reconciled the uncertainty Spanish decision makers had about economic and security interests by reinforcing their conviction that membership in European institutions would strengthen Spanish democracy.

The study answers the questions posed above. The Spanish government's eagerness to become part of Europe helped it to adjust to some of the unforeseen realities of European integration. Political linkages among European security, economic well-being, and responsibilities within NATO and the EC became transparent to Spanish decision makers. In the process, the Spanish government reassessed its interests in light of its continued support for European integration broadly conceived. Traditional security concerns were reconciled with the decision to remain in NATO and economic interests were redefined to coincide with the demands of strengthening the EC. The book draws implications for the process of European integration as it concerns other new democracies in Southern, Central and Eastern Europe.

Acknowledgements

This book is an outgrowth of my doctoral dissertation, written in the Department of Government at Cornell University. I would like to thank the members of my dissertation committee for their unwavering support during the researching and writing of this study. T.J. Pempel offered penetrating insight on the theoretical underpinnings of the project. Jonas Pontusson pushed me to defend the study's core propositions and, in the process, to weed out weaknesses and hone the analytical argument. Sidney Tarrow provided a wealth of knowledge on both the theoretical and empirical bases of the study. His frequent contributions were invaluable at every stage of the project. Above all, I want to thank my thesis advisor and friend Peter Katzenstein for his guidance, wisdom, and support. From the genesis of this project as a seminar paper, to its completion as a finished book, 'PK' has inspired me every step of the way. His intellectual rigor and generosity as a scholar served to propel me through proposing the thesis, conducting the research, writing the drafts, and polishing the finished product.

I owe an additional debt of gratitude to the numerous scholars who provided me with advice and guidance in the preparation of this book. In the Government Department at Cornell University I benefitted from input and advice of Professors Steve Jackson, Jim Goldgeier, Thomas Risse-Kappen, and Valerie Bunce who took time from their busy schedules to discuss my work. Amongst other scholars, Juan Linz, Robert Fishman, Lynne Wozniak, Trisha Craig, Modesto Escobar, Sofía Pérez, José María Maravall, Richard Gunther, and Juan Carlos Collado all provided valuable wisdom in helping me understand the intricacies of Spanish politics. Research assistance for the book was provided by John Von Osterheldt at the University of Wyoming and Morgan Allen at Willamette University.

My research in Spain was facilitated by the helpful staff at a number of institutions, libraries, government ministries, and archives. I was greatly aided by Professor Victor Pérez-Díaz, who welcomed me as a visiting scholar at the Instituto Juan March de Estudios e Investigaciones in Madrid. I would also like to thank the Instituto's librarian, Ms. Martha Wood for pointing me in the right direction and directing me towards the research materials I needed to complete this project. In addition, I would like to thank the personnel at Spain's Secretary of State for European Community Affairs and Ministry of Defense, and the Fundación Pablo Iglesias for their time and effort in aiding my research.

Financial support for this project was provided by the Cornell University Graduate School, the Council for European Studies, the McArthur Foundation, the Fulbright Program in the United States and Spain, the Mellon Foundation, the Western Societies and Peace Studies Programs at Cornell University, and by an Atkinson Grant at Willamette University.

List of abbreviations

AP	Alianza Popular (Peoples' Alliance, later PP)
CAP	Common Agricultural Policy
CDU	Christian Democratic Party (Germany)
CEEC	Central and Eastern European Countries
EC	European Community
EEC	European Economic Community
EFTA	European Free Trade Association
EMS	European Monetary System
ERM	Exchange Rate Mechanism
EU	European Union
IMPs	Integrated Mediterranean Programs
NATO	North Atlantic Treaty Organization
PASOK	Panhellenic Socialist Movement (Greece)
PCE	Partido Comunista Español (Spanish Communist Party)
PP	Partido Popular (Peoples' Party, previously AP)
PS	Partido Socialista (Socialist Party - Portugal)
PSF	French Socialist Party
PSOE	Partido Socialista Obrero Español (Spanish Socialist Party)
SEA	Single European Act
SPD	German Social Democratic Party
TEU	Treaty of European Union
UCD	Unión del Centro Democrático (Union of the Democratic Center)
VAT	Value Added Tax
WEU	Western European Union

1 Introduction

For decades, orthodox scholarly theories of international relations held that World War II in Europe provided evidence of the enduring role of power and interests in world affairs. Proponents of these theories maintain that the Wilsonian peace devised after the First World War proved unworkable when states with opposing interests used power to try and get their way. They argue that after World War II, peace in Europe could be insured only through the threat of force by the new keepers of the balance of power.

By the end of the twentieth century, however, a new generation of scholars has accepted the fact that a certain idea - the 'idea of Europe' - can provide the basis for cooperation, and eventual political integration, among the countries of the European continent (Gruender and Moutsopoulos, 1992; Heater, 1992; Nelson, Roberts, and Veit, 1992). This is not the first time that the idea of common identity has been proposed as a potential source of European unity. From the days of early Christendom to the rise of modern fascism, European leaders have put forward a range of ideologies that would form the foundation of a single political order which would unify Europe.

The difference between past and present, then, is not so much in the flow of European ideas, than in how these ideas are interpreted by academic observers. In the aftermath of World War II, with the experience of fascism fresh in the mind and the rise of communism a perceived threat, Western international relations theorists accepted the logic of the realist set of theories. This paradigm holds that states act according to their objective material interests which are derived either from the state of human nature (in the case of classical Realism) or from the structure of the international system (in the case of neorealism). Ideas, at worst, serve as a deliberate form of obfuscation of those interests by calculating leaders, and at best as mere justifications for material interests.

The creation and advancement of the European Economic Community (later the European Community, presently the European Union) has made it more difficult to adhere to the notion that ideas play no role in the creation of interests of

1

European states. Scholars now recognize that states' interests are not derived exogenously from the 'objective' structures of the international system, but are created endogenously through the internalization of framing ideas (Goldstein and Keohane, 1993). The 'idea of Europe' provides the basis by which European states' interests are currently formed. European integration, driven by the belief that peace and prosperity come from economic and political interdependence, is what dictates the calculations of European leaders.

Ideas as abstract beliefs serve as foundations for interest formation. How these ideas translate interests into policy, however, is a complicated process. In addition to ideas, scholars recognize that knowledge about specific issues helps state leaders devise policies that advance their interests (E. Haas, 1990; P. Haas, 1992). In the case of European integration, knowledge about the economics of monetary union, to take just one example, helps leaders create policies that will advance what they see as their interests in light of their acceptance of the desirability of the idea of European unification.

Knowledge about the logic of European integration is not limited to substantive issue-areas. Decision makers also acquire knowledge about the politics of European integration itself. The art of diplomacy actually is a set of accumulated skills reflecting an understanding of the rules of bargaining and negotiation agreed upon and shared by participants of the diplomatic process. These understandings, which comprise a body of knowledge, change over time. In order to benefit from diplomatic negotiation, one must learn this body of knowledge. The diplomacy of European integration is a distinct process, unique in the history of European foreign policy, and rests on consensual knowledge about the causes and effects of integrative policies and their impact on the interests of European states.

An heuristic case: The formation of European policy in post-Franco-Spain

In this book I will argue that knowledge-based claims about the politics of European integration provide the basis on which interests shaped by the idea of Europe are translated into policy. I derive this formulation from an exploratory case study of the foreign policy of post-Franco Spain. Following the transition to democracy, Spanish leaders were united in their agreement that economic modernization and democratic consolidation could come only through participation in the process of European integration. However, the support for the idea of Europe was accompanied by uncertainty over how best to secure Spain's interests in Europe. As Spanish leaders acquired knowledge about the politics of European integration, they better defined the policies to pursue their interests.

Historical debates within Spain over the merits of European integration frequently have been heated. The Spanish image of Europe has its basis in Spain's traditional isolation, which has been the norm since the fall of the Spanish Empire. This isolation was accentuated in the twentieth century by Spain's non-combatant status in both World Wars and came to a head under the first half of the Franco dictatorship. On the one hand, Franco used the isolation of Spain from the world community as a means to rationalize his particular brand of nationalist autarchy. On the other hand, he did not renounce his ultimate aspiration to end Spain's isolation. But Franco's desire to involve Spain more fully in European affairs could not overcome the widespread revulsion of Europe's leaders to the Franquist regime. As a result, membership in the two most important western European institutions - the European Community and NATO - was denied to Spain in Franco's lifetime.

The choices facing post-Franco governments concerning European integration revolved around Spain's forced exclusion during the previous forty years. Both within Spain and without, proposed Spanish membership in European institutions was viewed in the immediate post-Franco period as embedded in a larger political process of consolidating democracy in Spain. Given the inability to win recognition from Western military and economic alliances, the Franco regime developed alternative policies to full participation in European organizations. In place of membership in NATO, for example, Spain's leaders in 1953 signed a defense treaty with the United States. Likewise, Spain had to settle for associate member status within the European Community. The restoration of democratic government in Spain after Franco's death opened the doors to full participation in European institutions, but it also raised questions of how to undertake this integration without compromising Spanish defense and economic interests.

The dilemmas of European integration have been faced perhaps most dramatically by the Spanish Socialist Party (PSOE). Throughout the Franquist period the Socialist leadership argued forcefully in favor of Europe. These leaders felt that real political change meant a break with Spain's history of authoritarianism and social injustice by achieving a closer approximation to the Western European model. The former opposition forces to the Franco regime equated Europe with democracy, political openness, and social freedoms. Despite some early fiery Marxist rhetoric that likened the EC to the forces of international capitalism, the PSOE was firmly convinced of the beneficial effects European values would have on post-Franco Spain. European economic integration was also important to Western European leaders who agreed that it would serve to legitimate the return to democracy.

Nevertheless, the economic policies articulated by the Socialist Party leadership seemed to contradict its enthusiasm for European integration and its interests of modernization aside other European states. The PSOE's leaders publicly had endorsed a socialist agenda of increased state control of the economy and redistributive economic policies. Additionally, the PSOE's political leadership was not well-versed in economic theory or practice. In short, the position of the

PSOE at that time was unequivocally in favor of EC membership, yet its strategy for economic reform either reflected its radical past or were poorly defined. By the early 1980s it became obvious that continued economic growth could come only from closer ties to, if not membership in, the EC. This fact, coupled with the Socialists' uncertainty about the means and ends of economic development, led to tension between the Socialists' favorable image of Spain and their early economic agenda.

While the Socialists placed their faith in European economic integration, they were suspicious of closer military ties to the North Atlantic Treaty Organization (NATO). PSOE leaders identified NATO with American domination of European security. Given the history of U.S. military alliance with the Franco regime, the Socialists did not believe that closer security ties to NATO would further the objective of establishing democracy in Spain. On the contrary, certain prominent factions within the PSOE clung to the belief that Spain should identify its foreign policy with the non-aligned and Third World movements which had blossomed in the 1970s. In addition, Socialist foreign policy theorists argued that by joining NATO Spain would disrupt the European equilibrium of power. In other words, unlike economic integration, the Socialists did not believe that closer security ties furthered the cause of consolidating Spanish democracy.[1]

As far as specific defense policies were concerned, the danger of a Soviet invasion of Western Europe was not taken as a serious threat to Spanish security. Rather, the Socialists fully accepted the prevailing Spanish security doctrines; namely, that Spain must protect its southern flank against possible unrest spilling over from northern Africa, or Moroccan irredentist claims over the Spanish enclaves of Ceuta and Melilla (Marquina Barrio, 1985). Other security concerns included the defense of shipping lanes, protection of coastal waters, and modernization of the Spanish military. The Socialists also were concerned to keep Spain out of any hypothetical continental European armed conflict. Along with these traditional external security interests, the Socialists were preoccupied with internal security threats including Basque terrorism and possible disruption of the democratic process by a right wing military coup.

In short, in its years in opposition the PSOE had placed its faith in improving Spain via European economic integration. Yet its specific economic policy prescriptions either were poorly defined or based on claims at odds with prevailing EC doctrine. In contrast, the PSOE did not believe in integrating Spain into Europe's defense community, and clung to traditional conceptions of Spanish security policy.

The Socialists gained control of the government in 1982, and by 1986 their positions on NATO and the EC had undergone fundamental change. Negotiations for Spanish membership in the EC yielded results that were unpalatable to many economic sectors that traditionally had supported the EC. In addition, to effect modernization of the Spanish economy, the Socialist government implemented neoliberal economic policies at odds with the PSOE's previously stated redistributive plans. All this was undertaken in the name of preserving unity of action of European economic integration, an idea the Socialists still ardently endorsed. Regarding NATO, the government of the PSOE publicly acknowledged a fundamental change of heart. In 1984, President Felipe González presented parliament with a ten-point defense plan which, among other things, reaffirmed Spanish membership in NATO. González and his government argued that Spanish defense interests were served by remaining in the alliance.

The road to these policy changes was not an easy one. The euphoria of joining the European Community was tempered by the difficult process of conceiving of Spanish economic interests in different ways. The PSOE leadership continued to believe that membership in the European 'club' was the solution to Spain's economic ills. But the economic policies at stake underwent a painful process of redefinition. The Socialists learned that modernization entailed submitting many sectors of the Spanish economy to a period of renovation. Other sectors were forced to wait a long period before enjoying the benefits of EC membership and others were made uncompetitive. In addition, the Socialists had to reconcile themselves to much intransigence on the part of EC negotiators. The knowledge of how the EC operated in practice, the learning about Spanish responsibilities in an economically viable Common Market, and information about concrete benefits to be gained over the long term from making short-term concessions were powerful sources of enlightenment for the PSOE leadership (Alonso, 1985). In the end, the PSOE government arrived at the conclusion that these changes were beneficial and ultimately coincided with their belief that membership in the EC was the only way to achieve the vision they had of a modernized Spain.

Furthermore, after many years of opposing NATO membership, the Socialists found themselves looking at European military alliances differently. In this instance, what changed were the PSOE leadership's policy prescriptions for Spain's relationship to European security integration. Previously, the Socialists believed that NATO only reinforced the hegemony of the United States over Western Europe. In this light, they felt that Spain must stake out an independent defense policy, much as Yugoslavia had in Eastern Europe (Morán, 1980a). This option was precluded when the centrist Unión del Centro Democrático (UCD) government signed Spain's entry into NATO in May of 1982. Once in power, the Socialist government realized that to withdraw Spain from NATO would jeopardize European unity. This realization led to a reassessment of the Socialists' earlier tendency to disparage the western alliance. In October of 1984 the Socialist leadership declared publicly that Spain must remain part of NATO. This arguably was the most difficult foreign policy issue experienced by the PSOE government and culminated in the explosive 1986 referendum on Spain's continued membership in the Alliance. The government recommended that Spain stay in NATO and this position was approved by a narrow majority of the electorate.

In sum, changes occurred in the way Spanish Socialist government leaders thought broadly about European integration and in how they construed specific policies. In the case of economic integration with the EC, the PSOE leadership gradually identified specific economic strategies where, before, policy prescriptions had been either ill-defined or at odds with general EC practices. The resolution of economic uncertainty reinforced the continually favorable belief the Spaniards had of the beneficial nature of joining Europe. In the case of NATO, security interests were reconciled with Spain's long-term vision of Europe. Spanish leaders came to realize that Spain could not go it alone in securing its interests, and instead would benefit from greater European security integration.

Theory applied to the Spanish case

New knowledge assimilated by the Socialist government leadership allowed it to reconcile the earlier tensions that existed between its favorable ideas about European integration and its accompanying economic and security interests. In both the EC and NATO cases the Spaniards learned from other European elites about the intersubjective realities of European integration. Regarding the EC, economic interests were better defined and linked to the idea that Spain would benefit from adopting EC rules and time tables. In the case of NATO, the Socialists came to accept that Spanish membership in a unified European defense system would not jeopardize Spain's security interests. New knowledge, injected into situations of uncertainty, made sense of the relationship between political ideas and interests, and overcame the legacy of the PSOE's anti-Franco past. The Socialists learned that by admitting past errors and participating as full partners in European affairs they could forge a domestic political consensus and long-term electoral success. Most importantly, the Spanish Socialist government benefited from the knowledge that fulfillment of Spain's responsibilities within a unified Europe held the most promise for securing the country's economic and security interests.

Spanish foreign policy towards Europe in the post-Franco era serves as a good case in which to examine the role of ideas and knowledge in international relations. The history of Spain's membership in the EC and NATO has been analyzed from a number of different perspectives. Existing explanations tend to stress an interplay of fixed domestic constraints and incentives available for political actors to undertake economic and modernization and political democratization while maintaining electoral support. While not denying the domestic political environment, the findings presented in this study will show that the changes in Spain's European policies reflect a process of elite learning whereby domestic factors are manipulated by elites in order to create support for their chosen policy initiatives. Internationally transmitted knowledge about the direction of European integration provided clearer focus to the ideas Spanish leaders had about Europe and was responsible for their new conceptions of long-term political and economic possibilities in Europe and within Spain.

Current research on the role of ideas and knowledge in politics both informs this study and can be refined by it. Specifically, the Spanish case shows clearly how political ideas differ from political knowledge. It also shows how policies change when new knowledge reconciles tensions or uncertainty between elites' ideas and interests. The experience of Spain suggests a framework for understanding the interests of the leaders of emerging democracies in Europe and the ideas they have about European integration. The distinction between ideas and knowledge is not recognized by analysts employing these terms. Research on Spain presented in this book provides a way to illustrate and clarify the distinctions between these terms and make them useful tools for further research.

Spain's foreign policy is not simply a matter of economic or security interests narrowly defined, but is discussed in the light of the broader idea of integrating Spain into the European mainstream. I will show that the policies based on the ideas the Socialist government had upon taking office eventually proved unworkable as originally conceived. The idea of Europe was a lens for construing economic and security interests. But when the lens failed to focus on salient issues (the case of the EC), or where the lens was distorted (the case of NATO) the political leadership was left with a situation where ideas and interests were not mutually supportive. The resolution of this tension made creating new policies easier.

I am concerned in this book with how Spanish leaders reconstituted their interpretations of European integration and their perceptions of Spanish national interests. Consequently I do not take preferences and interests as exogenously arising but as endogenous to the process of foreign policy formation. It is not necessary to prove that ideas shaped Spanish policy as opposed to interests because ideas and interests are intertwined. The logic of this formulation is now well established in international relations literature (Goldstein and Keohane, 1993). Nevertheless, the empirical evidence supplied in this literature has been designed more to show that 'ideas matter' in policy implementation rather than tracing the process by which ideas matter over time.

As I have mentioned elsewhere (Marks, 1995), because ideas are posited as an element of identity formation and are therefore institutionalized on a broader level than that of individual decision makers, the presentation of evidence needs to be more descriptive and less compartmentalized into discrete statements about cognitive constraints. In this sense, research on ideas and foreign policy has more in common with the methodology of the emergent constructivist approach in international relations theory than with its predecessors in the field of belief systems and cognition. According to this approach, social identities are constructed through processes of societal interaction. Because societal interaction is ongoing, taking snapshots of ideas and interests at a single time is a risky endeavor. Inferences about the current significance of ideas and interests may be misleading if prior interactions are not taken into consideration. As I will show in this book, those prior interactions involve the transmission of bodies of knowledge that clarify and ideas and give concrete shape to interests.

The methodology I employ must uncover how ideas, knowledge, and interests are intersubjectively constructed over time. An approach that subjects pronouncements and writings of political elites to intense scrutiny, is best suited to this task (Moyser, 1988). Single statements or declarations may illuminate the conclusions a decision maker has drawn at a specific juncture. But these statements must be compared with past ones to uncover the evolution of thinking about particular issues (Woods, 1995). Analytical autopsies of elite thinking over time is the only way to uncover the interplay among ideas, knowledge, and interests.

Plan of the book

Most explanations of post-Franco Spanish foreign policy rely on analyses of the singular features of Spain's transition to democracy and the evolution of domestic political relationships. This book rests on the proposition that leaders' perceptions of states' interests are linked to changing knowledge-based claims about the nature of international order. Therefore, in Chapter Two I provide a brief historical review of Spain's past and show why traditional explanations of Spain's European policy are incomplete. I argue that Spain's historical relationship with the rest of Europe frames the country's recent foreign policy debates.

Chapter Three lays out the theoretical foundations of this study. Because traditional types of inquiry are inadequate to explain the Spain's external relations I turn to an examination of theories which focus on foreign policy responses to international change in general. I argue that the existing literature commits one or both of two errors: either it assumes that national interests arise exogenously and are fixed; or it fails to specify the steps by which interests are formed. I remedy this situation by positing a model of change based on the conceptualization of ideas, interests, and knowledge.

In Chapters Four and Five I present empirical material on Spain's post-Franco European policy. Chapter Four looks at the Socialists' evolving position regarding Spain's place in NATO. Chapter Five examines the process of negotiating Spanish membership in the European Community and the Socialists' role. These two chapters tell the story of the Socialists' changed thinking on European integration writ large, and Spain's responsibilities in this process. They also examine the domestic repercussions of the Socialists' European policies.

In Chapter Six I examine briefly Spanish foreign policy in the period since 1986, the year in which Spain joined the EC and the referendum was held that codified Spanish membership in NATO. I conclude that subsequent events verify the lessons I draw in the previous chapters. Chapter Seven provides a preliminary look at instances of other European states exploring increased ties to the process of regional integration. New European democracies and states with evolving relationships towards the EC and NATO may serve as future tests for the generalization of this study. Chapter Eight concludes with a review of the major findings of this book and a return to the theoretical debate.

This book does not provide 'proof' of a theory of theory of European integration. Rather, the Spanish case serves as a plausibility probe for a new way to conceptualize the role of ideas and knowledge in foreign policy. The case is useful in this regard for several reasons. First, Spain's present European policy was formed during a time of change and uncertainty. The end of the Franco dictatorship forced Spanish leaders to rethink nearly forty years of foreign policy. This uncertainty laid bare the process of policy reexamination, and thus provides a case where evidence is made visible. Second, post-Franco Spanish European policy evolved at the same time that European institutions were experiencing change given the revitalization of the integration process in the EC and the increased salience of European security institutions with the heating up of the Cold War after the Soviet invasion of Afghanistan and the election of Ronald Reagan in the United States.

Third, the Spanish case provides a point of comparison with the Central and Eastern European countries that are seeking membership in European institutions following the end of the Cold War. Similarly, the democratization of the formerly communist countries can be compared with Spanish democratization to gauge the role of domestic politics in the process of foreign policy formation. Thus, the conclusions drawn in this book should be taken as suggestive of a new way to think about European integration, and not as the final word. Further testing of the theoretical model presented here should be undertaken.

Notes

1   As with economic integration, European Socialist leaders for the most part believed that Spain's entry into NATO would be beneficial for the consolidation of Spanish democracy. This belief eventually would figure into the conversion of PSOE leaders' views on this matter.

2 The formation of European policy in post-Franco Spain in historical perspective

My purpose in this book is to explain a sea change in the foreign policy orientation of the Spanish Socialist Party (PSOE). This change implicated politics at both the domestic and international levels. However, neither the structure of the international system nor the preexisting constellation of domestic politics alone sufficiently explain shifts in the Spanish Socialists' European policy direction. Through an investigation of the changing historical perceptions of Spanish policy towards Europe, I will suggest a new theoretical approach which bridges the gap between international relations and domestic political strategy.

Existing explanations for the formation of European policy in post-Franco Spain

One way to approach foreign policy analysis is to treat the international context as a primary source of constraints. Spain's economic relations with the rest of Europe have been approached at this level on several fronts. One such approach situates Spain within the dynamics of core-periphery relations. Proponents of this approach indicate that any attempts to integrate Spain into the European economic system are constrained by the forces of global capitalism (Muñoz, Roldán, and Serrano, 1979; Vaitsos, 1982; Lipietz, 1987). The problem with this proposition is that it implies few options on the Spanish side. Yet, we shall see that Spain's leaders had considerable freedom of action which they exercised as they pursued membership in European institutions. Furthermore, theories which posit economic constraints on southern Europe overlook the fact that Spain, Portugal, and Greece have followed distinct paths in their European foreign policies. More sophisticated versions of the global political economy school grant greater volition on the part of Spanish leaders (Holman, 1996). Nonetheless, they still imply a sense of inevitability in Spanish policy choices which is contradicted by the uncertain fashion in which Spain's European policy unfolded.

10

Strangely, there have been no systematic attempts to apply traditional international relations theories to explain changes in Spanish security policy.[1] However, one could plausibly argue from a structural standpoint that Spain's position in the international system would determine its defense options. Analyses of this type would be unconcerned with specific policy changes in Spanish defense policy during the Cold War, as long as Spain remained in the Western bloc. Therefore, they are unsuited for the changes I seek to explain in this study because they underdetermine the specific shape that Spanish defense policy has taken.

In essence, theorists stressing international structures fail to see that the process of integrating Spain into the European community of nations has been an uneven exercise. Due to their opposition to the nature of the Spanish regime, Western European countries were only willing to allow Franquist Spain to participate selectively in European institutions. When democracy was established, European integration still progressed in fits and starts, reflecting the will of both European and Spanish leaders. Research also shows that explanations based on international structures fail to explain different outcomes in countries with similar international positions. Spain and Greece, for example, were similarly poised for EC entry but support for membership within Greece was far more divided than in Spain (Verney, 1990). Likewise, Portugal and Ireland - two comparably situated states in the European international system - have differed from Spain in their experiences with NATO.[2] Indeed, the wide variety of responses in other peripheral European countries cast doubt on the analytical power of explanations that stress uniform constraints and expected similar outcomes.

The process of reversal on NATO and EC policy involved a far greater role for interpersonal diplomacy than structurally based explanations would predict. Existing theories probably would be sufficient if the issue facing Spanish leaders was one of simply deciding 'yes' or 'no' on EC and NATO membership. Yet the intricacies of membership in both of these organizations requires an explanation that takes account of the decision making process.

One way to overcome the limitations of international structural explanations is to highlight domestic political considerations. This has been the primary focus of most accounts of Spain's Post-Franco European foreign policy. In the first place, researchers frequently have relied on electoral analyses when trying to explain the evolution of the Spanish Socialist Party. These authors have attributed moderate PSOE positions to shrewd politicking on the part of the Socialists and the tendency of the party to seek the electoral center (Gunther, 1986; Share, 1986; Pollack and Hunter, 1987). The emphasis is on how the PSOE altered its domestic and foreign policy prescriptions in a bid to reshape itself as a catch-all party.

As the Spanish case shows, however, the government during the period of democratic consolidation was less reliant on existing patterns of electoral support, and more successful at actively shaping public opinion in order to convince the

Spanish people of the wisdom of government policy.[3] This has been true for most political parties in Southern Europe.[4] In other words, European governments, including Spain's, are less captives of domestic interests narrowly conceived, and more shapers of the domestic national debate in order to forge greater European unity.

In addition to electoral theories, some researchers indicate that the interest groups which carried Spain through the democratic transition would continue to wield power in subsequent years (Lancaster and Prevost, 1985; Linz, 1981). Others emphasize the dynamics of the democratic transition in Spain and the legacy of moderation it instilled in those parties that successively weathered this process (Gunther, 1987). However, these types of interpretations are better designed to explain political behavior in established democracies where political forces are regularized and predictable and therefore may limit the creative ability of leaders to alter the political landscape. In newly democratized Spain, party and interest group support was a function of evolving political relationships. Therefore, it is unwise to apply ex post facto reasoning to explain the patterns that resulted.

The research I present in this book questions the responsiveness of elites to interest group pressures and points to explanations that account for cases where consensus is created in a top-down fashion. Indeed, the PSOE's high profile foreign policy initiatives actually clashed with its interests of appealing to a disenchanted Spanish electorate (Caciagli, 1984; McDonough and López Pina, 1984; Penniman and Mujal-Leon, 1985). Although the Socialists succeeded in establishing electoral dominance, their foreign policy actions seemed to have put the desired outcome in jeopardy (Gillespie, 1989, p.426). Regarding security policy, before 1984, the PSOE's anti-NATO position was a departure from the consensus that surrounded other volatile issues of the democratic transition and consolidation, whereas its reversal on NATO forced it to turn the tide of public opinion it had harnessed against NATO in the first place. In the realm of EC negotiations, the Socialist government made concessions that hurt many Spanish economic sectors, and the long-term benefits that economic structuring was expected to have might not materialize in time to vindicate the governments' actions in the eyes of voters and economic interest groups alike.

In short, prevailing explanations overlook the critical fact that the Socialists' preferences changed dramatically during the period between Franco's death and the resolution of Spanish membership in the EC and NATO. These changes then had to be sold to the electorate. In addition, this evolution of the PSOE's foreign policy positions reflects as much the party leadership's own maturation and evolving political philosophy as it does seemingly fixed electoral imperatives. Therefore, any explanation that fails to acknowledge these changed preferences is incomplete precisely because these changed preferences are what make the case so compelling.

Thus, if we hold constant the Socialists' goal of obtaining this electoral advantage, we are still left with a puzzle: Unless we impute perfect foresight to its actions, we must wonder why the PSOE chose a foreign policy strategy seemingly at odds with domestic political goals. Naturally, the strategies available to the PSOE were bound-up with its ability to manipulate foreign policy for domestic ends. More fundamentally, we must understand what the Socialists believed about foreign relations. Leaders cannot convince the electorate of the wisdom of their foreign policy choices unless they share this conviction themselves. I argue that the process by which PSOE elites have calculated their interests cannot be divorced from the meanings that these elites attach to action and foreign policy choice. Therefore, these meanings bear closer examination.

The Spanish Socialist Party and the idea of Europe[5]

In order to understand the policy turns of the Socialist government in Spain, one must have an understanding of the role ideas traditionally have played in Spanish political thought and practice. The Socialist leadership which took office in Spain in the fall of 1982 came to power with deeply held ideas about Europe and Spain's relationship with Europe. These ideas were supported by claims about the reality of world affairs which reflect the Spanish political experience. In short, when it took power in 1982, the Spanish Socialist Party fully subscribed to the notion that Spain must shed its traditional ways and become more like the rest of Europe.

Geography aside, Spain frequently has found itself isolated from the rest of Europe. Hapsburg Spain's empire was founded on conquest and Catholicism, while the reformation sweeping Europe was increasingly viewed from behind the Pyrenees as decadent and corrupt.[6] This was, in many respects, a continuation of practices established under the Spanish Inquisition - itself, a reaction against foreign influences in Spain. Some modern observers argue that the ultimate effect of this "purification" process was the eventual collapse of the Spanish Empire (Racionero, 1987, p.142). Under the conservative legacy left by Hapsburg Spain, Europe tended to be identified with modernization and knowledge, while Spaniards saw their own country, for better or worse, as a bastion of 'southern' tradition, Catholicism, and feudal honor (Marías, 1990, p.237).

During the Napoleonic invasion of Spain at the beginning of the nineteenth century, despite the fact that liberal Spanish reformers opposed French rule, conservative elements of Spanish society succeeded in equating all 'anti-Christian' reforms with French occupation and decadent Protestant European practices in general (Carr, 1973, pp.155-156). Thus, liberalism as espoused by Spanish patriots became identified, ironically, with foreign invasion and subjugation. Following the liberation of Spain from under Napoleonic rule, political schisms involved explicit references to these themes.

In the twentieth century, the debate over Spain's place in the world has continued to shape Spanish politics. The debate over the nature of Spanish identity is eloquently summed up in the contrast between the positions taken by two of Spain's most noted essayists of the twentieth century: Miguel de Unamuno and José Ortega y Gasset.[7] Unamuno and Ortega y Gasset were members of the so-called Generation of '98, a group of intellectuals, poets, novelists, playwrights, and essayists who reflected upon the nature of Spain in the wake of the disastrous defeat in the Spanish-American War (1898). Stripped of the last vestiges of the Hispanic overseas empire, Spaniards questioned how to construct a new Spanish identity.

For Unamuno, the new identity could be found in Spain's historical ties to the various roots of Spanish culture (Herr, 1971, p.29). According to Unamuno, the soul of Spain is embodied in the common Spanish people who trace their unique cultural heritage back to the pre-Christian era. With the introduction of foreign ways, Unamuno continued, Spanish culture became perverted. Therefore, when talking about Europeanization and seeking European influences, this was not to become like the rest of Europe, but to seek the essential Spain by rediscovering its roots.[8] In 1906, Unamuno wrote:

> I return to myself through the years, after having made pilgrimages throughout diverse fields of modern European culture, and alone with my conscience I ask myself: Am I European? Am I modern? And my conscience replies: no, you are not European, that which is called European; no, you are not modern, that which is called modern. And I ask myself again: And this about not feeling European nor modern, does this perchance bring up something about you being Spanish? Are we Spaniards, at base, not reducible to being European and to being modern?...Above all, and for what matters to me, I must confess that the more I meditate on it, the more I discover deep-seated repugnance that my spirit feels towards all that passes through the principal directors of the modern European spirit,...(Unamuno, 1968, p.926).

His were not retrograde notions, but arguments in favor of what made Spain special.

Ortega y Gasset, by contrast, argued that Spain's problems stemmed precisely from its historical uniqueness: Spain could solve these problems by becoming more like the rest of Europe.[9] Writing in 1910, Ortega y Gasset stated this theme starkly:

> Regeneration is inseparable from Europeanization: therefore as soon as one feels the reconstructive emotion, anguish, shame, and longing, one thinks of the Europeanizing idea. Regeneration is the desire; Europeanization is the means to satisfy the desire. Truly one thinks

clearly from the principle that Spain is the problem and Europe the solution (Ortega y Gasset, 1950, p.521).

The final words of this paragraph became among the most quoted of all of Ortega y Gasset's work.[10] The unique factors in Spain's history - its experience of Moorish occupation, its conquest of the western hemisphere, the Inquisition - were equated, in this view, with what was wrong with Spain. The only salvation could come from rejecting this path and becoming European.

The Spanish Civil War (1936-39) itself seemed the inevitable showdown between traditional, inwardly focused conservatives and progressive reformers favoring European liberal ideas.[11] In both cases, the image of Europe figured in the political visions which informed the ideological divide. These tendencies were seconded by outside observers who allied themselves with their Spanish counterparts (Carr, 1973, p.188). The result was the internationalization of the Spanish Civil War with its well-known consequences.

The preoccupation of present day Spanish democrats to increase ties with Europe represents an attempt to avoid the foreign policy mistakes of the governments of the Second Republic (1931-36) which made the Civil War possible. The irony of international relations during the liberal Second Republic was that the leaders of the various Republican governments, who all favored modernizing European values, lacked a coherent foreign policy to reinforce those values at home. The Republic's leaders chose to focus their energies on domestic reforms and ignored the changes that were sweeping the rest of the European continent.[12] In the eyes of modern observers, the inattention of Republic leaders to impending war in Europe created the conditions for the Republic's own demise (Maurín, 1966, pp.238-239).

Following his triumph in the Spanish Civil War, General Francisco Franco marshalled the symbolism of Spain's isolationist past to legitimize his brand of nationalist rule. He drew on Spain's unique history to glorify and legitimize the international isolation that was meant to punish him (Hill, 1969, p.202). In promoting isolation as a virtue, Franco was able to rely on the Spanish past which, as we have seen, frequently derided foreign ideas as corrupting of the Spanish way of life (Victor Pérez-Díaz, 1990, pp.8-9).

To the dictator's consternation, the price of this isolation turned out to be debilitating for the Spanish economy. Therefore, with the advent of the Cold War Franco was able to take advantage of rising superpower tensions and offer his solid anti-Communist credentials as an *entrée* to reestablishing diplomatic relations with the West. With the signing of a defense treaty with the United States in 1953, and Spain's entry into the United Nations in 1955, Franco began to lead the country back towards international respectability. These diplomatic achievements were accompanied by a gradual liberalization of political and economic policy, the latter orchestrated by the technocrat economists of the Catholic lay order Opus Dei (Casanova, 1983).

However, the influx to Spain of foreign investment, international aid under the auspices of the IMF and the World Bank, and tourists introduced Spaniards to those foreign ideas Franco had previously condemned. Large migrations of Spanish workers to Western Europe also provided a conduit for liberal ideas to seep into Spain. The dictator was then faced with the task of balancing these new ideas - which admittedly had accompanied rapid economic modernization - with the traditional foundations of Franquist rule. The more closely Spain came to fuller participation in international and European institutions, the more Franco needed to provide coherence to both Spain's new foreign experiments and changing needs at home. This was especially true for Franco's attempts to pursue closer ties to the emerging process of European integration. The following excerpt from a speech Franco gave in 1959 illustrates his calculations regarding foreign policy towards Europe:

> People speak today of the necessity of a union of European peoples. In reality, finding a suitable system of integration is an imperative of our age. We were not and are not indifferent to this demand. Within our constant ideology are principles that may be very useful in the illumination of the exact formula....We understand that the integration of European states can and must be conceived of in light of the unavoidable supposition of respect for the real and historical personality of each country within a unity of destiny. It is exactly this unity of destiny of the European peoples that can redeem the strength and stability of union within the necessary and unrenounceable variety [of nations] (*Pensamiento Político de Franco*, 1975, p.785).

The balance Franco tried to maintain was difficult given his inability to institutionalize a vision of Spain as a society apart from the rest of Europe (Boyd, 1989, p.189).

This perception was reinforced by the actions of other European states when the Franco regime applied for associate membership to the EEC in 1962. The European Parliament answered in the Birklebach Report: 'States whose governments do not have democratic legitimation and whose peoples do not participate in government decisions, either directly or through freely elected representatives, cannot aspire to be admitted into the circle of peoples which forms the European Communities' (quoted in Preston and Smyth, 1984, p.1). The Common Market's rejection of Franquist Spain's application for membership in 1962 helped convince the democratic opposition that democracy in Spain would be legitimated only through the imprimatur of approval of European institutions and organizations.

Despite Franco's attempts to control the flow of European influences and subordinate them to the more narrowly defined cause of economic progress, forces in opposition to the regime identified their cause with European democratic political ideas. These groups, including the leadership of the Spanish Socialist Party, accepted the prevailing wisdom that isolation from, and suspicion of, Europe established at various junctures in Spanish history, what had retarded the modernization of Spain.[13] Therefore, they continued to identify Franquist rule with conservative isolationism, despite the opening orchestrated by the regime in the 1960s. The opposition to Franco conceded that the Franco government could selectively import European economic practices to promote modernization. But the opposition also prescribed Franco's ouster and the wholesale adoption of European democratic political norms.

The Socialists viewed membership in the EC as a way definitively to end Spain's traditional isolation from the European mainstream.[14] The Socialist enthusiasm to be part of Europe was captured in an interview conducted for this project with a senior official at Spain's Secretariat for EC Relations, who argues that post-Franco Spain has accepted European integration as an article of faith: the faith that Spain should take its rightful place in Europe, and that Spain should not go against the current of history. Asked if this faith clouds Spanish leaders' judgement, the official replied that '*la fe es un don*' (faith is a gift) and that this faith favors the political will to participate in the project of constructing Europe.[15]

Yet, the pro-European orientation was not hegemonic in the Socialist party during the initial period after Franco's death in 1975. We can identify three additional foreign policy trends in the PSOE. First, for more radical factions within the party the idea of Europe meant not the adoption of capitalist market principles, but the opportunity to create a European-wide socialist transformation. Second, was the PSOE's Third World or "*Tercermundista*" orientation, which stressed increased ties to the South. Third, the leadership of the PSOE continued the tradition of seeking special ties with Latin America.[16] Given the Socialists' schooling in left wing theory while in clandestinity, these first attempts at forging an Iberoamerican sensibility focused on placing Spain in the forefront of demands by poorer nations within the larger North-South debate (Pollack and Hunter, 1987, pp.81-92; Roitman, 1985).

Like Europeanism, Pan-Hispanicism is a malleable idea that has taken on a variety of connotations in the 500 year long relationship between Spain and its colonies in the New World (Wiarda, 1986; Rosenberg, 1992). Following World War II, Europe's isolation of Franquist Spain forced Franco to pursue closer ties with Latin American states. In Spain, acceptance of the corporatist model that went along with the new 'Hispanidad' implied a whole range of political implications: 'Being "different" was a code word for supporting the Franco...regime, being "European" was a code word for opposition to them and for favoring European-style democracy' (Wiarda, 1986, p.231). Franco thus gave to his Latin American policy a connotation that would be adopted uncomfortably by elements within the Socialist Party.

Eventually, as they become more involved in politics following Franco's death, the young Socialists came to reject the *Tercermundista* rhetoric.[17] The PSOE's attempt at establishing a Latin American policy ultimately were overwhelmed by the European priorities of the party and, for that matter, the majority of Spaniards. The desire to modernize Spain through increased ties to Europe usurped any constructive role Spain could play in Latin America or in other regions of historical Spanish involvement. During the period of negotiations for Spanish membership in the European Community, the PSOE government promoted the idea that Spain could serve as a unique bridge between the EC and Latin America. This notion, accepted eagerly at first by EC leaders, largely has been abandoned, however, as the EC focused increasingly on resolving its own internal problems. To many observers, then, the whole hearted turn towards Europe represents a paradigm shift in Spanish thinking away from historic ties to Latin America and other parts of the world (Rosenberg 1992, p.133).

The task for the PSOE and other opposition groups during and after the Franco era has been to pursue increased Europeanization without duplicating the efforts of the Franco regime. This was especially true concerning membership in NATO. The Socialists' enthusiasm for membership in the European Community did not carry over to the Atlantic Alliance. The Socialists' opposition to Spanish membership in NATO stems in large part from their hostility towards the United States. This hostility was rooted in the Franco dictatorship's relationship with the USA, which has its origins in the defense treaty established between Madrid and Washington in 1953. The Socialists argued that the Treaty of Madrid bestowed legitimacy on the Franco regime by the outside world - legitimacy necessary to prop up the dictatorship and immunize it from increased external pressures (Berling, 1975, p.14). At the close of the Second World War, Franco stood alone as the sole surviving European dictator of those who rose to power in the 1930s, and Spain was branded a pariah state.[18] Therefore, when world events - i.e., the onset of the Cold War - induced the American government to recognize the Franco regime as a bulwark against Communism, the opposition to Franquism saw their hopes of bringing down the dictatorship through international ostracism greatly diminish. The Socialists' anti-Americanism was exacerbated by events of the post-Franco period. Washington's response to the attempted coup of February 23, 1981 - the greatest threat to Spanish democracy since 1975 - was treated casually by Secretary of State Alexander Haig who deemed it an 'internal Spanish affair' and chose to take no action to condemn the attempted military takeover.

As a consequence of the Socialists' distrust of the United States they rejected America's role as a positive force in European defense matters. NATO was viewed as a creature of American hegemony and not of European defense cooperation. In other words, the Socialists equated NATO with Atlanticism strictly defined. The old guard PSOE (the so-called 'historic' wing) supported NATO at its inception as a bulwark against Communist aggression (Gillespie, 1989, p.112). The latter-day PSOE was equally anti-communist, but rejected alliances with the West after the fight against communism became the source of legitimacy for the Franco regime within the Western camp. Therefore, it was hard for the Socialists to imagine that Spaniards could identify with the Cold War mentality of other Western European countries, especially if they did not benefit from other aspects the Cold War contract (Manera Regueyra, 1977, pp.58-59).

In addition to these perceptions, the PSOE's negative ideas about NATO also served the party's domestic political interests of gaining power by appealing to important sectors of the electorate. In the wake of Franco's death, this meant solidifying the PSOE's support among the Spanish left wing (Juliá, 1990, pp.269-270). This is not to say that the Socialist Party's opposition to NATO was rooted primarily in the desire to achieve dominance of the left. Even as late as 1980, the electorate did not consider the question of membership in NATO as a left-right issue.[19] Rather, the PSOE's anti-NATO position reinforced the party leadership's interest in consolidating the PSOE's appeal among left-leaning groups in order to create a new Spain. This was true for the generalized Marxism of the PSOE. In other words, whereas the PSOE's espousal of radical policies supported its interests of achieving hegemony on the left, it was also founded on the larger ideas the Socialists advocated for transforming Spanish society. Even after the PSOE gained hegemony of the left in Spain, it continued to oppose NATO membership on the grounds it was incompatible with the socialist vision of Spain.

Finally, the relationship between the Socialists' eagerness to join Europe, and their desire to maintain some sense of foreign policy autonomy within the West, was symbolized in the form of the coexisting deliberations over Spanish membership in the European Community and NATO. The implicit, yet changing, linkages between these issues presented the PSOE government with a test of the coherence of its European foreign policy. It is well established that the governments of other European countries perceived a positive relationship between Spanish membership in NATO and proposed admittance to the EC.[20] However, in the absence of formal enforcement mechanisms, this relationship must be seen in terms of the informal, not formal, links the Europeans perceived among the many facets of European integration.[21] Without a specification of the nature of these links, assertions that prudent decision making led to the Spanish government's reversal of its position on NATO present unwarranted assumptions about a rational calculus by government leaders.[22] Further, to assert that Spanish leaders merely adjusted their preferences fails to explain *why* these leaders should care if they damaged the integrity of NATO, especially given their long standing hostility towards the alliance. Therefore, as long as the evolution of the PSOE's views on NATO are overlooked, the linkages between the EC and NATO remain merely observed phenomena devoid of an explanatory framework.

Summary and conclusions

Post-Franco foreign policy has been influenced fundamentally by the ways that Spanish political elites conceive Spain's place in the world. For new political leaders, foreign policy can represent an uncharted policy realm. The way they approach international relations will necessarily involve the vague ideas leaders have about how the country fits into the world system. These ideas are based on understandings of a country's past. And these ideas are grounded in culture, symbol, and myth as well as recent events. Historical memory plays an important role in shaping political outcomes in Spain.

The Socialist Party leadership that emerged from Franquism was steeped in this historical memory. The majority of Socialists and other anti-Franco forces agreed that the true original sin of the dictator was that he closed Spain off from Europe and kept Spain isolated, backwards, and alone. The Socialists felt that only though becoming part of the European mainstream could they erase Franco's original sin.[23]

It is not difficult to see from this how the Socialist government rushed headlong into negotiations to join the European Community. On the other hand, the PSOE leadership resented the legitimation of the Franco regime motivated by American anti-communism. The anti-Americanism among the left that resulted from the Cold War recognition of Franco's Spain initially led the PSOE to embrace third world non-alignment of the 1960s and 1970s. Joining NATO under these circumstances was unthinkable. As with previous Spanish state leaderships, the resolution of this tension among competing visions of Spain's place in the world forms one of the interesting stories of post-Franco foreign policy. Existing explanations of the PSOE's European policy largely overlook these nuances in Socialist Party thinking and therefore imply a certain inevitability in Spain's policy towards Europe. This ignores the twists and turns of how this policy unfolded.

In sum, in the nexus between the international environment and Spanish domestic politics lies the Socialists' ideas about, and knowledge based claims on, the structure of European intersubjective reality. These ideas and knowledge-based claims, in turn, had a bearing on the Socialists' changing foreign and domestic policy strategy and interests. Indeed, only after we understand the PSOE's changed perception of European intersubjective reality can we comprehend its perceptions of political possibility and devise a strategy for exercising power in both the international and domestic spheres.

Notes

1   The accounts of Spain's relationship with NATO that do exist employ mostly historical description and make few theoretical claims (see for example Gil and Tulchin, 1988; Maxwell, 1991).

2 Portugal was a charter member of NATO, Ireland has continually resisted membership in the Alliance.

3 One former member of the PSOE government indicated in an interview that the party focuses its attention on shaping public support for its programs and only responds to public opinion polls before elections.

4 Kevin Featherstone argues that relations between Southern European socialist parties and the EC, for example suggest 'the elitest influence on the parties' policies on Europe; the lower ranks in the party structures have obeyed the lead from above. The party leaderships have enjoyed considerable domestic leeway, in political terms, when seeking to manage their relations with the rest of the EC' (Featherstone, 1989 p.268).

5 Portions of this section appeared in M. Marks, 1995.

6 This distrust of changes in the rest of Europe was embodied in the rule of King Philip II (ruled 1556-1598). Philip II set out to purify Spain of what he saw as the contaminating effects of Europe under the Protestant Reformation (Menéndez Pidal, 1950, pp.218-224).

7 I would like to thank Pedro Schwartz, José María Maravall, and José Victor Sevilla for their thoughts and advice on this subject.

8 'They have said and repeated to us - and I have said and repeated on my own part - that we must Europeanize ourselves. I retract that; Europeanize ourselves, no, because Europe makes us small; universalize ourselves is better, and for that matter Spanishize ourselves [*españolizarnos*] is better still' (Unamuno, 1968, p.725).

9 'We ask for nothing more than this: fasten upon Spain the European point of view....The European words, which we have silenced throughout three centuries, will come forward at once, crystallizing in an epic song. Europe - asleep in France, exhausted in Germany, weak in England - will have a new youth under the powerful sun of our land. Spain is a European possibility. Only viewed from Europe is Spain possible' (Ortega y Gasset, 1950, p.138).

10 In numerous interviews I conducted among Spanish opinion makers, the expression 'Spain is the problem and Europe is the solution' was repeated with great frequency.

11   The sources of the Civil War are many, and a rich body of evidence can be marshalled to support one explanation against another. Changes in Spain's class structure brought about by the gradual erosion of aristocratic privilege contributed to the rise of popular demands for increased power, to be sure. See, for example, Malefakis, 1970; Brenan, 1943; Preston, 1983. However, the historically-based antagonisms between progressives and conservatives clearly informed the unfolding of events.

12   The period of the Second Republic coincided with European attempts to revive the languishing League of Nations in order to oppose Japanese aggression in Manchuria and the Italian invasion of Ethiopia. Nevertheless, the Spanish government was uninterested in taking part in these operations. When Japan invaded Manchuria in 1931, Madrid showed no interest in joining the League's condemnation. One exception was Spain's ambassador in Geneva, the renowned internationalist Salvador de Madariaga, whose pleas for support fell on deaf ears at home (Carreras Ares, 1981, p.44).

13   One Foreign Ministry official related in an interview that the combination of Spain's decline after the sixteenth century and forty years of isolation under Franquism produced the overriding idea that Europeanization means democratization.

14   In a personal interview I conducted, a member of an influential Spanish political family and former senior government official revealed that Prime Minister Felipe González and Vice Premier Alfonso Guerra were rural country folk who were genuinely ashamed of Spain and its conditions compared to the rest of Europe. The desire to be European was fundamental for these leaders with humble rural backgrounds.

15   This was related in a personal interview.

16   Robin Rosenberg argues that Felipe González 'expressed reservations about the European project. Membership in the EEC would not necessarily require NATO membership as long as French Socialism was there to support Spanish accession to the Community....Open and unabashed sympathies for the Palestinian and Polisario causes signaled a new, more activist, non-aligned stance for Spanish foreign policy. Latin America, where the Socialist International already was working in conflict resolution, would be the main target of Spanish diplomatic resources within this new framework' (Rosenberg, 1992, p.141).

17   'The importance of Spain's Europeanization during the 1980s is that it represents a major shift in Spanish priorities. The identification of the Socialist government with the European project and European standards may even be deemed a typically un-Spanish phenomenon....As early as 1983, the Madrid press was debating "a radical pro-Western turn in our foreign policy"' (Rosenberg, 1992, pp.132-133.   Rosenberg cites *Cambio 16*, June 27, 1983).

18   Dr Antonio Salazar, the authoritarian leader of Portugal, rose to power in the late 1920s and was not considered by European leaders on a par with Franco, Hitler, and Mussolini.   Portugal stayed neutral during World War II and Salazar's policies were not deemed as offensive as the other totalitarian states.   Indeed, Salazar's Portugal was a charter member of NATO.

19   A 1980 public opinion survey found that whereas 28 per cent of respondents characterized pro-NATO positions as part of a definition of the right, 48 per cent responded that this was not an issue they used to distinguish left from right (Maravall, 1982, pp.110-111).   See also, Treverton, 1986, p.8.

20   In 1984, German Chancellor Helmut Kohl was overheard in an 'off-the-record' conversation saying: 'One cannot hope to sell olives in the European marketplace and not contribute to its defense' (*Cambio 16*, 28 May 1984, p.39).

21   Emilio Rodríguez points out: 'The EC and NATO are independent institutions and therefore the Europeans never explicitly, or formally, made Spanish integration in the Community contingent on permanence in NATO' (Rodríguez, 1988, p.65).

22   Eusebio Mujal-Leon argues that the PSOE 'stumbled' upon the EC-NATO connection in its negotiations to win Common Market membership (Mujal-Leon, 1986, p.210).

23   One economic advisor to former Prime Minister Felipe González related in a personal interview that after democracy was restored, whenever a parliamentary deputy proposed this or that policy he would argue, 'this is how they do things in Europe' when making a point.

3 Analytical perspective: ideas, interests, and knowledge

As I discuss in the previous chapter, traditional theories which emphasize international structural conditions overlook the evolution of Spain's changed relations with the rest of Europe. Explanations that stress the interests of Spanish political elites begin to rectify this problem by adding considerations of political agency. However, even if we accept that Spanish Socialist leaders made strategic calculations, we are still left with the question of why preferences changed so dramatically in such a short period of time. The most promising approaches to compensate for these failings are offered by theories of international institutions and current analyses emphasizing the role of ideas, knowledge, and interests. I will present a framework that incorporates elements of these new approaches but modifies them in two fundamental ways. First, the framework specifies the sequential steps by which international norms form the bases for a country's foreign policy. Second, it emphasizes the distinctions between ideas and knowledge and their separate roles in shaping leaders' responses to international change.

A first cut: international institutions, regimes, and norms

In moving beyond structural explanations to understand the formation of Spanish foreign policy, a satisfactory model will be one that takes into account domestic political history, the role of leaders, and international influences. International institutions offer a good way to conceptualize these features.[1] Institutions have received a great deal of attention in recent theorizing, and the word has become a slippery term. Robert Keohane has provided one of the best clarifications of the institutional debate by dividing the approach into two camps (Keohane, 1988). On the one hand are what Keohane calls 'rationalist' approaches, which characterize institutions as organizational routines and formal arrangements for establishing international cooperation.[2] This usage stresses institutions as intervening variables between state interests and international cooperation, with institutions providing ways of reducing transaction costs and increasing the availability of collective goods (North, 1981; Keohane, 1984; Aggarwal, 1985); Axelrod, 1984; Oye, 1986). As James March and Johan Olsen maintain, institutions contribute order to the political world and establish rules of behavior, norms, and roles by which individuals understand their duties and obligations (March and Olsen, 1984, pp.741-744). However, a rationalist institutional approach is of limited use for describing Spanish-European relations: Spain's leaders did not use international regimes merely to advance a set of pre-existing interests, but rather, defined their interests through interactions with other states in an institutional setting.

More appropriate for the Spanish case is what Keohane calls the 'reflectivist' approach (also known as the 'constructivist' or 'structurationist' approach). This type of analysis portrays institutions as sociological expressions of 'values, norms, and practices [which] vary across cultures' (Keohane, 1988, p.389). In this approach, institutions are based on socially constructed norms (Young, 1990; Barnett, 1993, 1995; Ashley, 1986; Wendt, 1987; Cox, 1981). Actors' interests are not based on some objective standard, but are continually created as society creates and recreates itself. In his critique of a systemic theory of international relations, John Ruggie argues that what matters is not only the structure of the international system, but the 'principles on the basis of which the constituent units are separated from one another' (Ruggie, 1986, p.142). The main problem with the reflectivist approach in interpreting Spain and Europe is that it underspecifies the way that post-Franco Spain joined an international society of states (Western European democracies) from which it had been previously excluded.

International regimes theory offers one way to cut across the rationalist-reflectivist divide, by attaching both organizational and normative elements to arrangements designed to foster international cooperation (Keohane, 1984). In the standard definition, regimes are composed of shared norms, rules, principles, and decision making procedures (Krasner, 1983). Of these four elements, John Ruggie and Friedrich Kratochwil emphasize the role of norms, pointing out that 'what distinguishes international regimes from other international phenomena (from strategic interaction, for example) is a specifically normative element' (Kratochwil and Ruggie, 1986, p.767). Kratochwil later suggests a way in which we might understand change as a function of acceptance of a normative template that gives meaning to specific economic and security interests: The key is not to view norms as causal variables, but as common sources of understanding akin to constitutional law (Kratochwil, 1989, pp.61-64).

Martin Heisler and Robert Breckinridge have advanced an interpretation of Spain's relationship with the EC and NATO based on regime theory with a special emphasis on norms. Heisler and Breckinridge's main hypothesis is as follows:

A domestic regime shaped in part by the normative and interactional templates of an international regime is more likely to lead to conformity with the latter and to do so in a more systematic, normatively and institutionally supported fashion than could be expected from merely issue-specific, case-by-case determinations of actors' *ad hoc* interests (Heisler, and Breckinridge, 1989, p.9).

In the process of confirming this hypothesis the authors make two findings about Spain and the EC: 1) Internalization of international EC norms led to the consolidation of democratic political arrangements in Spain and, 2) the EC regime, itself, became more robust as new member states incorporated the regime's norms (ibid, pp.18-19). The authors make more limited claims about security norms given the tendency within NATO away from collective goals (ibid., p.22). Perhaps because of this limitation, Heisler and Breckinridge restrict their claims.[3] But their argument is plain: Normative precepts of international regimes can be the basis for domestic political development and democratic consolidation.

This is a cogent argument but it raises a number of questions about institutions and the behavior of state actors: Do domestic regimes simply absorb international norms from the institutions in which they are embedded? If not, what aspects of domestic politics make state leaders susceptible to the influences of international institutions, regimes, or norms? How are the normative elements of international institutions assimilated by decision makers? How are any tensions between norms and interests resolved, both domestically and within the international regime? Heisler and Breckinridge are correct that Spain's accession to the EC and NATO was prefaced on the normative preferences of member states. But I believe they have left gaps in both the theoretical framework and historical picture. These gaps include the steps by which Spanish leaders approached the EC and NATO with preconceived ideas, the process of learning, the assimilation of new knowledge, and the redefinition of ideas and interests in light of new knowledge.

In order to fill the gaps left by regime theory, I specify the steps between how institutionalized international norms become part of domestic policy creation.[4] A focus on international norms as independent variables unnecessarily reduces political leaders and their political strategies to a residual category endowed with little or no volition (Klotz, 1995, pp.460-462). It also minimizes the role of leaders' ideas about politics that they bring with them when they conceive political interests. Instead, I argue that we cannot understand how these norms translate into state actions without looking at the role of the agents who transmit norms through the process of socialization. To do this I place an emphasis on the relationship between ideas and interests in the formation of foreign policy and the interpretation of international norms through knowledge based claims. In the process, I fill in the steps of foreign policy creation which include the ideas that inform leaders' world views, the claims that underlie these ideas, leaders' perceived political interests, and how new knowledge can often change the relationship among them.

Ideas and knowledge and their separate effects on the conception of interests

Instead of imagining a direct relationship between norms and outcomes, the Spanish case shows that the definition and redefinition of interests involves a series of steps between the origination of ideas that national decision makers hold when they think about the world, the grounding of these ideas through a knowledge base, the conception of interests, and the assimilation of new knowledge about normative expectations in international systems which alters existing ideas and interests. Leaders' perceive their political interests as logically connected to their ideas about the world and their understanding of the political universe. But dramatic changes in domestic or international political conditions can undermine leaders' understanding of political realities and create tensions between previously compatible ideas and interests. When these situations arise, new knowledge, often transmitted though international interactions, can help decision makers reestablish the consistency they previously recognized between ideas and perceived interests. New policies normally follow these periods of clarification.

Ideas

The nature of ideas in politics has gained a great deal of attention in academic circles in recent years. As of yet, no single definition has emerged, nor is there agreement on what causal role ideas play in the political process (Jacobsen, 1995; Yee, 1996). Judith Goldstein and Robert Keohane have offered the most wide ranging treatment of ideas and foreign policy. They posit three categories of ideas, and three causal pathways in which ideas influence political outcomes.[5] Given the complicated typology that results from such an expansive treatment of ideas, in this book I limit myself only to a conception of ideas suggested by the Spanish case.

By 'ideas' I mean the generalized images political actors bring with them to a yet unexplored new problem. These images often are grounded in cultural myth, symbols, values, beliefs, and historical discourse deeply ingrained in society. In this sense, I treat ideas as abstract, yet deeply held, beliefs that approximate what traditionally have been called 'ideologies' or 'culture' in the political realm (Sartori, 1969; Geertz, 1973; Hunt, 1987; Schulman, 1988; Howard, 1989; Scarbrough, 1990).

There are those who while recognizing the role of ideas in foreign policy, contend that leaders simply use ideas as a justification for actions taken on the basis of material interests (Garret and Weingast, 1991; Garrett, 1992). Rather, I maintain that when leaders are faced with uncertainty and new circumstances, they turn to ideas not to justify decisions already made, but as guideposts in the policy making process. The vantage point of leaders is important for understanding why ideas are not merely used as justifications for policies. When leaders are faced with new and uncertain situations, they will more likely be motivated by deeply held beliefs than by fleeting strategic concerns (Staniland, 1991). For example, Spanish foreign policy makers in the post-Franco era were convinced that they needed to construct a European policy because they believed in the 'idea of Europe'. Yet 'Europe', for Spanish leaders, lacked precise meaning in practice - there was no blueprint for action or strategy for achieving precise ends.[6] Rather, the Socialists relied on the idea of 'Europe' as an ideal - a utopian vision based on the desire to overcome years of Spanish isolation, and nurtured by the inexperience of formerly radicalized elements of the Spanish opposition.[7]

Interests

By interests, I mean an actor's set of preferred outcomes. Robert Reich argues that whereas ideas are based on motivations of the social good, interests reflect narrowly construed self regard (R. Reich, 1988, p.3). By contrast, I maintain that ideas do not 'compete' with interests as causal variables when explaining political events. Decision makers attach interests to their political ideas (Diggins, 1986; J. Hall, 1993). John Kingdon maintains succinctly:

> If one could specify a set of cases of policy making, for instance...in which one could clearly predict (or postdict) one outcome on the basis of self interest and a contrary outcome on the basis of ideas, then one could test which explanation seems to hold over those cases, how frequently, and under what conditions (Kingdon, 1990, p.47).

Unfortunately, this optimal situation rarely exists: 'Ideas and self interests are...inseparable in principle; different, but inseparable. People need to attach meaning to their behavior, even if that behavior is motivated by self interest' (ibid., p.5) In practice, individuals adopt interests in tandem with ideas since both phenomena are situationally generated. Stated another way, ideas shape the way individuals perceive their political and interests within the confines of structures, situations, events, or circumstances.[8] In other words, as long as ideas are based on the perceptions of individuals and collectivities, it is impossible to disentangle ideas from the circumstances in which they are embedded (Goldstein, 1989).

Therefore, because ideas and interests are bound together, and because we normally associate interests with policy creation, we cannot divorce ideas from their policy implications (Douglas, 1986; Staniland, 1991). For example, in Spain, the idea of Europe as a model has competed periodically with the idea of a pan-Hispanic commonwealth, a notion that recurs throughout modern Spanish history (Wiarda, 1986). Indeed, certain attempts were made to connect this idea to a set of policy prescriptions. These attempts came into conflict with opposing interests based on the competing idea of European integration as a source of political inspiration.

Knowledge

Complementing the political ideas that leaders adopt to help them simplify the world and their perceptions of political interests is a fund of knowledge that allows leaders to order the world and explain their perceptions of political reality (Adler, 1987; S. Reich, 1990). Much recent literature has equated the terms 'idea' and 'knowledge. Yet, knowledge is distinct from, and complementary to, ideas in the policy creation process. I prefer to reserve the term 'knowledge' for use in the sense described by Ernst Haas: Knowledge expressly implies specialized and specific understanding about a particular issue or problem. In this regard, Ernst Haas's definition of 'consensual knowledge' is an especially good one. He defines consensual knowledge as:

> Generally accepted understandings about cause-and-effect linkages about any set of phenomena considered important by society, provided only that the finality of the accepted chain of causation is subject to continuing testing and examination through adversary procedures (E. Haas, 1990, p.21).

In other words, whereas ideology and ideas are frequently - though clearly not always - portrayed as vague generalities, knowledge implies comprehension of truths, facts, or accepted explanations of particular processes. In a broad sense I accept this definition of knowledge as specific agreement, shared among peers, of any cause and effect relationships.[9] Furthermore, Haas stresses that knowledge is politically salient when it is consensual; that is, it 'is the sum of technical information and of theories about it that command sufficient agreement among interested actors at a given time to serve as a guide to public policy' (E. Haas, 1990, p.74).

Despite the strength of Haas's formulation, its limitation derives from the fact that Haas sees knowledge as something that *informs* politics, as opposed to something *of* politics. In fact, most if not all of the recent literature on ideational politics sees ideas as framing a specific policy issue (Jacobsen, 1995; Woods, 1995). Like Haas, these analyses are limited to scientific and quasi-scientific agreement. In other words, ideas and knowledge are still treated largely in an instrumental sense since they are conceived as tools that inform, and provide solutions in, a specific policy issue.

Instead, I allow for the possibility that not only does scientific or technical knowledge influence politics, but also there is something we can call *political knowledge*.[10]   In politics, knowledge certainly applies to data, findings, conclusions, etc. available to decision and policy makers. However, it also refers to any theory of politics, economics, or policy making that leaders confront when considering political choices. Leaders' abstract ideas about the world, and the nature of international relations specifically, are underpinned by understandings of the cause and effect of any actions taken in the practice of world politics and diplomacy (Herrmann, 1985; Blum, 1993). As Elisabeth Prügl writes: '[Social] structures reproduce only through the practices of *knowledgeable* agents. Stuctures and agents cannot exist without each other. Actors draw on the rules which make up structures in their everyday routines, and in doing so they reproduce these rules' (Prügl, 1996, p.15, emphasis added). Thus, the way that decision-makers understand political conditions and options themselves, constitute a type of knowledge in the course of governance. In other words, knowledge (or knowledge-based claims, as I will also refer to this concept) is an expression of the shared perception of political reality.

Even within a narrow definition of knowledge there are still many variants of knowledge in political situations. Most important for this study, foreign policy knowledge involves understanding of the policies and preferences of the leaders of countries that deal with one another. Concerning requirements for Spanish EC entry, for example, the European Council of Ministers spelled out in 1983 at the Stuttgart Summit the specific linkages between internal EC reforms and the southern enlargement to include Portugal and Spain (*Bulletin of the European Communities*, 1983, pp.18-24, 90-93). This represented knowledge of certain economic responsibilities Spain faced in order to join the European Community. In the NATO case, European leaders made clear to Spanish officials the political ramifications of withdrawal from NATO. In this case, Spain's leaders learned what Spanish membership in NATO meant for the long-range plans for European integration. The problem for Spanish leaders in the early 1980s was how to construct a coherent foreign policy. This required a knowledge about the functions of European institutions and the expectations that European leaders had of new member states.

Summary of key concepts

In short, ideas and knowledge are distinct concepts. Ideas reflect broad conceptions about the political universe based solely on conviction, expectation, or faith. In a loose fashion, they may be equated with Thomas Kuhn's notion of 'intellectual paradigms' (Kuhn, 1962). That is to say, ideas are the cultural equivalent of academicians' intellectual frames of reference. Knowledge, on the other hand, is more like scientific theory. It implies a much more rigorous set of rules or laws explaining the nature of how the world works.

The relationship among ideas, interests, and knowledge, and their effect on policy in a single state can be summarized as follows. Politics and society are constituted by three elements: ideas, material interests, and knowledge based claims. Ideas are the abstract beliefs that provide generalized political orientations. Material interests motivate action. And knowledge based claims are the rules that define political reality. In times of normal politics, the knowledge base that guides leaders is submerged or taken as a given for the sake of simplifying decision making. By the same token, ideas serve as abstractions or assumed beliefs about the political universe. Both phenomena inform the definition of interests (Hurwitz, Peffley, and Seligson, 1993). Leaders rely on both ideas and knowledge when calculating preferences.[11] When tensions surface between ideas and knowledge-based claims, the definition of interests may change. Only by recognizing this can we understand the dynamics of changing interests *over time* that are so central to the political process.

During times of intense domestic or international political upheaval, the bases of foreign policy decision making are no longer submerged or taken for granted. This is notable when old assumptions are challenged because of tensions that emerge among old understandings of political reality. During these periods, leaders unpack the three components of ideas, interests, and knowledge that guide them in foreign policy formation. The need to distinguish broad ideas from specific knowledge is evident: Because leaders' interest perceptions are shaped both by ideas and knowledge, to conflate the latter two categories undermines attempts to trace the process by which leaders' perceptions are altered during periods of tension and change.

Ideas, interests, and knowledge during periods of uncertainty

The relationship between ideas and interests is constantly evolving (Ferguson and Mansbach, 1991; Yee, 1996). If policy creation is the aim, I argue that new knowledge can offer clarification when the ever changing equation relationship between ideas and interests fails to yield satisfactory results. The question then is: Under what political situations does new knowledge act as a catalyst for change? Above all, leaders engage in a process of knowledge search during periods of uncertainty, when the relationship between ideas and interests is in flux. Ole Holsti has suggested seven situations in which decision makers' are receptive to new knowledge. These include non-routine situations, decisions made at the top of the government hierarchy, policies requiring long-range planning, ambiguous situations, circumstances of information, unanticipated events, and circumstances in which complex cognitive tasks associated with decision making may be impaired (Holsti, 1976, p.30). This list is a good starting point for considering the political circumstances under which ideas come under scrutiny and clarifying knowledge is welcome.

Knowledge is important because it can reconcile tensions, ambiguity, or inconsistencies within ideas, or between ideas and interests or existing knowledge-based claims. Using Holsti as a guide, this section describes situations of uncertainty in which tensions, ambiguity, or inconsistencies might arise and why new knowledge may be welcomed. I begin with quandaries of ideas and move on to problems between ideas and interests. In each instance I cite examples from the Spanish case.

Uncertainty of ideas

First, because an idea may be simply a vague notion, founded on cultural or societal myths, people will be receptive to knowledge that will help relate the idea to empirical reality. The Spanish Socialists' idea about Europe was based, in many respects, on the oft-quoted observation by the famous Spanish essayist José Ortega y Gasset: 'If Spain is the problem, Europe is the solution' (Ortega y Gasset, 1950, p.521). Europe represented a sort of cure to Spain's economic backwardness. Specifically how the cure would be administered, however, was not at all clear. Knowledge about what Europe really means would offer clarification. Second, there may exist internal inconsistencies in the idea as currently perceived; or groups of ideas held by a single society occasionally may come into conflict with one another (King, 1973b, p.422; Stryker, 1980, p.73; Barnett, 1993, 1995). For example, certain Spanish leaders favored the idea of Spain becoming more European while continuing to espouse the idea that Spain could speak for the concerns of underdeveloped Third World nations.

Third, the nature of the idea itself may be one that stresses learning and openness. In many post-communist countries, for instance, the operative political idea currently enjoying acceptance is precisely the idea of opening to the rest of the world. That is to say, there is not only a willingness to learn from other political systems, but this idea is what is driving current developments. In the Spanish case, the idea of Europe was directly related to Spain's gradual emergence from decades of isolation. The opening to Europe was paralleled by the openness to new knowledge. Fourth, people likely will assimilate new information when ideas do not correspond with perceived reality (Staniland, 1991). As Emanuel Adler points out: 'Beliefs and expectations are based on the perception of reality, not on reality itself' (Adler, 1987, p.16). In Spain, Socialist Party hostility towards NATO frequently was based on the perception that NATO was a creature of United States hegemony. The reality was that the leaders of most of the Alliance countries considered NATO essential for maintenance of European unity, despite the obvious American influences. Finally, ideas may become so enshrined that they no longer hold any practical meaning (Berman, 1991). Spanish ideas of Europe as economic savior were of little use the more the EC made clear its requirements for Spanish entry.

Uncertainty in the relationship between ideas and interests

The second set of circumstances in which new knowledge may be welcome by decision makers involves situations where tensions arise between ideas and knowledge based claims reflecting uncertainty over interests. The relationship between ideas and interests is a dynamic one and subject to change. Ideas create broad expectations - they present political elite with loose frameworks for interpreting events. Yet these ideas are connected to knowledge based claims, which may be submerged during times of political stasis, but are challenged during times of change.[12]   And because knowledge based claims undergo change, interests are therefore not fixed.   Under various circumstances of uncertainty or rapid change, tensions or inconsistencies may increase. It is the resolution of these tensions through the introduction of new knowledge that reestablishes the harmony between ideas and interests that characterizes periods of normal politics.[13]

Uncertainty is especially important in the Spanish case.   Spain's membership in the European Community and NATO coincided with the period of democratic consolidation.   The process of democratization may open political space for this type of fundamental foreign policy reorientation.   Additionally, the rise of the Spanish Socialist Party to power in 1982 represented the arrival of a new class of political elite that desired a break with the past, and whose ideas about Europe - pro and con - were a function of its experiences under the Franco dictatorship (Pérez-Díaz, 1990, p.1).   Likewise, the PSOE's perceptions of how to secure Spanish economic and defense interests reflected its radical past, political inexperience, and uncertainty about the specific nature of Spain's post-Franco national interest (Share, 1989, p.141).   Furthermore, during the immediate post-Franco years, Spain sought membership in a variety of international organizations that was denied during Franquist rule.   The more Spain became integrated in international organizational frameworks, the more likely its leaders would be exposed to information about the norms and agreements that underpin these organizations, perhaps challenging previous foreign policy beliefs. Finally, Spain negotiated membership in NATO and the EC at a time of change in the international system.   Heightened Cold War tensions, and efforts to reconcile the 'Eurosclerosis' plaguing the EC, made this period one of fluidity in European affairs (Sandholtz and Zysman, 1989; Moravcsik, 1991).

How knowledge reconciles uncertainty

During periods of uncertainty, the relationship among ideas, existing knowledge based claims, and interests may be subject to change.   First, political actors must reconcile their past experiences with current political problems (Goldstein, 1989;

Blum, 1993). Tensions may arise between ideas formulated under distinct historical situations and interests reflecting the changed political environment. Leaders with full knowledge of present political responsibilities then can better reconcile their past ideas with changing interests. The Spanish Socialists' political ideas reflected a radical past and clandestine opposition to dictatorship. These ideas did not always reconcile easily with political interests in a newly democratic state (Gillespie, 1989, p.219). Second, decision makers may be open to new knowledge in periods of uncertainty about interests (Rothstein, 1984, p.735). Ideas may be the lens through which interests are perceived. However, altered political conditions may render the ideas-interests relationship imperfect or obsolete. This tension may be caused by the fact that while people perceive that the idea and interests do not entirely mesh, there may be no better solution than the one at which they have already arrived (Goldstein, 1989, p.71). For example, Spanish Socialist officials were quick to feel the tensions between favoring the idea of European integration and their perceived interest of withdrawing from the Western security apparatus, but they were unsure of how to resolve this tension.

Third, leaders in the initial stages of formulating policy in a particular issue area may discover that the ideas they hold are not completely consistent with the policies they contemplate implementing. Michael Hunt observes: 'It is important...to accept the view that the relationship between ideas and action is not rigid. The simple idea or set of ideas on which policy may initially rest invariably has to leave room for...nonideological considerations...' (Hunt, 1987, p.16). The Spanish Socialists' distaste for joining the European security alliance would not be reconciled easily with the policy of controlling the Spanish military by increasing its ties to other Western armies. Since the policy rested on these other 'nonideological factors,' new knowledge about these factors may help clarify or rectify the tension between the policy and prevailing ideas.

Fourth, knowledge claims based on past experiences are often inapplicable to new situations. As Ernst Haas writes:

> Decision-making models that are supposed to draw on the lessons of history, that are predicated on the assumption that actors deliberately learn from prior mistakes, are badly flawed because the lessons of history are rarely unambiguous: different actors certainly offer varying and equally plausible interpretations of past events that often mar decision making in the present (E. Haas, 1990, p.32).

Therefore, we can understand disputes within the Spanish Socialist Party over the likely effects on Spanish and European security if Spain were to join (and later exit) NATO. These disputes rest on different understanding of military history and Spanish defense. Finally, as political conditions change in established issue areas, inconsistencies between the ideas and interests may arise where before there was complete harmony (Kratochwil, 1989, p.62). The EC's evolving agricultural policy, for example, challenged Spanish agricultural interests that were formulated with the idea of Europe coming to Spain's economic salvation.

The sources and transmission of new knowledge

Having established what circumstances lead political elites to assimilate new political knowledge, we must examine the sources and means of transmission of this knowledge. Some psychological models argue that individuals, under the proper circumstances, are particularly susceptible to new information (Phares, 1976; George, 1979; Davies and Parasuraman, 1981; Fiske and Taylor, 1984; Kowert, 1992).[14] However, in this book I am interested in the formation of coherent policy over an extended period of time (E. Haas, 1980; Levy, 1994). Therefore, I do not attempt to predict how Spanish decision makers acted at certain specific junctures, and am not interested in knowledge defined as discrete information.[15] Rather, I intend to explain how Spanish leaders were socialized into European political reality over an extended period of time.

Furthermore, change of ideas and knowledge based claims reflect cultural socialization which cannot be reduced to individual cognition. As Charles Taylor writes:

> It is not just that the people in...society all or most have a given set of ideas in their heads and subscribe to a given set of goals. The meaning and norms implicit in these practices are not just in the minds of the actors but are out there in the practices themselves, practices that cannot be conceived as a set of individual actions, but which are essentially modes of social relation, of mutual action (Taylor, 1979, p.48).

Therefore, leaders may approach new knowledge claims not as personal predilections, but as constitutive of societal evolution. In this regard, leaders' ideas are connected to their perception of national, not personal, interests (Plamenatz, 1971, p.16; Scarbrough, 1990, p.103, Klotz, 1995, p.460). Therefore, to focus solely on the psychology of individuals in isolated situations ignores the larger societal setting (Bruner, 1986; J. Johnson, 1992, p.25).

In the case of NATO, the Socialist leadership accepted new knowledge that gave serious challenge to their preconceived ideas about the nature of the alliance. They did this with little psychological anguish because the new knowledge reinforced the ideas about European integration writ large with which all of Spain was so preoccupied. In the same vein, the Socialists accepted knowledge about their responsibilities in the EC despite the fact that this challenged short run Spanish interests. Spain's leaders confronted this new knowledge over the course of EC negotiations, not in a single situation, and it did not require immediate response by the individuals involved. Rather, it was framed within the idea of European integration that informed much of the political debate in Spain and which formed the basis of the PSOE's opposition to Franquism and eventual rise to power as a new set of political elite.

Additionally, we must take into account the sources of new knowledge over time. Knowledge is generated from all directions. But national leaders most likely will be exposed to, or learn from, knowledge to which political ideas have directed them (Coats, 1989, p.113). Joseph Nye shows how international regimes can contribute to learning by providing information and channels through which norms and principles are internalized by regime members (Nye, 1987, p.400; see also Argyris and Schon, 1978). More importantly, the type of problem with which leaders are presented will indicate the nature of the knowledge involved which, in turn, will indicate the source of advice they seek. For example, when politicians are assembling a political agenda that requires knowledge about current domestic initiatives, they might seek the advice of domestic policy advisors and aides. Likewise, problems of designing a political campaign that involve knowledge of electoral trends imply sources of this knowledge in the form of purveyors of polling data.

Closer to the focus of this thesis are complex problems requiring expert knowledge and implying sources of this knowledge in specialized communities (Spengler, 1970, p.143). These types of expert groups exist, for example, in economic policy-making (H. Johnson, 1981; Weir and Skocpol, 1985; P. Johnson, 1991) and scientific or environmental issue-areas (Gilpin and Wright, 1964; P. Haas, 1990; Peterson, 1992). Peter Hall and Kathryn Sikkink contend that these communities must be institutionalized within governments or international relations for them to be influential in the policy-making process (Hall, 1986; Sikkink, 1991). Indeed, institutions are not merely organizations where behavior is routinized, but cognitive constructs which shape actors sense of identity prior to observed behavior.

The Spanish experience with the EC and NATO involved foreign policy issues that necessitated knowledge of policies and preferences of the countries in question. This type of knowledge would be available not so much from expert or 'epistemic communities' (P. Haas, 1992), but through traditional diplomatic channels among and between the international political leadership (Singer, 1972; Barnett, 1993). Far more plausible than the notion that knowledge simply 'flows' to national elites or is 'made available' as a public good through international regimes, the concept of interpersonal channels would seem to conform more closely to observed fact.[16] As Robert Keohane writes: 'Effective intergovernmental regimes facilitate informal contact and communication among officials. Indeed, they may lead to "transgovernmental" networks of acquaintances and friendships' (Keohane, 1984, p.101). For example, in the Spanish case, the leaders of the Socialist government were in constant communication with key political leaders throughout Europe. These communication links were the means by which Spanish leaders were apprised of NATO and EC interpretations of priorities *vis-à-vis* Spanish membership in the two organizations. Thus, a focus on the interpersonal relationships and elite contacts of socialization is in order in this case.

John Ikenberry and Charles Kupchan identify three ways that norms may be internationally transmitted: First, norms are often transferred through normative persuasion, as core states transmit ideas to peripheral elites. Second, new norms might be transferred through external inducements. Third, core states may internally reconstruct peripheral states' domestic political institutions (Ikenberry and Kupchan, 1990, pp.290-293; see also Barnett, 1995). However, Ikenberry and Kupchan reduce socialization to power dynamics found more frequently in realist theories of international relations:

> Hegemonic control emerges when foreign elites buy into the hegemon's vision of international order and accept it as their own - that is, when they internalize the norms and value orientations espoused by the hegemon and accept its normative claims about the nature of the international system (Ikenberry and Kupchan, 1990, p.285).

The problem with this formulation is that one cannot easily disentangle true normative shifts from out-and-out coercion. A better approach is supplied by Thomas Risse-Kappen, who argues that 'the transnational promoters of foreign policy change must align with domestic coalitions supporting their cause in the "target state" to make an impact' (Risse-Kappen, 1994, p.187). More importantly, Ikenberry and Kupchan fail to see that true international socialization occurs when *both* 'strong' and 'weak' states - however these categories are defined - develop new international norms of conduct (Taylor, 1979, p.48). Thus, as knowledge about European integration was transmitted throughout Europe, Spain was an active participant in this constitution of political reality.

The importance of distinguishing ideas and interests: disaggregating international socialization

In the previous subsection I suggest that a socialization process characterizes interaction among states. Yet, we still must disaggregate the sequential steps by which actors translate international interactions into national foreign policy. As I argue above, leaders of any particular country approach foreign policy issues with a set of abstract ideas about the nature of politics that reflect historical memory, past circumstances, conceptions of national identity, and responses to perceptions of structural and systemic reality. A set of knowledge based claims underpins these ideas, but these claims are submerged during stable periods for the sake of convenience and the demands of normal daily politics. Leaders perceive political, economic, and security interests in light of these ideas that

37

guide their political undertakings.

If we apply this framework to the totality of interactions among states in an international system, we can conceptualize the international transmission of knowledge among states and how it affects the ideas governmental leaders have about international relations and their perceptions of interests. For an individual state interacting in an international system, internationally transmitted knowledge reconstitutes the relationship among domestic ideas, interests and preexisting knowledge based claims. We can expand this process, then, to represent for all states interacting in an international system the construction of international society over time. Just as domestic society is upheld by a reinforcing relationship among ideas, interests, and knowledge, international society is based on these three elements as well. When uncertainty or other conditions described in this chapter weaken these elements that hold together the fabric of international society, international society can be reconstituted through the transmission of shared knowledge among states much as this process occurs on the domestic level. This knowledge is supported by unifying ideas and shapes conceptions of material interests. Thus, the sequencing of steps involved in the construction of international society made up of many states is the same that which occurs for a single state socialized into the international system. This formulation helps avoid the nebulous way that international socialization is portrayed by most constructivist theories of international relations.

Finally, to paraphrase the title of Ernst Haas's book, in the construction of international society, countries need not be powerful in the sense of possessing economic wealth and military might, if *knowledge is power* (E. Haas, 1990). Spanish Socialist Party leaders in post-Franco Spain could be both international learners, and domestic policy strategists, if they couid successfully link new knowledge about European integration to the successful implementation of changed interests at home. And, as I will discuss in the conclusion to this book, the indication of a state's international power is measured by the degree to which its leaders monopolize agenda setting and the construction of consensual knowledge regarding the outcomes of foreign policy decisions. In short, the power of new knowledge emanates from its ability to allow leaders to reconcile ideas with interests in a coherent cognitive package from which policy ultimately flows.

Summary

In this chapter I have presented a theoretical framework to explain the formation of Spanish foreign policy towards Europe in the 1980s. Both structural international relations theories and rational actor approaches make rigid assumptions of interests and responses that do not capture what transpired in the Spanish case. The constructivist approach to international institutions assumes the importance of international norms in shaping national foreign policies, and is therefore a good starting point in developing a framework to explain the Spanish case. Still, it must be modified so that it can specify the steps by which established norms shape interests. Uncertainty and change can precipitate a process by which old ideas, knowledge, and interests become uncertain or come into doubt. When this happens, leaders may adopt institutionalized international norms through a process of learning. They may also share in the construction of intersubjective reality through the transmission of consensual knowledge based claims.

Two theoretical innovations are suggested in this chapter. First, the framework I develop specifies the steps between international norms and Spanish foreign policy using Spain's relations with Western European institutions as an example. Elites approach international relations with a broad set of abstract foreign policy ideas. These ideas are based on a set of knowledge based claims which reflect the country's recent or distant history, culture, and political memory. Perceptions of national interests are based on these ideas and claims. Interests may appear to be exogenously arising, but closer examination shows they are constructed along with leaders' political ideas. Then, as contact with the changing international environment increases, the reinforcing relationship between ideas and interests can weaken and uncertainty increases. Finally, knowledge about normative expectations in international institutions leads to a reconstruction of political ideas and interests along established lines. Policy creation is the outcome of this process.

Second, knowledge need not merely elucidate technical aspects of policy areas. Knowledge about politics itself, and the practice of international politics and diplomacy specifically, is a crucial link in the socialization process by which interests are constituted through ideas. What both of these insights demonstrate is that international socialization can be discerned empirically by disaggregating the steps by which it occurs and specifying the causal claims that underpin worldviews. In other words, specifying the distinction between ideas and knowledge, and treating knowledge as something more than technical expertise, provides the basis for empirical testing so necessary in this field of international relations research. The next two chapters provide this sort of empirical evidence in the case of European policy in post-Franco Spain.

Notes

1   Regardless of which approach to institutions one chooses, it is important to make a distinction with formal international organizations. The European Community and NATO are formal arrangements reinforced by organizational routines and rules which exist within institutions of socially constructed norms, but are not coterminous with them.

2　　　　Here, Keohane sees institutions as international regimes, which are value neutral mechanisms that provide a purely 'functional' role in fostering international cooperation (Keohane, 1984).

3　　　　'Our argument does not hinge on finding a neat alignment of domestic regimes along some apposite lines in one or more international regimes. Rather, we suggest that the shape and prospects of the former probably would be very different without the presence, characteristics and eventual accessibility of the latter...' (Heisler and Breckinridge, 1989, p.29).

4　　　　In order to avoid a lengthy debate on norms, I simply accept Martha Finnemore's definition of a norm as 'a rule-like prescription, which is both clearly perceptible to a community of actors and which makes behavioral claims upon those actors' (Finnemore, 1993, p.566, fn# 1).

5　　　　Goldstein and Keohane offer three categories of ideas: 1) 'Worldviews' ('conceptions...embedded in the symbolism of a culture'); 2) 'Principled beliefs' ('normative ideas that specify criteria for distinguishing right from wrong'); and 3) 'Causal beliefs' ('beliefs about cause-effect relationships') (Goldstein and Keohane, 1993, pp.8-10). The authors also posit three ways ideas influence politics: 1) Ideas as 'roadmaps' that help minimize uncertainty; 2) Ideas as solutions to coordination problems; and 3) Ideas embedded in institutions that 'play a role in generalizing rules and linking issue areas' (pp.13-24).

6　　　　There is ample support for the notion that the 'idea of Europe' exists only as an abstract generalization. As Paul Howe observes: 'European leaders have...directed attention to Europe's potential *future* as a thriving economic partnership, free of the internecine violence that had plagued the continent for much of the past few centuries....These ideas about the future have the same mythical qualities Smith identifies in the historical musings of nationalists: their focus is hazy,...they exaggerate fact, and they attach great political importance to the events they selectively highlight' (Howe, 1995, pp.31-32).

7　　　　As Manuel Blanco Tobío writes: 'One of the great motivations of the change [to democracy in Spain] was homologizing with Europe, with its democratic political system and its way of life. Europe, throughout the transition, has been the point of reference, the horizon of Spanish aspirations, and we were re-acquainted with her, following so many hates or indifference, like a date with liberty' (Blanco Tobío, 1979, p.214).

8   Kathryn Sikkink sums this up nicely: 'Ideas are the lens, without which no understanding of interests are possible. Ideas transform perceptions of interests' (Sikkink, 1991, p.243). See also P. Hall, 1989; Wendt, 1992.

9   In defining knowledge in this fashion, I create a separate word for what Goldstein and Keohane see as simply one category of political ideas (Goldstein and Keohane, 1993). In many ways, the choice of words is arbitrary. Goldstein and Keohane's third category of ideas - ideas as 'causal beliefs' - approximates my category of 'knowledge'. However I prefer the more explicit analytical distinction so as to isolate the influence that new knowledge plays in altering leaders' generalized images about the world and the interests they perceive support these images.

10   The closest Haas comes to this is a category loosely classified as 'operational' knowledge (Haas, 1990, p.23). This applies to organizing information about political problems (for example, nuclear energy). But it does not encompass something as broad as knowledge of the political world in which such 'problems' are embedded.

11   Therefore, Ernst Haas is incorrect when he argues that interests may be defined by *either* ideas *or* knowledge: 'Interests need not be informed by knowledge at all. Ideology may be the source of interest, unaided by any notion of technical information - structured or unstructured, consensual or disputed' (Haas, 1990, p.75). (Haas uses 'ideology' where I employ the term 'ideas.')

12   Because I take knowledge of the world to be based on claims of reality, people normally justify their ideas not by laying out every notion they have of cause-and-effect relationships, but by arguing that 'that's just the way things are.' However, they may be forced to re-examine their claims of reality if 'the ways things are' suddenly are not as they always have been.

13   Whether or not changed ideas are made to conform with existing interests, or if new definitions of interests are harmonized with existing ideas, the crucial role of knowledge is to re-establish harmony in instances where leaders perceive tensions between the ideas that guide policies and their interest perceptions. I would like to thank Peter Katzenstein for helping me with this formulation. For a case in which interests are altered although political perceptions of the 'self' remain the same, see Katzenstein and Tsujinaka, 1991, p.139.

41

14   I am grateful to Paul Kowert for his advice on this subject.

15   Ernst Haas argues that 'the term *knowledge* is more appropriate than *information* because it implies the structuring of information about whatever topic engages [an] organization in conformity with some theoretical principal' (Haas, 1990, p.74) (emphasis in the original).

16   Everett M. Rogers's landmark work, *Diffusion of Innovations*, which shows how new technological concepts or practices spread through the scientific community, is an apt analog for how political knowledge spreads. Diffusion of innovations takes place on several levels including interpersonal channels that are 'effective in persuading an individual to adopt a new idea, especially if the interpersonal channel links two or more individuals who are near-peers...' (Rogers, 1983, pp.17-18).

4 The NATO dilemma in Spanish foreign policy

The debate over Spanish membership in the North Atlantic Treaty Organization (NATO) represents the most divisive foreign policy issue in post-Franco Spanish politics. Whereas the period of democratic transition was marked by a surprising degree of consensus at both the elite and popular levels, the proposal of the government of the Unión del Centro Democrático (UCD) in 1981 to seek NATO status for Spain ruptured this consensus by introducing an issue over which Spanish leaders had fundamentally opposing views.[1] At the heart of the matter were deeply held ideas about Spain's relationship to the European and Atlantic defense apparatus. The perceptions of Socialist Party elites about Spanish defense interests were bound up with the ideas they had about Spain's proper role in European security matters.

In this chapter I will argue that the changes in the Socialist position regarding NATO membership were the result of a learning process that challenged earlier PSOE perceptions of Spanish defense interests. At the time when NATO membership was initially proposed, the Socialists' ideas about the alliance and their perceptions of Spanish defense interests formed a coherent whole. However this coincidence of ideas and interests became tenuous when the Socialists won control of the government. The new tension made the PSOE government leadership receptive to knowledge about how other NATO members evaluated Spanish membership in the alliance. Prime Minister Felipe González's 1984 ten point plan for Spanish security policy reflected the new situation, and the 1986 referendum on continued Spanish membership in NATO granted the government popular approval of its policies.

The Socialists' defense related interests and knowledge based claims about NATO

The situation of Spanish security

Spain's Socialist Party leaders perceived threats to Spanish security along traditional lines. Immediate security interests involved the defense of Spain's southern flank. Spain's two semicolonial enclaves of Ceuta and Melilla remain exposed to Moroccan irredentism (Marquina Barrio, 1985). Socialist Party militant Enrique Múgica acknowledged Spain's vulnerability along this front:

> In the north of Africa, Ceuta and Melilla could suffer diplomatic, economic, military, and even armed threats... At this time the Moroccan monarchy finds itself subjected to profound erosion by not accepting solutions to the difficult socio-economic problems posing the country and problems that exist as a consequence of the defeats it is suffering in its expansion into Western Sahara; this is not the first time that Hassan II has launched foreign adventures to redirect domestic attention and dissatisfaction that could break down his absolute power [at home] (Múgica, 1980, p.152).

Other security concerns of the Socialists included deterrence against African irredentist claims against the Canary Islands, defense of shipping lanes along the Canaries-Baleares axis (including the Straits of Gibraltar), protection of the Bay of Biscay, the creation of a domestic arms industry, and the devising of a unified defense strategy among the three services.

The Socialist leadership also was interested in preserving the Cold War balance of power in Europe based on the bipolar system. The Socialist position on non-alignment was framed by PSOE foreign policy architect Fernando Morán. According to Morán, this meant not shattering the equilibrium that existed between the two superpower blocs. Morán argued that if Spain stayed away from NATO, southwestern Europe would counterbalance Scandinavia in European security arrangements by Spain paralleling Sweden's self-declared neutral status (Morán, 1979, p.371). Formal Spanish membership in NATO would disrupt this bipolar balance and alarm the Soviet bloc.[2]

The PSOE's reasons why membership in NATO would not secure Spanish defense interests were summarized in the party's resolutions of the 29th Congress in October of 1981:

> 1. NATO does not guarantee the integrity of Spanish territory, in that the North Atlantic Treaty excludes parts of Spain's territory from the Atlantic defense system.

44

2. NATO does not cover Spain's security and defense needs, in that the scenarios of risk and threats facing Spain lie outside the purview of the Treaty.

3. Participation in NATO signifies an increase in the risk of the nuclear destruction of the Spanish people.

4. The expansion of NATO to include Spain would provoke the reaction of the other military bloc leading to the strengthening or enlargement of the Warsaw Pact and an increase in tensions and the risk of war in Europe (del Arenal and Aldecoa, 1986, p.312).

These were the elements stressed by PSOE leaders in parliamentary hearings on proposed NATO membership during the same month (Pollack and Hunter, 1989, p.100). The Socialists bolstered these arguments by drawing on knowledge based claims on what would transpire in Spain joined the alliance.

In PSOE thinking, Spanish needs in protecting its interests in northern Africa would not be insured in the event of Spain joining NATO (Treverton, 1986, pp.14-15; Preston and Smyth, 1984, p.19). According to Fernando Morán: 'We can advance the idea that if a conflict is presented as the result of a colonial situation, the Western countries - members of NATO or not - will not lend enthusiastic diplomatic support' (Morán, 1980c, p.146). The Socialists' interests of protecting Spain's territories on the northern coast of Morocco were bound with their distrust of American intentions. The UCD government had the same defense interests, but believed that they would better be served by Spain's inclusion in NATO. The Socialists' position differed fundamentally, arguing that the Americans would pursue their own agenda in northern Africa at the expense of local interests (Aguirre, 1983, p.37).

Other territorial interests that the Socialists thought would not be served by joining NATO included Spanish sovereignty over the Canary Islands. Here the logic was somewhat different from that concerning Ceuta and Melilla. It was not so much that NATO would not consider the Canaries an integral part of Spain - and therefore could not guarantee their defense - but that any connection between Spain and NATO would imply that the Canaries *were* part of the Atlantic Alliance. This, in turn, would provoke undue suspicion in neighboring African states. Fernando Morán explained the dilemma this way in 1979:

Our argument, shared with the representatives of the distinct Canaries political groups, is that the ascription of the Canaries to NATO would unleash a political campaign on the part of the countries of the OAU [Organization for African Unity], which would create a great deal of tension. The other possibility would be a NATO base [in the islands] which would convert the Canaries into an authentic aircraft carrier off the coast of Africa. The situation of the Canaries with respect to Cape Verde and Madeira would contribute to rarefy the situation (*El Socialista*, 14 October, 1979, p.8).

By referring to the American bases on Madeira and Cape Verde Morán presented NATO as a military organization devoted to far more than simply the defense of Europe, and presumably a creature of U.S. interests. He also assumed that Spanish membership in NATO would jeopardize Spain's traditional favorable standing with the African-Arab world (the Canaries are located off the coast of Mauritania). The idea that NATO simply reinforced an American agenda also jeopardized the Spanish interest of recovering Gibraltar. According to Fernando Morán: 'Procuring Gibraltar in exchange for it being a NATO base is to renounce Spain's own strategic role: it is perpetuating a situation of inferiority' (Morán, 1980a, p.106). The interest of securing the territorial integrity of Spain were therefore tied to the Socialists' belief that NATO was an inherently threatening organization to more than the communist world.

Spanish security and the European balance of power

PSOE opposition to NATO membership was also based on the party's perception of European defense realities. Spain had little to gain from involvement in either World War and, as the Socialists saw it, had no compelling interest in Cold War concerns which were the domain of superpower rivalries. To involve Spain in this context would run counter to Spanish interests and only embroil the country in disputes that were not its own. Felipe González argued:

> From a military strategic point of view, the incorporation of Spain into NATO would convert our cities, our towns, our communication links, our airports into principal targets of Warsaw Pact missiles without a single benefit in return, not military, nor in respect to our interior security, even less in the socioeconomic realm (*El Socialista*, 10-16 December 1980, p.9).

Ironically, the Socialists argued that Spain's bilateral defense arrangements with the United States would *not* make the country a primary target of Soviet attacks in the case of superpower conflict, presumably because maintenance of the existent defense treaties with the USA would not alter the European balance of power. Only the formal insertion of Spain into the NATO apparatus would violate the interests of keeping Spain distant from Cold War conflicts.

The Socialists thus made dire predictions of a disruption of the present balance of power in Europe if Spain joined NATO. In the first place, Spanish alteration of the current equilibrium would destabilize the bipolar balance of power, and destabilization of any kind would increase the likelihood of war. In the second place, Spain would pay a high price by alienating the Soviet Union and its allies (Morán, 1980a, p.120) Felipe González also presented the NATO decision in terms of the PSOE's perceived interest that the world would be better served by the absence of military blocs. His negative ideas about NATO dovetailed with this articulated interest:

> And there should not be the slightest doubt that we are against military blocs. Not against NATO specifically, I have said it a thousand times. Some people would like if we were opposed to NATO, but we are not. We are for the disappearance of military blocs. And naturally, in this philosophy of the disappearance of military blocs it does not seem logical to introduce ourselves into one... (*Diario de Sesiones del Congreso de los Diputados* {Comisión de Asuntos Exteriores}, 6 October 1981, p.1854).

It is interesting to note that González seemed to equate the disappearance of military blocs with the easing of East-West tensions. This was not an idea shared throughout Europe, where memories of the instability bred by multipolarity were still fresh.

Fernando Morán also argued that Spain should avoid becoming a satellite state in the Western defense system (Morán, 1980a, p.25). He argued that the West's isolation of Franco led Spain to pursue a foreign policy of 'substitution', exchanging relations with Spain's natural sphere of relations - Europe - for an idiosyncratic relationship with Latin America and the Arab world (Holman, 1996, pp.97-98). Nonetheless, Morán maintained these:

> Alternatives may have been created under specific circumstances does not mean that under the current circumstances - more genuine and adapted to Spain's social and cultural structure - cannot be developed and yield appreciable results.... Integration into NATO and the sacrifice of important dimensions of our possible foreign actions would not improve our international activity (Morán, 1980a, p.109).

The idea of avoiding satellization, then, was bound up with the sense that Franquist rule represented a period of lost opportunities, and that post-Franco Spain should not squander those opportunities by merely becoming an extension of superpower (i.e., American) interests. The PSOE therefore opposed Spanish membership in the Alliance based on the Socialists's unique vision of Spain as a neutral and/or non-aligned state.[3]

Spanish security and domestic politics

The Socialists' distrust of the U.S. also led them to believe that internal Spanish security interests would not be served by membership in NATO. Certain analysts had postulated that closer ties between the Spanish military and foreign armed forces would modernize the military and sway it away from internal political meddling (Ballarín, 1979). But the Socialists did not see how this could be possible, given that NATO was headed by the United States, which had been sympathetic to right wing dictatorships in Europe (Holman, 1996, p.111, fn#7). Fernando Morán argued:

> The Spanish Armed Forces do not need to enter NATO to demonstrate, as they are demonstrating, a composure and exemplary democratic sensibility. But, in any case, the Greek Colonels executed a *coup d'etat* in accordance with a NATO plan; the Portuguese army was a genocidal army when it was in NATO, and when Portugal rejected this system and installed different principles, it was not exactly due to a NATO doctrine, rather due to a doctrine which was not exactly NATO's (Morán, 1979, p.369).

By the same token, the PSOE did not think of NATO as an international institution supporting democracy. In the party's famous 1981 publication *50 Questions About NATO*, one question asks, 'Are all the members of NATO European countries with parliamentary democratic regimes?'. The answer, of course was 'no' - that authoritarian regimes like Portugal, Turkey, and Greece under the Colonels were all part of NATO whereas democratic Ireland, Switzerland, Sweden, Finland, Austria, Malta, and Cyprus all were not (*50 Preguntas Sobre la OTAN*, 1981, pp.5-6).

Therefore, the decision in 1981 by the centrist UCD government to seek NATO membership provoked concerted opposition by the PSOE. In light of the Socialist idea that NATO was an expression of American hegemony, PSOE Secretary General Felipe González laid blame for the government's decision on pressures from the United States.[4] Strangely, the Socialists' campaign against Spanish entry in NATO was waged under the purposefully ambiguous slogan: '*OTAN: de entrada no*' - a Spanish play on words which can mean either 'NATO: no to entry' or 'NATO: not at the outset', but implying maybe in the future. In fact, much has been made of this slogan by academic observers. Otto Holman argues that it was part of a PSOE strategy of 'calculated ambiguity' to allow the party to reverse itself at a later date (Holman, 1996, pp.103-104, 108-110). However, Javier Tusell argues that even with this ambiguity, 'without a doubt it was interpreted unequivocally as a testimony of pacifism and reluctance to involve Spain in a militarist NATO' (Tusell, 1988, pp.15-16). Furthermore, Benny Pollack and Graham Hunter argue that the PSOE's 'opposition was not based on ideological conviction but, following the advice of [Fernando] Morán, it resulted from an objective consideration of how both Spanish national interests and the cause of world peace would best be served' (Pollack and Hunter, 1987b, p.159). Thus, we can conclude that whereas the 'OTAN: de entrada, no' slogan was ingenious in hindsight because of its cheeky use of the Spanish language, a preponderance of the evidence shows that the cupola of the Socialist Party was genuinely opposed to NATO membership based on ideological conviction and perceptions of Spanish defense realities.

The breakdown of Socialist opposition to NATO

During the Socialists' early experience in office they were confronted with inconsistencies in the ways they thought about Spain's foreign policy orientation. The PSOE's opposition to NATO, for one, was based on its traditional dislike for American foreign policy. However, the other European members of NATO perceived the Alliance as a trans-Atlantic partnership whose task was the maintenance of peace in Europe. Given that the Spanish Socialists hoped to insert Spain into the European mainstream, the PSOE leadership soon saw inconsistencies in their vision of NATO which rejected the strong sense of partnership held by other European governments.[5] Even before the PSOE took office, its leaders contemplated how they could reconcile the party's anti-Americanism which was not shared by its European counterparts.

Additionally, the idea that Spain should refrain from military alliances conflicted with the history of Spanish decline during periods of isolation. This ambivalence between playing an active role in world politics and fear of the corrupting role of outside influences is a recurring motif in Spanish political culture. This was true in the twentieth century as in earlier times. As I mention in Chapter Two, Spain's self-imposed aloofness from European politics in the 1930s indirectly brought about German and Italian aggression in alliance with Franco's forces against the Second Republic (Carreras Ares, 1981). Furthermore, at the same time that PSOE leaders acknowledged the benefits of neutrality during both World Wars, they recognized that this neutrality came at the price of being excluded from post-war reconstruction. Felipe González noted the irony when he contrasted Spain's exclusion from the Marshall Plan on account of its fascist government with the lopsided 1953 USA-Spain defense treaty (*Diario de Sesiones del Congreso de los Diputados*, 28 October 1981, p.11394). The Socialists' prescription that Spain should now opt out of NATO thus came into conflict with their vision of modernization and democratization through increased external contacts.

The modernization-through-foreign-policy thesis was advanced by members of the UCD government and other parliamentary groups in favor of membership in NATO. For example, UCD Foreign Minister José Pedro Pérez-Llorca argued:

> Entry into NATO involves breaking with the tradition of isolation. And it also contributes to bringing a country to the point where it no longer is lost in self-absorption - meaning Spain's obsession with its own problems.

49

In my opinion, entry into NATO is a positive factor in raising up our country through the means of stability and normalcy (*ABC*, 8 September 1982).

At the same time that the Socialists' were suspicious of NATO, they were not insensitive to this argument. And this resulted in a degree of tension. Perhaps more important, the PSOE's foreign allies echoed the position of the pro-NATO forces within Spain.

The Socialists also had to reconcile the idea that Spain should avoid falling under the influence of the United States by joining NATO with the fact that Spain *already* was involved in a bilateral relationship with the USA by means of the 1953 defense treaty. Some Socialists began to argue that membership in NATO would give Spain a larger voice in deciding defense policy and lessen dependence on the United States. This was a theme argued by the pro-NATO forces in Spain. Foreign Minister Pérez-Llorca claimed:

> Entry into the Atlantic Alliance supposes a step in the direction of Europe, it implies that the relations of defense cooperation which up to now we have had only with the United States are going to be shared with a group of democratic, free, sovereign, and independent countries. ...[This step] inserts our bilateral relationship with the United States into a multilateral forum in which we can count on the contribution, help, and solidarity of interests of the European countries (*Diario de Sesiones del Congreso de los Diputados*, 28 October 1981, p.11387).

Six months before Felipe González's public endorsement of continued NATO membership, PSOE member of parliament José Miguel Bueno admitted:

> In such a situation of neutrality, without dedicating more budgetary efforts to defense than is now dedicated, Spain would have to modify its present defense model. It would have to adopt a model of *total defense* with armed forces equipped with fewer ground forces but supplied with more powerful and modern arms systems, with a more rapid mobilization plan, and with much more active air and naval defenses (Bueno y Vicente, 1985, p.216, emphasis in the original).

These realizations made the Socialist government re-examine the ramifications of membership in NATO as opposed to other options, which included bilateral ties with the United States and a unilateral defense position in Europe.

In this light, the PSOE leadership was faced with its previous conviction that NATO membership would jeopardize Spain's standing in the Third World and how this reconciled with their perceptions of Spain's immediate defense interests. In terms of the Third World orientation, the Socialists' political ideas reflected a radical past (Share, 1989, p.141). The PSOE represented the rise of a new class of political elites in Spain, a generation whose ideas about the country's place in the world were a function of its experiences under Franco (Pérez-Díaz, 1990; Rodrigo, 1995a, pp.59-60). Certain Spanish leaders favored the idea of Spain becoming more European while continuing to espouse the idea that Spain could speak for the concerns of underdeveloped Third World nations. The problem was that Spanish leaders perceived very real security threats emanating from north Africa, for one, and would be left alone to face these problems outside of the NATO framework. Therefore these leaders experienced uncertainty as to whether they could belong to both the European and non-aligned camps.

Socialist perceptions of NATO as a Cold War organization also contained no prescriptions for how Spain could carve out a security role outside this framework. The United States government's increasing willingness to negotiate the withdrawal of American forces in Spain made the Socialists take a second look at NATO as a source of collective defense. On the one hand, PSOE leaders had warned that Spanish entry into NATO would disrupt the European balance of power. On the other hand, neutrality was not a viable option and the PSOE had tied Spain's democratic fate to closer relations with Europe. As the leader of the Catalán party Convergencia i Unió (CiU) pointed out in the Cortes:

> Fifteen parliaments in the western world [the members of NATO] must each say yes for the membership of Spain in the Treaty organization to be ratified. Evidently, if these countries have any fear that this will provoke an alteration in the international system, capable of leading to a war that would affect them, very possibly one of them could say no. In this regard we depend on what this very important jury of fifteen says (*Diario de Sesiones del Congreso de los Diputados*, 28 October 1981, p.11367).

Since the Socialists' idea about Europe was based, in many respects, on the perception that Europe represented a sort of cure to Spain's political backwardness, they became uncomfortable opposing Spanish involvement in NATO on the grounds that it did not contribute to the process of democratization. To the contrary, they came to realize that destabilizing European peace would perhaps thwart their desire to tie Spain to European democracy.

Socialist leaders, looking in retrospect, recognized these inconsistencies and tensions. This was especially true in the period between President González's parliamentary speech advocating continued membership in NATO and the 1986 referendum. In a 1984 press conference with Belgian journalists, a reporter asked González: 'Sometimes I get the impression that Felipe González is a bit of a prisoner of Señor President of Government, as much in the personal aspect as in the political aspect, faced with the wishes and political ideals of hard reality ... no?' González's response was telling:

51

The second aspect is true, the first is not....I think that we must accept things as they are.... Between what is ideal for some and what one is obliged to do as President of the Government there is always a distance that must be traveled. And one always travels it with certain sadness, with certain personal drama....However, I think that one must assume the responsibility of the presidency of the government in function of what is the reality of the country without losing sight of what one perceives as utopia, but doing it realistically. I think that in this, we Socialists are obliged to conduct a type of internal revolution because we are becoming a little sclerotic with ideas....To be a conservative of the right is coherent; to be conservative with an ideology of the left is an internal contradiction (*Actividades, Textos y Documentos...*, March 1984, p.140).

PSOE elites recognized the task of convincing the electorate that the Socialist Party had changed its view owing to the contradictions it now acknowledged.[6]

New knowledge about Spain's responsibilities in Europe

The most important thing the Socialists learned about NATO was how their European partners thought about the alliance. Not having experienced foreign occupation in World War II, and not having been faced with the threat of Soviet aggression, the Spanish Socialists initially were insensitive to the perceptions of European NATO states that the Alliance was a positive feature in establishing post-war stability within the continent. To change this, European leaders shared with their Spanish counterparts their conviction that unity within NATO counted for far more than simply codifying American Cold War prerogatives.

Linkages between the Spanish decision on NATO and European security issues

European leaders argued that a Spanish withdrawal from NATO would injure the alliance. More important were the linkages the European leaders drew between defense issues and European integration broadly conceived. To begin to understand the PSOE leadership's change of heart, we need to look to Prime Minister Felipe González's visit to Germany in May 1983. On that trip, Chancellor Helmut Kohl and Foreign Minister Hans Dietrich Genscher asked for Spanish support on the deployment of U.S. Pershing II Missiles in Europe - the so-called 'Euromissiles' - and a Spanish commitment on NATO. Their argument to the Spanish leaders was this: Unless Spain tacitly supported the missiles and committed itself to NATO, it would cause a rift within the western defense alliance and aggravate the popular unrest in Europe over the deployment of the Pershings. In other words, a Spanish withdrawal from NATO would encourage the anti-Pershing demonstrators and give courage to other NATO members - most notably Greece - also to consider leaving the alliance.[7]

González's visit to Germany was preceded by a similar trip made by Foreign Minister Fernando Morán in February. In Bonn, Genscher made the same pitch to Morán as Kohl made to González. A senior member of Germany's diplomatic corps, who was present at the February encounter, relates that instead of berating Morán and threatening him with repercussions for Spain, Genscher moved the focus of the issue away from Spanish problems, putting it in terms of *German interests*. He told Morán that if Spain should leave NATO it would cause problems for the German government because it would send a very dangerous signal. For one thing, it would give *carte blanche* to the government of Andreas Papandreou in Greece to do the same thing. Second, it would send a signal to the restless pacifist public opinion movement in Germany right when the Euromissiles issue was a major political matter. Genscher was very concerned that the Euromissiles be deployed, and he linked this German interest to the PSOE's early opposition to Spanish membership in NATO. Genscher asked Morán: 'please, don't create difficulties for us'.[8] Although Prime Minister González was the first to appreciate the German point of view,[9] Morán's eventual acceptance of the German position was especially important since he (Morán) had been one of the most staunch opponents of Spain's entry into the alliance in 1982.[10]

Knowledge about the full ramification of a Spanish withdrawal from NATO was multi-faceted. In each instance, what was important was the understanding of the cause-and-effect relationship between Spain's threatened exit from the alliance and the repercussions for European politics. Fernando Morán demonstrated comprehension of this relationship regarding the repercussions for European governments with respect to the Pershings issue and the Spanish threat to withdraw from NATO:

> In the year of deployment of the [Pershing] missiles, 1983, which augured to be a tense year, a decision of this type [to decide to convoke a referendum on membership in NATO], with a referendum in process (which [the 'no' vote] would have won with 85 per cent of the votes), would have provoked an explosive effect in Denmark where the Parliament did not want the missiles deployed, perhaps in Greece, perhaps in Turkey...(*La Vanguardia*, 25 March 1984).

In other words, in early 1984 Morán was hinting that the Socialist government had already made the decision to continue Spanish membership in NATO *as early as the late winter/early spring of 1983*; that is, within the first six months of taking control of government (Treverton, 1986, p.11).

Of course, Spain had no direct involvement with the Pershing missiles and the PSOE, in its short period in office, had been able to minimize debate over the NATO issue. So opening up these issues seemingly was not in the interest of the

Spanish leadership. If anything, tacit support for the Euromissiles appeared to run against the PSOE's previously stated positions (George and Stenhouse, 1991, p.76). But González and his advisors understood fully the implications of threatening the unity of Europe. A Europe that lost unity would paralyze other areas of European integration and therefore almost assuredly slow down Spain's EC application process. A nonunified Europe also would offer far fewer benefits to Spain even in the event of Spain joining the Community. This argument was used subsequently by the government to justify its decision in the run-up to the 1986 referendum.[11] Thus, this new knowledge of the direct consequences of a Spanish withdrawal from NATO resonated with the Spanish leadership and, more importantly, enabled it to re-think the idea it had of the alliance as a function solely of American interests.

The Socialists showed themselves predisposed towards these arguments. While PSOE leaders might turn a deaf ear to American appeals to stay in the alliance, the cozy ties between the Spanish Socialists and their German counterparts made Bonn's appeal especially compelling (Maxwell and Spiegel, 1994, p.34). Furthermore, the splits in the Socialist government between hardline NATO opponents and more pragmatic members of the cabinet (Rodrigo, 1995a, p.61) began to dissolve as the repercussions of a NATO withdrawal became evident (Holman, 1996, pp.109-110). Even the initially anti-NATO Foreign Minister Fernando Morán changed his position. Speaking in Parliament, regarding increased superpower rivalry and public opposition to the installation of the Euromissiles in Western Europe, Morán declared:

> In these circumstances, the Socialist government will not do anything to debilitate, or give the appearance of debilitating, the West's position, and it will not do anything to debilitate the position of the Alliance, of which Spain is a member, not by its own will, but as a member as a matter of inheritance and succession of the previous government...(*Discursos y Declaraciones del Ministro de Exteriores...*, 1984, p.168).

This was not simply a piece of information that a Spanish withdrawal from NATO would jeopardize the alliance, but rather part of the larger learning process the PSOE leadership underwent as it confronted the political equation of popular opinion and stable foreign policy in Spain as in the rest of Western Europe (Mujal-León, 1986, p.227). Angel Viñas, advisor to Foreign Minister Morán, expressed this comprehension in a 1984 interview:

> I can think...of countries that see themselves confronted with relatively important opposition, although it may be diminishing, as is the case of the Netherlands, Denmark, or even England or West Germany; and [they] have faced this opposition in some cases calling new elections, as in Germany, England and Italy.... These countries would not look favorably

upon a Spanish government that withdraws from the Alliance. They would probably be disposed towards passing us the bill in one way or another (Albuquerque and Gomáriz, 1984, p.16).

Felipe González also spoke later of a learning process on foreign policy matters:

> The transition from a dictatorship, which carried with it a great deal of ideological accumulation, to a position which is the position of the European left in its entirety, maintaining the peculiarities each of us has, occurred in Spain in a very rapid fashion and was led by the Socialist Party (Calvo Hernando, 1987, p.182).

This learning process indicates how the Socialist leadership came to accept the European worldview.

Of course, one could argue that the major states within NATO simply exerted pressure on the Spanish government, threatening to withhold EC membership that if Spain withdrew from the Alliance. However, one should take seriously statements made by Felipe González:

> When one uses the word 'pressure' one is utilizing very heavy artillery. That which is confirmed is the satisfaction of European governments because we are in NATO...,[Some governments] might not like that we hold a referendum [on continued membership in NATO], it worries them and they are concerned, but they are extraordinarily respectful and tactful [on this matter] (*El Socialista* {Extra XXX Congreso}, 13 December 1984, p.3).

Indeed, what went on behind closed doors is hard to know, but Fernando Morán's memoirs give some indication. According to Morán, German Foreign Minister Genscher expressed understanding of the Spanish predicament at the same time as he stressed the importance of Spain staying in NATO. At the January 1984 meeting of the Conference on Security and Cooperation in Europe (CSCE) in Stockholm, Morán asked Genscher 'what importance do you Germany attach to Spain's permanence in NATO?' Genscher replied:

> If the previous Spanish government had not joined NATO, the issue would not be so important. There would be other ways to link Spain to the general interest. But if you leave now it would have more moral and political than military effects, of certain importance....But look, you must be in the Alliance in your own specific way....We need two things: defense and *detènte*. You must be [in NATO] in such a way that does not harm the Alliance, but that does not create obstacles to *detènte* (Morán, 1990, p.269).

55

This logic was repeated by PSOE member of parliament and Vice President of the Defense Commission in the Cortes, José Miguel Bueno, who stated publicly:

> One of the principal reasons why the other members of the Alliance argue [that Spain should stay in NATO] is that our exit would deliver a hard blow to the *morale* of NATO, which would translate into an increase in weakness and would carry with it a disequilibrium between the blocs that is neither desirable nor beneficial (Bueno y Vicente, 1985, p.218, emphasis in the original).

Bueno admits that Spain is 'constantly being *counseled* not to denounce the Atlantic Pact' (Ibid., p.218, emphasis in the original). Most important, however, is the fact that the government submitted NATO membership to a popular referendum *after* Spain joined the EC. Community states were advised that this would be the case.

Indeed, when speculating on the supposed pressure NATO states exerted on Spain to stay in the alliance, we should remember that Spain had some bargaining chips of its own. European members of NATO wanted Spain to remain in the alliance, after all. Spanish leaders could threaten to withdraw unless Spain's demands on EC membership negotiations were addressed (Marquina Barrio, 1991, p.41; Story, 1995, p.43). Spanish ambassador to Germany, Eduardo Foncillas, recalled that:

> Although the government and especially Fernando Morán wanted to keep both topics separated formally, in Germany they saw things differently. I think the Germans understood that if Spain did not enter in the EC it would have been difficult to keep her in NATO, and they were conscious that the Spanish political process had to culminate in the total integration of Spain into the Community (*El País*, 27 February 27).

Thus, the construction of European political realities was a process in which Spain was not necessarily the object of European power.

The new knowledge about the repercussions of a Spanish withdrawal from NATO also challenged the idea that Spain somehow did Europe a favor by staying out of the alliance. PSOE foreign policy experts, led by Fernando Morán, previously had believed that if Spain joined NATO it would disrupt the delicate equilibrium of Cold War Europe. However European leaders impressed on the Spanish leadership the importance of maintaining the alliance in the face of unrest over the deployment of the Pershing II missiles.[12] The Spanish Socialists were impressed by this reasoning and developed new ways of thinking about the European balance. Above all, the Socialist government gradually understood that the only way to ease Cold War tensions was through strengthening, not weakening, the Atlantic component of the bipolar system

(Bueno y Vicente, 1984, p.40). Speaking in Parliament prior to the 1986 referendum on Spain's membership in NATO, Felipe González argued:

> By being in Europe and in the Atlantic Alliance, Spain, in defending itself, defends Europe, and Europe, in defending itself, defends Spain. Security, in short, is guaranteed but, at the same time, permits us, as a sovereign country and as player of this European role, to act actively, decidedly, and in an autonomous fashion in favor of world peace in all conflicts that present themselves (*Diario de Sesiones del Congreso de los Diputados*, 5 February 1986, p.12036).

More to the point, Elena Flores argued:

> If no [international] equilibria were disrupted [when Spain entered NATO], then if we leave NATO, yes, certain equilibria will be broken. I am not saying that the politics of blocs will be weakened - I wish it were that way -, rather, the Atlantic Alliance will be weakened, with all the good and bad effects that may have (Arrojo, et.al., 1984, p.58).

The PSOE always had been opposed to military blocs and resisted Spanish membership in NATO on these grounds. By 1984, we can see that Socialist leaders no longer believed that Spain's status affected the existence of blocs but, rather, would cause international instability and jeopardize the position of the West.

The Socialist reversal on NATO and Spain's security dimension

Also important was what the Socialists learned from their European counterparts about the consequences of pursuing a neutral defense strategy outside of NATO. In September of 1984 Western foreign ministries were taken by surprise by renewed efforts by Lybia and Morocco to establish a union along the lines of the defunct United Arab Republic once forged between Egypt and Syria (Gillespie, 1995a, p.163). An article in *El País* cited an unnamed highly placed Socialist leader who argued that Spanish membership in the 'Atlantic Club' (NATO) would constitute a 'factor of dissuasion' in the case of any Maghrebi threat against Spanish interests in northern Africa. Official sources conceded that PSOE members had 'polled' the leaders of various countries concerning Spain's membership in NATO with regards to the Lybian-Moroccan initiative (*El País*, 4 September 1984, p.10). If the government wished to shore up its defenses of Spain's southern flank, then it might have to dispense with the sanguine notion that Spain enjoyed some sort of 'special relationship' with the Arab world. European leaders convinced the Spaniards that membership in an alliance of collective security took precedence over Spain's quirky policy towards North

57

Africa. Furthermore, Spain could ease tensions with its southern neighbors more easily through NATO than by relying on bilateral ties with the United States or attempting to deal with the Maghreb countries on a unilateral basis (Mujal-Leon, 1986, p.229).

Significantly, the treaty of friendship between King Hassan II of Morocco and Libyan leader Colonel Muammar Qadhafi revealed the web of reinforcing relationships among countries in Europe, North Africa, and North America, and Spain's place within this set of formal and informal alliances. As reported in the Spanish press, Qadhafi's visit to Morocco was designed to reconcile differences with the king and 'was based on a principle as realistic as this: 'You [Qadhafi] don't help the Polisario Front with arms and money, and I [Hassan] won't send my troops to Chad, as Reagan and Mitterrand ask me, to fight against yours"' (*Cambio 16*, 27 August 1984, p.46). The new friendship between Tripoli and Rabat put into stark relief Spanish foreign policy possibilities that depend on where Spain is positioned *vis-à-vis* NATO and other military and non-military alliances. Although few people took seriously the proposition that the Libyan connection would embolden King Hassan to order an assault on Ceuta and/or Melilla, a pair of journalists pointed out: "one must remember that for the Colonel [Qadhafi] the Canary Islands, Ceuta and Melilla are colonies to be liberated; and, although there are those who say the Colonel was only joking in bad taste, he also said the same about Andalusia' (*Cambio 16*, 10 September 1984, p.41). This talk conjured up historical memories in Spain of the Moorish occupation which lasted for over five centuries before the expulsion in 1492.

While few people in Spain took seriously the notion that Morocco's newly found friendship with Lybia would make an attack on Spain's overseas territories imminent,[13] there was a renewed sense that Spanish foreign policy could not be conceived outside the framework of regional defense institutions including NATO, or European organizations like the EC (López Garcia and Nuñez Villaverde, 1994, p.133). The United States and France for years had maintained steady support for Morocco but recently improved relations with Algeria. Meanwhile, tensions between Rabat and Algiers had festered owing to the latter's support of the Polisario Front which was fighting to liberate the Western Sahara from Moroccan control.[14] In its years in opposition, the Spanish Socialist Party supported the Polisario Front as part of its promotion of Third World liberation movements. The PSOE quietly moved away from the Polisario Front, however, when it took power and sought improved relations with Morocco. Yet, by moving away from its support of the Saharan rebels, the Socialist government in Spain risked its friendly relations with Algeria, the Polisario Front's main backer. The 1984 treaty between Lybia and Morocco, therefore, introduced yet another ball to those the Madrid government was already trying to juggle in its North Africa policy.

The European and Atlantic implications of the new fluidity of Maghreb politics was not lost on Spain's leaders. By 1984 the Socialists had begun to realize that

France would not allow Spain to join the European Community if the concessions for the latter's agricultural industry would injure North African economies. The Paris government maintained a studied diplomacy in Maghrebi affairs. The Libyan-Moroccan pact therefore presented new problems for France (*The Economist*, 15 September 1984, p.39). The Spanish leadership also wondered what the recent events meant for relations with the United States. Morocco was a firm ally of the USA, and the former Mayor of Melilla said that he was convinced that before King Hassan 'sat down...with Qadhafi, he had asked permission from the United States and, therefore, what happens will be what the Americans want' (*Cambio 16*, 3 September 1984, p.26).

Within this tangled web, the idea that Spain's 'special relationship' with the Arab world would enable it to pursue a foreign policy apart from the Atlantic Alliance gradually was revealed as an illusion. Elena Flores, a member of the PSOE's Executive Committee and specialist in foreign policy matters observed: 'Effectively, the defensive coverage of NATO does not extend to North Africa, but it can act as a factor of deterrence, because if there is a war in North Africa, the territory of peninsular Spain will be seen as affected, and that scenario is conceived within the Treaty' (Arrojo, et.al., 1984, p.64). Angel Viñas, one of Fernando Morán's top advisors wrote regarding defense strategies in the Western Mediterranean:

> Our political, diplomatic, economic, cultural, and military apparatus is adapted with the aim of deactivating or neutralizing the eventual centers of 'autonomous' conflict that might surface in that zone and 'negotiate' in and with the Atlantic Alliance the corresponding division of labor (Viñas, 1984a, pp.28-29).

Viñas's view reflects the changed way that Spanish leaders accepted a positive role for extra-Spanish forces in protecting Spain's southern security interests.

Assessment of the learning process

What the PSOE government learned about NATO was not simply individual pieces of information but a collection of interpretations that led to an understanding of cause and effect relationships in the sense described by Ernst Haas (E. Haas, 1990). As Pollack and Hunter write:

> The government sought to explain its conversion by declaring that in opposition they had not been fully conversant with all the facts relating to NATO membership. Prior to 1982 socialist defence policy had therefore been formulated without fully comprehending the profound implications of Spain remaining outside the alliance (Pollack and Hunter, 1989, p.102).

The entirety of what the Socialists learned and how this changed their ideas about NATO is summarized in a document issued by a special committee of the PSOE executive council formed in 1985 to examine the party's position on foreign relations. The section on NATO was designed to establish the arguments the party would make in the proposed referendum on NATO membership planned for early 1986, and is worth quoting at length:

> This project of peace and security responds to the process of reflection and experience of the Government, during which it has carefully analyzed the internal conditions of our country and its needs as much as its foreign projection and international circumstances.
>
> This process of reflection and experience of three years of our country in the Atlantic Alliance has permitted to verify that some of the considerations of our party made during the parliamentary debate over entry of Spain into the North Atlantic Treaty [October 1981] did not conform to reality.
>
> Thus, one can confirm that the membership of Spain in the Alliance has not implied any reduction in the exercise of our sovereignty nor our decision making capability. On the contrary, the possibility to exchange points of view within the system of periodic consultations with the allied countries has made it possible for our opinion to be heard and considered. From this one can derive the conviction that the defense of international peace and security can be more efficacious and active in a forum where Spain is present and can make its voice heard defending its interests and opinions.
>
> One can equally confirm that our membership in the Alliance has not affected our relations with third countries; we have reinforced our ties of friendship and cooperation.
>
> Our contention that the entry of Spain into the Alliance would alter the established equilibria did not take into account the situation of international equilibria beginning with the fact that Spain already formed part of the system of Western security through the bilateral agreement with the USA and that signing the North Atlantic Treaty did not add a single substantial change to the de facto situation.
>
> On the contrary, an eventual exit of Spain from the Alliance *would* suppose a political alteration of the equilibria established with our entry and, by consequence, an increased fragility of the Atlantic Alliance in favor of the Warsaw Pact.

In other words, the policy of defense which has as its objective national security cannot be conceived in isolation, rather it must contemplate wider considerations of a political nature, of arms control, and in conclusion, of countries cohabitating [despite] differences (*Una Política de Paz y Seguridad Para España*, 1985, pp.40-41).

These 'findings' represent a stunning admission by top officials within the PSOE executive that what they learned about NATO fundamentally challenged their previous beliefs.

Outcomes of the Socialist government's learning process

Ideas about NATO and Europe

Having assimilated this sort of knowledge, the Spanish Socialists had to reassess their ideas about NATO. First, the PSOE government no longer perceived of NATO solely as a creature of American domination. Rather, the Socialists thought of NATO as a function of increased European unity. Responding to the arguments of an opposition leader in the Spanish Cortes during the debate over the proposed NATO referendum in 1986, Felipe González proclaimed:

Again you are endeavoring to confuse things... saying that NATO, in essence, is thought of as a payment for services that one must give to the Americans, or that the Americans are hegemonic in NATO by virtue of their power. But it is the Europeans who solicited the creation of the Atlantic Alliance, and not the reverse (*Diario de Sesiones del Congreso de los Diputados*, 5 February 1986, p.12032).

The PSOE leadership previously believed that NATO was an American dominated military alliance, unconnected to other facets of European integration. This changed so that the PSOE government now saw NATO linked inextricably to the process of creating new European institutions.

As the preceding section on the PSOE learning process suggests, the greatest connections were with the European Community. Following González's October 1984 pronouncement of his 'Decalog' on Spanish security he appeared on British television saying that although entry into the EC did not imply integration into NATO's integrated military command structure: 'Nonetheless, I admit as logical that, when one wants to share the destiny of a group of countries like those in Western Europe, one shares it in all senses, including those that refer to security and defense' (*El País*, 20 November 1984). The message that González conveyed, and that he hoped to use later to persuade Spaniards of the wisdom of his decision, revolved around the idea of NATO as an integral part of constructing the European project. González further maintained that there was no direct connection between NATO and the EC:

> I think there is not a single linkage [between membership in NATO and the EC] from the juridico-institutional, juridico-political, or juridico-international point of view....[The logic employed] is the following: if you want to participate in the economic-political-social-cultural institutionalization of the countries of Western Europe, from here one logically derives that you would also want to participate in the problems of collective security of Western Europe. This reasoning is difficult to refute logically, but each country dispatches it in function of its interests and sovereignty (*Actividades, Textos y Documentos...*, November 1983, p. 1062).

Spain's prime minister continued to assert Spanish interests, but presented a vision of NATO that contrasted starkly with the previous ideas he expressed about the alliance.

One of the most striking changes made by the PSOE leadership in its thinking about Europe was the original idea that European economic and security integrations could somehow be treated separately. In the widely distributed 1981 party publication, *50 Questions about NATO*, the PSOE maintained:

> It is not necessary to be a member of NATO to join the Common Market. They are too different things. NATO is fundamentally a military organization. The Common Market is basically commercial and economic. The [UCD] government conditioned its entry into NATO on Spain's membership in the Common Market. To relate both things is an error of principle and to publicly utilize the trade-off and its fundamental change of decisions constitutes a political and diplomatic peccadillo and a fraud played on the public (*50 Preguntas Sobre la OTAN*, 1981, pp. 6-7).

As we have seen, the PSOE would reverse itself completely on this logic. Regardless of American dominance over NATO, and regardless of the peculiar nature of the EC as a tariff union, the major European powers always intended that increased economic integration would improve the chances for peace in Europe. They also continued to believe that the American military presence could insure the peace necessary for economic progress.

The Europeans did not threaten to exclude Spain from the EC because they believed that Community membership was essential for the consolidation of democracy in Spain. On the other hand, continued Spanish membership in NATO was not critical to Alliance defense strategy. Rather, Spain's withdrawal would do more to damage the internal morale of NATO and exacerbate growing political cleavages within the Alliance than undermine its military strategy

(Treverton, 1988, pp.136-137). The European leadership conveyed to the PSOE government the interconnected nature of all these elements: The importance of maintaining cohesion within NATO to foster the unity of Europe, the unity of Europe as a precondition for successful economic integration, and the beneficial aspects economic integration would have on consolidating democracy in Spain. Therefore, the Socialists' perception of NATO as a security institution with no relationship to other aspects of European integration (especially economic aspects) was no longer operative in light of this new knowledge.

Ideas about Spain's place in the world

The Socialists also were able to discard the idea that Spanish membership in NATO would jeopardize Spain's ability to act as a voice for developing nations' concerns or its special relationship with Latin America and the Arab world. Increased ties with Europe meant linkage among economic, defense, political, and social issues. The more the Spanish government tied its fate to European integration, the more it would rely on European security institutions to solve its defense problems, especially relating to north Africa. This led to a diminishing of the PSOE's non-aligned project.

In addition, confronted with what a Spanish withdrawal from NATO would mean to European security, the Socialist government no longer believed that Spanish membership in the alliance disrupted the existing balance of power. The PSOE leadership always had an interest in maintaining the peace in Europe. But it believed that Spanish inclusion in NATO would be counterproductive to that end. After learning about how the major European powers viewed the situation, especially as regards their own internal problems, the Spanish Socialists experienced a change of heart.

Resolving the tension between ideas and interests

The decision to maintain Spanish membership in NATO signaled a change in PSOE ideas about the Western defense alliance. This change resolved the tension the Socialists experienced when they began to realize that opposition to NATO ran counter to Spanish defense interests. The Socialist government continued to direct resources and attention to core Spanish security areas, primarily the defense of the southern flank, control over Ceuta and Melilla, and protection of sea lanes along the Canaries-Baleares axis.[15] The assumption that NATO membership would lead to increased concern paid to East-West tensions and Cold War military priorities was not fulfilled. On the contrary, the codification of Spain's membership in NATO allowed the Spanish government to pursue reductions in the American military presence in Spain. President González also re-stated his insistence that Spain would not belong to NATO's integrated military command structure because it would reduce Spain's freedom of action in protecting its traditional security interests.

In fact, one of the things the government leadership learned during the first period in office was that the United States and other NATO countries were not insistent that Spain become part of the Integrated Military Command Structure. According to a senior military official in Spain, although Spain's NATO counterparts were happy that Spain stayed in the alliance, they reassured Spanish leaders that the best solution for everyone was for Spain to remain outside of NATO's military command.[16] From May 1982 on, there were many negotiations between Spain and NATO on this issue. All of the strategic command areas to which Spain had an interest were already jealously guarded by other NATO countries. The United Kingdom had control over the Straights of Gibraltar (GIBMED), Portugal had control over IBERLANT, and France had control over the defense of the Bay of Biscay (Heiberg, 1983). In addition, countries Italy, Greece, and Turkey had protected strategic command interests that would come into play if the Integrated Military Command Structure issue was re-opened. Therefore, for NATO and Spain alike, it was just as well that Spain stayed out of the integrated command. The military commands are not purely military. They have political backdrops as well. Spain would have opened a Pandora's Box by looking for changes in the integrated military command structure. If Spain were to take control over one or more of the strategic commands in its purview, then the UK, Portugal, France, and even Greece and Turkey would have had to face changes that challenged their traditional interests. No one wanted this. In other words, by staying out of the Integrated Military Command Structure, Spain actually reinforced the unity of the European status quo in NATO. Spain's non-participation thus resolved many problems of NATO unity.

An additional security interest articulated by the PSOE Foreign Minister Fernando Morán was that Spain should not disrupt the balance of power between the two military blocs. Originally the Socialists argued that to maintain this equilibrium Spain should not join NATO. Later they declared that this interest could only be secured if Spain stayed within NATO.[17] Foreign Minister Morán put it this way:

> The decision that ultimately will be taken shall be, in the Spanish government's opinion, that which produces the greatest benefits to Spanish national interests. But it is necessary to underline that Spain does not have a narrow or provincial conception of these interests: Spain is part of Europe and the Western world, and one Spanish national interest constitutes the contribution, for one thing, to peace and stability of Europe and to Western security for another (Morán, 1984a, p.27).

In terms of strategies to insure European stability, a senior PSOE theoretician related in an interview for this project that staying in NATO could have beneficial effects: In the long term, PSOE leaders could see that by strengthening Europe's defense they could strengthen Spanish interests by advancing the causes of *detènte*, disarmament, etc. These were the long term benefits of 'globalizing' Spanish interests by staying in NATO.[18] Thus we see that not only did the interest of not disrupting the existing balance of power remained the same, but was now situated within a broader conception of means for advancing it.

Alongside these interests of international security, other defense related interests perceived by the Socialists were reconciled with the PSOE's new conception of Spain's place in European security. One important interest was the modernization of the Spanish armed forces. In addition to modernizing the armed forces through subjecting them to governmental authority, orienting troop deployment away from internal control to potential external threats, and putting into place a plan of modernization and professionalization, former Defense Minister Narcís Serra suggested that a fourth measure involves greater opening to foreign influences:

> Any process of homologization requires mutual acquaintance [and] contact. In accord with the process of incorporation of Spain in the European Community, we have designed a plan of aligning Spanish with European defense and initiating contacts and signing bilateral accords with almost the totality of the democratic countries of Europe (Serra, 1986, p.177).

This change of strategy to meet constant interests could not have occurred had the governmental leadership not thought about NATO in new ways.

Conception of new policy and PSOE strategy

Felipe González's 'Decalog'

The resolution of the tension between ideas and interests through the assimilation of new knowledge was expressed in the Socialist government's policy agenda in defense matters in general and towards NATO specifically. The policies adopted were spelled out in Prime Minister González's 1984 State of the Nation address as enumerated in the so-called Decalog (*Diario de Sesiones del Congreso de los Diputados*, 23 October 1984, pp.7069-7070). This ten-point manifesto had the following components:

1) Spain should remain a member of NATO

2) Spain need not be incorporated into NATO's Integrated Military Command Structure

65

3) The USA's military presence in Spain should be reduced gradually

4) Spain's policy of prohibiting nuclear weapons in its territory should be continued

5) Spain adheres to the Comprehensive Test Ban Treaty and allows inspections by the International Atomic Energy Agency which is sufficient, but the government does not exclude the possibility of signing the Nuclear Non-proliferation Treaty

6) Spanish participation in the Western European Union is desirable, though not pressing at this point

7) Advances must be made to return Gibraltar to Spanish sovereignty

8) Spain must continue actively pursuing global disarmament

9) Spain is, and should continue, developing bilateral defense cooperation agreements with other European countries

10) The Unified Strategic Plan that Spain is devising should form the basis of consensus in internal and extern: defense matters.

These policies do not reflect any major alteration in Spanish defense interests as perceived by the Socialist government. The return of Gibraltar, the nuclear-free status of Spain, the reduction of the American military presence, and development of a unified Spanish defense plan were all interests articulated by the PSOE before it took office and before it changed its position on membership in NATO. The other points of the Decalog show that the Socialist government felt Spanish defense interests could be served even when NATO membership figured into the equation. But the ideas about European security enunciated by González in the Decalog do indicate a major shift away from the past. The decision to stay in NATO clearly reflected the diminishing, if not the disappearance of the Socialists' hostility towards the Alliance.

The 1986 referendum on NATO

Prime Minister González's 1984 Decalog represented the first time the government publicly advocated continued Spanish membership in NATO.[19] No further action by the government was necessary to formalize the status quo. Yet González insisted on following through on his 1982 campaign promise to hold a referendum on the question of Spain's status in NATO. This was a gamble on the part of a leader who had staked his political career on avoiding such direct confrontations with public opinion. Furthermore, what may have been an electorally advantageous strategy in 1982 turned out to be a serious liability later in the PSOE government (Treverton, 1986, p.12). Public opinion figures indicated that at the time the government reassured its NATO allies on the Pershing issue (and began its public move towards advocating staying in the alliance), a majority of Spaniards had reservations about Spain's continued membership in NATO.[20]

One of the key foreign policy planks of the PSOE's October 1982 campaign platform was a promise to hold a popular referendum on Spain's recent (May 1982) entry into NATO. The PSOE attached no specific date for the referendum but in its campaign document vowed that, should the party win control of government, 'it will at a first moment freeze the negotiations on [Spain's] integration into [NATO's] military organization. At a second moment, it will uphold the promise made by the PSOE to convoke a referendum so that the Spanish people may decide the issue of our membership in NATO' (*Por el Cambio*, 1982, p.47). However, upon assuming power the PSOE government leadership decided to postpone indefinitely the promised referendum. In a March 1983 press conference Prime Minister González argued that:

> When someone...agitates, and gets in a hurry, about this question [NATO], I must say that, having made the decision to brake the military integration [into NATO's unified command structure] we will take the necessary time to study our defense needs and, naturally, so as not to harm the interests of that part of the world in which we are included. We do not want to create any added disequilibria or tension. We will have the patience to produce a decision of the highest responsibility for this government (*Actividades, Textos y Documentos...*, Año 1983, p.221).

Assuming that the argument presented in this chapter is correct and that government leaders had decided by mid-1983 that Spain should remain in NATO, then we can assume plausibly that González and his advisors decided to delay the referendum so as to convince the Socialist Party and the electorate of the wisdom of this decision.[21]

By 1984 the government was deeply divided over the NATO issue. Supporting González's pro-NATO position were Defense Minster Narcís Serra and Economics Minister Miguel Boyer, whereas González was opposed by his confidant and Deputy Prime Minister Alfonso Guerra, and cabinet ministers Javier Solana (Culture), José María Maravall (Education), Ernesto Lluch (Health) and Luis Yáñez, the director of the Instituto de Cooperación Iberoamericano (Mujal-Leon, 1986, pp.221-222; Rodríguez, 1988, pp.64-65; Rodrigo, 1995a, p.61; Holman, 1996, p.109). The governmental leadership also had to win over dissenting factions within the PSOE. This was accomplished at the 30th Congress of the PSOE in December 1984.[22] The PSOE leadership had done such a good job at creating anti-NATO feelings in the 1970s and early 1980s that a sizable portion of the Socialist Party was strongly opposed to Spain staying in the alliance. González's attempts at winning over or purging anti-NATO voices in the Socialist Party actually helped accomplish one of his interests: presenting the PSOE as a party of state interests as a means of displaying the PSOE's maturity and undercutting the opposition. González argued: 'The Government of the Nation has a national responsibility to transcend the limits of its own party and, consequently, to have the floor to say, and in due course the President will say, in the defense of what I think are the legitimate national interests' (*El País*, 15 September 1984, p.11).

In addition to needing to convince his own cabinet and party of the need for Spain to remain in NATO, González could not count on public support for his position. During the PSOE's campaign against NATO membership the party created an anti-NATO sentiment among the masses that was difficult to reverse. González continued to delay the referendum, waiting until March of 1986. Yet, as late as 23 February 1986 a poll in *El País* showed only 25.2 per cent of respondents in favor of continued Spanish membership in NATO with 34.2 per cent against, 17.9 per cent vowing to abstain, 19.1 per cent answering don't know or no answer, and 3.6 per cent expressing no opinion (*El País*, 23 February 1986, p.14). The right of center opposition party Alianza Popular (AP) party hoped to derail the entire referendum process by calling for massive abstention from the planned popular vote. The intention of the AP's leader, Manual Fraga Iribarne, was to de-legitimize the PSOE government by calling on people to stay away from the polls.

The decision by the government leadership to convoke the referendum therefore was a risky gambit designed to win approval for its actions. Public opinion polls continued to show that the pro-NATO position was not accepted by more than half the electorate and many of González's close advisors tried to convince him not to hold the referendum.[23] In this regard, the popular vote on NATO soon became less a test of the government's decision on NATO than a referendum on the PSOE's record in office. The question as put to the public in the referendum read: 'Do you consider it expedient that Spain remain in the Atlantic Alliance according to the terms established by the Government of the nation?' If the 'yes' vote prevailed, then the Socialists would have a mandate to continue their policies and would be strengthened for the 1986 general elections.

The government played on Spain's recent accession to the European Community in order to stress the good work it already achieved and the linkages between the benefits Spain would receive through membership in the EC and the need to fulfil Spain's European obligations. Thus, as Benny Pollack and Graham Hunter point out, the government attempted to harness a '*voto de miedo*' (vote of fear), warning that 'abandoning NATO would be detrimental to the modernisation and future well-being of the Spanish economy' (Pollack and Hunter, 1989, p.104). Speaking in Bilbao, Economics Minister Carlos Solchaga argued that 'it is not likely that we would have the same treatment from those who are now our partners in the EC if our position were to withdraw the promises that they understand we are obliged to maintain in the realm of security' (*El País*, 1 March 1986, p.17).

However, one should remember that this '*voto de miedo*' strategy was implemented *after* Spain was firmly within the EC. Therefore, the strategy of the government was to solidify its domestic hegemony, rather than try 'play the NATO card' against its EC partners. Felipe González later confirmed the supposition that, had the government lost the referendum, he would have lost his mandate to govern. Yet he contended it was more important that the Spanish public not make the wrong decision:

> [In the event of a 'no' vote] I would have ended my mandate, and I would not have undertaken the task of carrying out what the 'no' implied. Not because I would dare to defy [public opinion], but because I think it would be the wrong path for Spain. And I think there must be some coherence in a democracy [between what the people want and what the leaders do] (Calvo Hernando, 1987, p.184).

If González was able to convey his beliefs about what was best for Spain to a domestic audience, then this strategy would be deemed a success. It was a risky strategy precisely because it was based on the government's beliefs, and not on a firm preexisting base of support for Spanish membership in the alliance.

As with the PSOE's appeal to the left in the immediate post-Franco period, the moderation of the party's positions must be understood as part of a fundamental ideological shift, where the capturing of voters was an outcome and not the linchpin of some opportunistic strategy.[24] In other words, the PSOE leadership was motivated by ideological considerations that now were reinforced by its interests in holding onto the Spanish electoral center. The PSOE was confronted with the task of changing public opinion on NATO to establish consensus around the government position. The degree to which this flexibility, pragmatism, or confusion could be translated into policy is a reflection of the PSOE's success in transmitting what it learned to the voters.

The PSOE won a 'yes' vote on continued NATO membership in the 12 March 1986 referendum by the slim vote of 53 per cent in favor, 40 per cent opposed, and 7 per cent of the ballots invalid; however, only 60 per cent of the electorate turned out to vote. This represented the outcome of skilled salesmanship by the government leadership to a suspicious population. The point simply is that the enactment of NATO policy reflected elite level decisions that later were submitted to the public for approval, but only *after* government leaders undertook a campaign to convince the public of correctness of these policies. However the government was not entirely successful in silencing all potential criticism, as the referendum campaign showed.

Summary

Appreciating the sequence of events in the Socialist government's shift on NATO requires first understanding how the PSOE leadership thought of NATO before it came to power. The Socialist elite equated NATO with American domination. In addition, the clandestine origins of the Socialist leadership fostered a belief in the dependency and non-alignment theories which were in vogue with the political left of the day. Finally, the PSOE's foreign policy brain trust, led by Fernando Morán was convinced that Spain must stake out an independent foreign policy in a bipolar Europe. Given its generalized suspicion of the United States, its education in Marxist Third World teachings, and their belief that Spain did not belong within the European system of military balances the PSOE leadership therefore could not conceive of a democratic and socialist Spain in the Western military sphere. These ideas reinforced PSOE security interests which revolved around knowledge based claims of maintaining Spain's autonomy to deal directly with immediate security threats and avoiding military entanglements or becoming a satellite of NATO or the United States.

These ideas, interests, and knowledge-based claims shaped the Socialists' position on NATO from the vantage point of political opposition. When the PSOE took office its leadership was confronted with the way other European states conceived European integration. The governments of these states did not construe integration in the same compartmentalized fashion as the Spanish. To them, the creation of the European project not only linked together economic and security matters, but also forged a new European identity based on norms of unity around which these issues would be decided. Therefore, the European states did not see a possible Spanish withdrawal from NATO as a purely defense related move. Rather, they perceived that it threatened the larger project of European union.

For the Spanish government, this was not merely information about what would happen to Spain if it left NATO. European states refrained from making direct threats to withhold EC membership should Spain leave the alliance. Moreover, the immediate effects of a Spanish withdrawal would be felt not in Madrid but in other European capitals, where the governments would be faced with similar anti-NATO sentiments among electorates which had grown dissatisfied with increased Cold War tensions of the early 1980s. Faced with popular unrest, European governments would be distracted from efforts to create economic and political union within the EC and other regional institutions. Therefore, the negative ideas the Spanish leadership had about NATO - ideas based on a distrust of American military hegemony - were replaced with the knowledge that NATO meant far more to the leaders of other European states. Most importantly, they were faced with the knowledge that disruption of unity within the alliance would create a potential domino effect by which European consensus on a whole host of issues would come under attack.

Replacement of the PSOE's perceptions of NATO with knowledge about how the alliance was part of the larger project of European integration constituted a process by which Spanish leaders came to share their European partners' socially constructed reality of linkages among seemingly disparate issues. They no longer viewed NATO negatively, nor did they see continued Spanish membership in NATO as inherently damaging to Spain's defense needs. The sequence of events also reveals how the Socialist government operated ahead of public opinion and actually was able to use the temporary lag between elite and mass perceptions to further its domestic political interests. The Socialists were forced to convince the electorate to back continued membership in NATO, but by doing so they were able to present the party as a mature party of state able to cope with issues affecting the national interest. The government's definition of the national interest was codified by the yes vote on the NATO referendum, establishing a precedent which has enabled it to act in a similar fashion on other pressing foreign policy matters.

Notes

1   Fernando Rodrigo argues that the notion that there was consensus surround Spanish foreign policy in the immediate post-Franco period is a myth that is not supported by the facts (Rodrigo, 1995, pp.50-52). While I agree with Rodrigo's assertion, the myth is still widely accepted by Spaniards who opposed the decision by the UCD government in 1981 to pursue NATO membership.

2   To the claims the PSOE made against NATO membership, Richard Gunther adds that the Socialists were opposed to the economic costs of modernizing the military to meet NATO standards and that NATO membership would not only contribute nothing to Spanish security, but would also jeopardize European peace and Spain's relationship with Latin America (Gunther, 1986, p.26).

3   The resolutions of the PSOE's 1981 party congress described Spain as 'a western European nation, a middle-to-high power, linked historically and culturally to a large continent which is Latin America [Iberoamérica], and with good relations with the Arab world' (del Arenal and Aldecoa, 1986, p.313).

4   Felipe González took pains to point out that the Spanish government's decision to join NATO took place fifteen days after the Reagan administration took power in Washington (*Diario de Sesiones del Congreso de los Diputados*, 27 October 1981, p.11337).

5   Reflecting on this period, PSOE theorist Ludolfo Paramio observed later: 'It is said that the dictatorship, having disappeared, it is not easy to know who is the enemy; and for lack of something better, NATO and the United States appear to offer that point of reference against which we can define ourselves. Naturally, this creates a serious problem: A country that is evidently Western in its social and political schema, and can in the short term accentuate these characteristics even more with its integration into the EEC, should now define the identity of its left by taking an "anti-Western" position' (Paramio, 1985, p.4).

6   Writing in 1985, leading PSOE theoretician Ludolfo Paramio argued: 'It is a paradox but it is this way: those who think that the PSOE has moved to the right look for a unifying identity in the form of anti-Americanism and anti-Westernism' (Paramio, 1985, p.4). This anti-Westernism, apparently, was no longer viable.

7   At a 1984 meeting with leaders of the Catalán Socialist Party, Defense Minister Narcís Serra argued that one of the reasons the government was inclined to maintain NATO membership was the fear manifested by certain other European governments that a Spanish withdrawal would produce similar movements in their countries (El País, 27 November 1984, p.1).

8   This information was related to me in a personal interview with a senior member of Germany's diplomatic corps. This account was corroborated in an interview I conducted with a former Minister in the Socialist government. European leaders asked Felipe González's government: 'How can we accept the Euromissiles - with all the domestic opposition we face - and not expect Spain to carry its share of the defense burden?' Apparently Spanish leaders came to see that the answer to this question was that Spain must carry its burden by staying in NATO.

9   In 1984, Felipe González justified the softening of Socialist anti-NATO rhetoric arguing: 'what worries us is facile demagogy that results from not being directly affected by an issue [the Euromissiles] and initiating a campaign for domestic consumption that hurts our allies' (Actividades, Textos y Documentos... March 1984, p.139).

10   Following González's May 1983 visit to Bonn, the Spanish press reported tensions between the Prime Minister and Fernando Morán. Morán was said to be displeased with the evolution towards a pro-NATO position. He admitted that differences existed within the cabinet, yet conceded that, as far as the Euromissiles were concerned, 'one must be careful not to inconvenience the Germans on this issue' (Cambio 16, 6

June 1983, p.35).

11   For example, Defense Minister Narcís Serra claimed in 1985: 'Access [to technological knowledge] would be reduced, not to zero, but to a considerable degree, if we were not a member of the Alliance. That is to say, to have important industries, not only from the point of view of jobs, but with advanced levels of technology to produce other items other than arms systems, passes through integration with Europe and remaining in the Alliance' (*El País*, 20 January 1985).

12   West German Chancellor Helmut Kohl used strikingly similar logic in explaining why Germany should not leave NATO: 'Whoever today looks for unilateral disarmament of the West and the Federal Republic's exit from NATO to avoid the threat [of war] will only succeed in destroying the equilibrium that assures peace in the face of the power of a totalitarian system' (Kohl, 1983, p.88).

13   Fernando Morán devotes only one paragraph in his memoirs to the Hassan-Qadhafi meeting at Oujda (Morán, 1990, p.359). He argues that the new alliance caused more alarm in the media than in official circles, and that the government situated the Lybia-Morocco initiative within larger developments in northern Africa.

14   In the Spring of 1975, King Hassan II orchestrated the 'Green March' to wrest control of the Spanish Sahara from Spain. Faced with the domestic crisis of Franco's failing health, Madrid hastily decolonized the territory during the winter of 1975-76. A treaty granted interim administration to Mauritania and Morocco until a permanent status for the Western Sahara, as it was renamed, could be found. However, the Algerian backed Polisario Front demanded immediate and full independence. Mauritania signed a peace treaty with the Polisario forces in 1978 while Morocco continued to clash militarily with them over control of the region. At this writing, the issue is still not resolved, although a United Nations sponsored plan to allow for a Saharan referendum on the territory's status has been proposed and delayed various times.

15   Spanish leaders still perceived little Soviet threat. As Angel Viñas observed: 'One must underline the fact that Spain's vulnerabilities from the point of view of the normal tension of the East-West conflict are few' (Viñas, 1984a, pp.26-27).

16   The following analysis is based on an interview I conducted with a senior official in Spain's Ministry of Defense.

17   A PSOE foreign policy manifesto declared: 'The permanence of Spain in the Atlantic Alliance constitutes our specific contribution to European security and equally to its stability in that it avoids any alteration in the current established equilibria' (*Una Política de Paz y Seguridad Para España*, 1985, p.49).

18   Personal interview.

19   González won the approval of his party to advocate NATO membership at the PSOE's 30th Congress in December 1984.

20   A March 1983 public opinion survey conducted by the government sponsored Centro de Investigaciones Sociológicas asked, among other questions: 'If a referendum were held tomo₁.ow, would you vote in favor or against definitive membership in NATO?' The responses were: 13 per cent in favor, 49 per cent opposed, 8 per cent saying they would abstain, and 30 per cent don't know or no answer (*Revista Española de Investigaciones Sociológicas*, April-June 1983, p.245).

21   The PSOE, acting as an agent, endeavored to convey the government's position to the population at large as in its 1985 document *Una Política de Paz y Seguridad Para España*, in which the authors admit: 'The Party, for its part, has wished to develop...the points contained in the Resolutions of our 30th Congress and the "decalog" so that public opinion on the policies of peace and security for Spain can be widely known and diffused and can count on the support of the whole of society' (*Una Política de Paz y Seguridad Para España*, 1985, p.47).

22   In an oft-quoted passage from Felipe González's speech at the PSOE's 30th Congress, the Prime Minister declared: 'If we want to become integrated into Europe we must stand by during good times and bad (*hay que estar a las duras y a las maduras*). We must share the collective security of the western world in which we live' (*El Socialista*, {Extra XXX Congreso}, 15 December 1984, p.3).

23   One highly placed foreign diplomat told me that he warned González that following through on the promised referendum could be political suicide.

24   As Donald Share observes: 'Just as González had purged his party of its Marxist ideological baggage in 1981, the president now [1984] was convinced a majority of party delegates that NATO membership was necessary for "external and internal stability." This development is

particularly surprising, given the fact that opinion polls continued to show a majority of Spaniards opposed to NATO membership' (Share, 1986, p.190). Share cites *The Economist* (10 November 1984) regarding public opinion polls on NATO membership.

5 Negotiating Spanish membership in the EC

The Socialist government's change from opposition to support of Spanish membership in NATO represented a major policy shift. This shift was based on lessons of responsibilities in a unified Europe. By contrast, Spanish membership in the European Community seemingly demonstrates consistency in Socialist positions.[1] However, I will show that the negotiations by which Spain became a member of the EC did involve an evolution in Spanish foreign economic policy.[2] The Socialist government abandoned an approach that stressed narrow conceptions of national interest in favor of a position favoring long term economic health by strengthening the economic viability of the Community.

As with the NATO issue, the Socialists' preoccupation with overcoming Spain's traditional international isolation created an opening for learning about the realities of European integration. New knowledge about the mechanics of internal EC politics enabled the Socialists to resolve the tension between the positive ideas they had about Europe and the difficulties of undertaking fundamental economic reform. First, the Socialists' favorable image of Europe made them susceptible to arguments that an economically strong Europe implied economic benefits for Spain, despite the concessions the Spanish might have to offer. Second, the PSOE government learned that by making concessions on the terms of EC membership they could improve relations with Spain's future EC partners as well as with third party states. Third, by sacrificing short run economic gains for domestic interest groups that traditionally supported the PSOE, the government determined it could raise the long term standard of living for a larger portion of the population. This reinforced the party's trend towards a social democratic electoral strategy. Fourth, the Socialists learned that by making tough economic decisions they could solidify the PSOE's status as a party of state and the only political force capable of dealing with the responsibilities that come with long term European integration.

The Socialists' initial positions towards the European Community

The early economic agenda of the Spanish Socialist Party

The overwhelmingly favorable ideas the Socialists had about membership in the European Community were supported by very real interests and knowledge based claims. Socialist Party leaders favored the EC because they perceived European institutions as the antithesis to the authoritarian institutions of the Franco regime. However, what specific set of economic policies should replace Franquist economic structures was a source of debate within the PSOE. Looking at the clandestine origins of the party, one possible solution could be found in the Marxist economic theories popular during the 1960s and 1970s. The economic policies advocated by the PSOE before it took office aimed at increased state control of the means of production, labor friendly legislation, and redistribution of wealth (Gunther, 1986, p.16). At the party's 27th Congress in 1976, the PSOE defined itself as 'socialist, because [our] program and action are directed at the triumph over the capitalist mode of production by taking political and economic power and socializing the means of production, distribution, and exchange by the worker class' (Conte Barrera, 1977, p.149).[3] While much of the language used in PSOE pronouncements was rhetoric aimed at staking out a position on the left, it nonetheless expressed the party's economic agenda of extensive redistribution of wealth away from the oligarchic class to the workers and other disenfranchised classes (Hershberg, 1991, p.4).

The PSOE began to drift towards the right on economic and other issues following its surprisingly good showing in the 1977 national elections. This drift found its internal expression at the party's 28th Congress in 1979 where the debate over the PSOE's Marxist label exploded into the national media.[4] After having reaffirmed the party's principles at the PSOE 27th Congress in 1976, conflicting opinions were offered as to what direction to take in the wake of the 1977 vote. The faction led by party Secretary General Felipe González favored dropping the Marxist label. Richard Gillespie argues that 'before 1976 the party had never considered it necessary to adopt the label "Marxist" since the maximum program embodied in its Declaration of Principles was so self-evidently of Marxist inspiration' (Gillespie, 1989, p.338). But the electoral impulses of the party's leadership forced the debate back into the open. At the 28th Congress, the 'minimalist' position, led by González, prevailed and the 'Marxist' label was removed. The party was re-christened as 'a federal and democratic class-based party of the masses which assumes Marxism as a critical instrument of analysis to transform society, as well as being constituted by other Marxist and non-Marxist contributions' (*La Vanguardia*, 30 September 1979). Still, the resolutions of the congress continued to call for such things as collectivization of the means of production and, in this sense, the public face of socialism in Spain did not always present a consistent image.

77

The economic agenda of the Spanish Socialist Party and the European Community*

The economic agenda of the Spanish Socialist Party and the European Community

Turning to the PSOE's view of proposed membership in the EC, the positions the Socialist leadership considered appropriate to adopt in negotiating membership in the European Community corresponded to the party's domestic economic program (Mesa, 1982, p.11; Pollack and Hunter, 1989, p.97). During the Franco regime, the democratic opposition was careful to argue that although the dictator had opened Spain to economic ties with the West, the political Europeanization of Spanish life would be a way to overcome the injustices of authoritarian rule. The existence of the European Community which pointedly excluded fascist Spain was evidence that the EC could be counted on to enforce more than purely economic cooperation among member states. Early Socialist conceptions of the EC, then, focused less on the free trade aspects of the community and more on its role as an institution to which European democracies belonged (*Exprés Español*, January 1976, p.4). Aside from the perceived economic benefits of European integration, the former opposition forces to the Franco regime equated Europe with democracy, political openness, and social freedoms. Speaking in Mannheim at the 1975 Congress of the German Social Democratic Party, PSOE Secretary General Felipe González declared:

> For many sectors of the Spanish population, the democratic alternative consists in achieving a system of liberties homologous to the European systems, and in addition to this exists the objective of incorporating Spain with Europe, in whose framework Spain finds itself geographically, politically, economically, and culturally (*Exprés Español*, January 1976, p.10).

Despite some earlier fiery Marxist rhetoric that equated the EEC with the forces of international capitalism, the PSOE leadership was firmly convinced of the beneficial effects European values would have on post-Franco Spain.

Whereas the PSOE's leaders saw the EC as an expression of European democratic values, they were careful to avoid embracing the capitalist elements of the Community which would impinge on the party's radical economic claims. The Socialists wanted to remove economic structures in Spain which supported the old privileged classes and oligarchic financial, industrial, and agricultural forces which controlled the economy. The initial perception was unclear as to how EC membership would aid in this endeavor.

The Spanish economy under Franco was marked by intense protectionism shielding uncompetitive industries. Although the PSOE leadership wished to eliminate Franquist economic institutions, it did not want to hurt those sectors that would be unable to survive in a less protected environment. This can be seen in the PSOE's original position towards EC membership talks. The party's economic agenda was laid out in 1980 in a document entitled *Estrategia Económica del PSOE*. This short book recommended that negotiations for entry into the EC should follow along the following lines:

a) Negotiations for entry must take as a basis the 1970 accord established between Spain and the EC. There should be no net loss to Spain with regards to this accord. Negotiations must build on the 1970 agreement so that any Spanish concession in one area be compensated by EC concessions in another.[5]

b) There must be no provisional status. Spanish entry should result in full membership in all EC institutions.

c) The rhythm of the negotiations should follow the resolution of technical problems....Decisions made in the course of the talks should include the consultation and participation of the different sectors affected, especially the major unions and employers' organizations.

d) Transition periods should be adapted to the needs of the Spanish economy. The necessary restructuring of the Spanish economy should be treated as a priority.

e) An effort at regional and sectoral planning is necessary so as to coordinate Spanish policies with Community measures. The Autonomous Communities should participate in the elaboration of these studies.

f) The agricultural sector must carry out as soon as possible the removal of obstacles to trade, establishing the adjustments necessary to overcome serious problems that result [from] integration.

g) In the industrial sector, a transition period is necessary for the most vulnerable branches of production and those which employ the greatest number of workers. Too rapid lowering of tariff levels could result in an aggravation of the economic crisis and have negative repercussions for employment.

h) The principle of the free movement of labor must be established from the moment of Spanish entry into the EC.

i) Spanish workers already living in Community countries must not be the object of discrimination with respect to local nationals.

j)   Introduction of the Value Added Tax (VAT) must be the object of study so as to fix a transition period that will not create insurmountable problems (*Estrategia Económica del PSOE*, 1980, pp.74-76).

On the one hand, these guidelines seemed to reinforce the interests of the PSOE as a party that stood for traditional concerns of the left. Measures that protected labor were emphasized, and stress was placed on the conviction that long term economic restructuring should not entail short term hardships. On the other hand, the guidelines were tentative in nature, highlighting broad goals and recommendations, presenting an agenda that stopped short of technical specifications on how the objectives are to be obtained. In this regard, the interests of the PSOE regarding membership in the EC reflect left of center goals, but uncertainty as to specifics, and a generally positive attitude towards membership in the Community. More important, they show how the Socialists held the seemingly conflicting interests of eliminating Franquist economic practices by immersing Spain in the EC, but protecting those sectors that inevitably would be threatened under the free trade practices of the Community (*El Socialista*, 11 February 1979, p.5).

Certain sensitive industries typified the types of areas where tensions arose when the Socialists' enthusiasm for EC membership was confronted with the negotiations process. The fishing industry was one of those sectors where the PSOE's positive ideas about the EC confronted conflicting beliefs about what membership would accomplish. The Socialists were determined to protect the status of Spain's immense fishing fleet.[6] Given the positive ideas they had about the Community, people within the PSOE thought they could protect Spanish fishing rights and build on the agreements Spain had signed with the EC (*El Socialista*, 14-20 January 1981, p.23). They also desired to formalize Spanish fishing rights which, up to then, were governed by an elaborate system of bilateral agreements with various states. This was important because 'the state of depletion found in the fishing grounds directly off the Spanish coast has traditionally implied that present fishing under the jurisdiction of third countries has had considerable significance' (González Sánchez, 1980, p.736). The goal of the Socialists was to maximize benefits already enjoyed by the Spanish fishing industry while normalizing these third party agreements by inserting Spain into the Community's Common Fishing Policy.

Space does not permit a review of all economic areas that were be affected by Spanish membership in the EC. However, the fishing example is illustrative for what it reveals about the Socialists' perceptions. The interests of Spain's massive fishing sector had to be compromised in return for expected long term benefits of EC membership. We now turn to how this realization came about.

The emergence of doubts about membership in the EC

In much the same way as tensions arose between the negative ideas the PSOE leaders had about NATO and their perceptions of Spanish defense relations with the West, the Socialist government leadership was also confronted with inconsistencies between its positive ideas about the EC and its loosely defined economic positions. The government found that the benefits it anticipated from membership in the Community did not coincide with the sacrifices the EC states expected Spain to make. Uncertainty over economic policies came to a head during this period. The PSOE leadership was confronted with its notions of the EC as a bastion of democracy, which produced positive feelings about the Community, and the rhetoric of its radical past, which cast the free market aspect of the EC in a negative light. Although the leaders of EC states self consciously attach normative values to the Community, the EC in practice also serves as a customs union designed to lower the internal barriers to the free movement of goods, capital, and labor across national lines. The PSOE's enthusiasm for the normative element of the EC as a source of democracy came up against these economic realities.

Cracks in the Socialists' perspective

The failure of the French and Greek socialist examples in the early 1980s was a prelude for the decisions that would confront the PSOE (Holman, 1996, pp.77, 142). The leadership of the Spanish Socialist Workers' Party is composed of a generation of young anti-Franco organizers who were attracted to Marxist thought, among other underground political and economic teachings, in authoritarian Spain. However, the abandonment by Mitterrand and Papandreou of their socialist experiments in France and Greece - experiments that fell short of radical redistribution of resources or wide spread nationalizations - was a blow to the PSOE's belief in the validity of any variant of left wing economics.[7] The party's leadership had maintained close ties with the French Socialist Party (PSF) and took the example seriously. Just as Paris was unable to stake out a deviant economic model within emerging European convergence, the Spaniards became wary of trying an experiment that was falling increasingly out of favor with other European states.

Spanish Socialist leaders also were quick to feel the tensions between favoring the idea of European integration and their perceived economic interests, which became threatened as the EC's requirements for entry became known. Although the other EC states supported membership for Spain as a means of supporting Spanish democracy, their economic interests revolved primarily around maintaining the health of the Community. The experience of Greek accession had taught Community members that expansion of the EC must take repercussions of EC enlargement on existing economic arrangements more fully into account. Thus there existed a conflict of perceptions when the Spanish Socialists believed the Greeks made too many concessions in order to win EC membership, and Community leaders felt that they had not sufficiently protected EC interests when allowing Greece to join.

Realizing the value of EC membership and its costs

Proposed Spanish membership in the EC was framed within the debate of the presumed beneficial effects on Spanish democracy. By the early 1980s it became obvious that continued economic growth in Spain could come only from closer ties to, if not membership in, the EC (Wiarda, 1981, pp.30-31). The issue then became one of pursuing a hard line EC membership and continuing to protect the interests previously defined, or softening those positions in the face of probable Community intransigence. The Socialists argued that modernization of the Spanish economy was necessary whether Spain joined the EC or not. However, no one wanted to risk the latter route. Therefore, the prospect of concessions on Spanish demands loomed imminent.

The EC's evolving agricultural policy, for example, challenged Spanish interests that were formulated with the idea of Europe coming to Spain's economic salvation. Agricultural policy within the EC historically has been the forum for some of the largest disputes, and these ongoing clashes of interest served as a sobering reminder to the problems Spanish entry would face. Spanish agricultural exports already were the focal point for intra-Community conflict. These disputes intensified during Spain's membership talks. For instance, in the Spring of 1984 the Spanish government protested a proposed increase in agricultural tariffs. The German, Dutch, and British governments supported the Spanish position because higher tariffs would mean higher consumer prices for fruits and vegetables. The French and Italian governments, on the other hand, wanted to protect domestic growers (*El País*, 30 April 1984). Spain could count on its EC application to provoke similar disputes, dampening Madrid's enthusiasm for the benefits membership was supposed to bring.

The biggest source of tension was uncertainty. What was uncertain was whether EC membership would help secure the twin goals of reinforcing Spanish democracy and modernizing Spain's economy. Looking back at the period when Spain was trying to win membership in the Community, the full ramifications of joining the Community were not even fully discussed in Spain (Featherstone, 1989, p.254). Spanish Secretary of Commerce Guillermo de la Dehesa admitted:

> During the years of negotiations for EC membership, Spain tried to assess through innumerable studies of all kinds what the impact of entry into the E.C. would be for its economy and its social system. The results of these studies were diverse: some concluded that Spanish entry into the Community would have a disastrous effect on its economy, others foresaw

a positive growth in the medium run and others were neutral (de la Dehesa, 1986, p.52).

In an interview conducted for this project, a highly placed member of the PSOE's economic section, explained that during the period of negotiations it was virtually impossible to calculate the costs and benefits of entering the Community; there was no exact formula for figuring out the costs and benefits when one was talking about modernizing an entire economy.[8] Given this uncertainty, the stage was set for the Spanish leadership to accept the Community's logic on Spanish membership.

New knowledge about Spain's responsibilities In Europe

For a party like the PSOE, which had not held power in over 40 years, which looked to Europe as a panacea, which was faced with the enormity of negotiating membership into the European Community, whose leadership's formative years were spent in hiding, and whose leaders' ideas were shaped under dictatorship, knowledge about the normative expectations within the EC would go a long way towards resolving uncertainty over negotiations with the Community, and better defining economic interests.

During the negotiations period the Socialist government was confronted with EC member states' conceptions of how to fit Spain into the Community. As with the case of NATO, this learning process cannot be characterized simply as a re-ordering of preferences by the Socialist government. Rather, the process of entering into the Community was one of slowly adopting the existing members' socially constructed norms. Norms are translated into changed policy as they are revealed to actors through the transmission of knowledge. Knowledge, to reiterate, makes social relationships and the linkages among salient political issues transparent to policy makers. Therefore, what Spanish leaders learned were these social relationships and linkages among issue that constitute the normative base of the EC.

Negotiating Spanish membership in the EC

The general conditions under which Spain would be permitted to join the EC were spelled out by the Community prior to the PSOE's electoral victory. The European Council and the EC Commission concluded that the Community must get its economic house in order before any Iberian expansion would occur. The EC single-handedly was not going to solve Spain's economic ills, and EC officials refused to let Spanish and Portuguese membership threaten the economic viability of the Community (Morán, 1990, p.61). This was made explicit in a European Commission communication to the European Council at the latter's

December 1982 summit in Copenhagen:

> The Commission clearly stated, particularly in its 'General considerations', that 'a return to sufficiently rapid and lasting growth is a major condition for resolving the serious economic policy problems which have to be overcome' and thus on it depends 'the reciprocal capacity of the applicants and the Community to overcome the obstacles arising from restructuring and intensified competition' ('Problems of Enlargement', 1982, p.6).

Shortly after the PSOE's assumption of power, Foreign Minister Fernando Morán explained the government's position on EC membership to parliament, emphasizing the importance of maintaining the health of the Community over purely parochial Spanish concerns:

> To remain patriotically on horseback of the 1970 Agreement and at the same time not negotiate, nor attend to, nor correct, nor adjust is, shall we say, not only an extremely ambitious vision... but also an absolutely utopian one....I will not deceive anyone or do I desire to create illusions. There exists an implicit relation between the stabilization of the Community and the advancement of negotiations with Spain....The will to maintain the Community is the basis for a possible and probably common will to widen the Community (*Diario de Sesiones del Congreso de los Diputados*, 23 March 1983, pp.925-932).

The congruence between the EC's position, and that adopted by the Socialist government in Spain, is easily established. What remains to be shown is that the Socialists responded directly to their increased knowledge of EC norms and not the imperatives of assuming power.

The 1983 Stuttgart summit: the norm of issue linkage

At the July 1983 Council of Ministers' summit in Stuttgart, the heads of state of the ten EC member countries spelled out the general conditions under which Spain and Portugal would be allowed to join the Community. The Stuttgart summit codified the principles of the Copenhagen declaration: In essence, unlike Greece's entry in 1981, no additional southward expansion of the EC would take place until the Community solved the chronic problem of financing of EC activities and addressed serious imperfections in the Common Agricultural Policy (CAP) (*Bulletin of the European Communities*, June 1983, pp.18-25). According to Fernando Morán, the government in the Spring of 1983 received from German Foreign Minister Hans Dietrich Genscher advance notice of this agenda for the upcoming Stuttgart summit (Morán, 1990, p.165; see also Story, 1995, p.39). The Germans were not alone in stressing the need to solve EC problems before

Spain could join the Community. The resolution of French demands over Community policy on fruits and vegetables just prior to the Stuttgart Summit implied a linkage between this issue and the EC's southern expansion (Morán, 1990. p.244). Part of what was imparted to the Spanish government, then, were the norms of curing the internal problems of the EC and moving beyond the 'Eurosclerosis' that had plagued the Community since the 1970s. This cause-and-effect logic was reflected in an address to parliament by Fernando Morán just prior to Stuttgart:

> I am going to limit myself to offering an objective account of the question because...the Spanish government is interested in an increase in Community resources in that if the Community's resources increase there are more possibilities for increased financing; if there is financing, there is reform of the CAP; if there is reform of the CAP there is discussion of the agriculture chapter, and if there is a decision on the agriculture chapter, there is [Spanish] membership (*Diario de Sesiones del Congreso de los Diputados*, 25 May 1983, p.1054).

The Stuttgart summit solidified the impression of the Spanish leadership of what was necessary to join the EC. In his October 18, 1983 letter, sent to the ten heads of state of the EC countries, President González signaled his acceptance of the Stuttgart summit formula for Spanish membership (*Actividades, Textos y Documentos...*, Año 1983, pp.842-843). This was an important move because it illustrated González's comprehension of EC priorities, namely, that no expansion of the Community southward would take place until and unless it solved the problems inherent in EC finances and the Common Agricultural Plan. This became the de facto position of the Community for the remainder of the negotiations period with Spain. The only problem was that the Community itself had not reached closure on resolving the fundamental problems plaguing the EC and that whose resolution was a precondition for Spanish and Portuguese membership.

The Stuttgart summit only identified the problems facing the EC but did not solve them. The crisis of Community finances, for instance, dates back to the 1970s but became a serious obstacle in the early 1980s after the government of Margaret Thatcher took office in Great Britain and began to object to EC formulas the prime minister found unfavorable to British interests. In order to solve the chronic problem of financing the Community and mollify British concerns, the European Commission issued a Green Paper on EC finances in early 1983. This Green Paper proposed four areas from which increased finances might be raised: 1) Adding a degree of progressivity to revenues paid from national collection of the Value Added Tax (VAT); 2) Directly taxing member states progressively on the basis of GDP; 3) Reforming the way revenues are generated from agricultural sources (proposed as a provisional measure); 4)

Linking revenues to other non-agricultural issue specific areas (*Bulletin of the European Communities*, January 1983, pp.9-13). As the Commission itself conceded, each of these possible sources of increased financing posed political obstacles in that they would burden different member states depending on the specific formula chosen.

Developments after Stuttgart: issue linkage and Spanish membership in the EC

In light of the discussion above, we can see that the debate over financing reform really was a debate over the nature of the EC and its purpose in general. We can understand this as a clarification in the social norms by which the Community was constructed: National interests must be fulfilled by strengthening the EC as a whole. Spain's proposed membership, then, was inextricably linked to this process of redefining the EC's identity and links between the Community's structures and member state interests. This was laid bare six months after Stuttgart at the failed Athens summit In December 1983. There, the goals of the Green Paper on financing and the first step made at Stuttgart seemingly faced derailment. Press accounts attributed the failure of the Athens summit largely to disputes over the British position on financing the EC (*The Economist*, 10 December 1983, pp.41-42). However, in a joint news conference in which the leaders of the ten EC states performed a public autopsy on the failed talks, Dutch Prime Minister Ruud Lubbers 'stressed that the breakdown was not due solely to the British problem but was also attributable to the southern European countries, which wanted a new North-South distribution of income in the Community, and to the financial difficulties of the Member States' (*Bulletin of the European Communities*, December 1983, p.8). Indeed, the theme of the Athens Summit was that of a Community which had lost cohesion and was plagued with selfish interests on all fronts.

How, then, did the resolution of these disputes affect proposed Spanish membership? Settlement of the problems which led to the Athens failure involved reestablishing the normative framework by which national self interests were transformed into a new agenda of cohesion. This cohesion would be achieved by identifying states' interests with the process of issue linkage within the EC. If each state perceived it could reap long term gains through tying short term concessions to EC reforms, then integration could go forward. Gaston Thorn, President of the Commission, re-stated these principles (which originally had been proposed at Stuttgart) at the end of the Athens Summit:

> The Community must be afforded the resources essential to ensure its development; a lasting solution must be found for the budget problems; the common agricultural policy must be allowed to perform its role more effectively; available resources must be efficiently managed; the accession of Spain and Portugal must be made possible. This means an end to the

clash of conflicting national interests on too many single isolated issues
and a return to the procedures of the Treaty, the only ones which can
make the superior interest of the Community central to the debate (*Bulletin
of the European Communities*, December 1983, p.9).

Thorn showed that what was really being debated were not isolated issues, but
the identity of the EC and the commitments member states would make towards
nurturing that identity:

> So I wonder whether the main cause of the Athens *débâcle* is not the lack
> of genuine agreement on the scope and meaning of European
> integration.... What sort of Community do we want? What are our plans?
> How is it that the questions on which the European Council foundered in
> Athens are the same ones that caused the deadlock at Lancaster House in
> 1981? (ibid., p.13).

The breakdown of Athens, then, was not simply one of failure to reach agreement
on mediating conflicting interests of member states, but of defining what were
state interests in the changing Community environment by reinforcing the norms
of the EC.

These norms of issue-linkage were in evidence throughout the remaining period
of negotiations on Spanish membership. For example, at the 1984 Winter summit
of the Council of Ministers at Dublin, the issue of Spanish and Portuguese wine
production was unblocked when the EC Ten reached (at least temporary)
agreement on Mediterranean agricultural production. Greek Prime Minister
Andreas Papandreou threatened to block wine agreement (which involved the
compulsory purchase of wine surpluses at below market prices) unless funds
proposed under the stalled Integrated Mediterranean Programs (IMPs) were
released. Although *The Economist* argued that the type of parochialism implied
by Papandreou's threats would be inevitable 'so long as the EEC is a collection
of states with their own national interests to defend,' the Greeks eventually did
relent to preserve the unanimity necessary for the Iberian expansion (*The
Economist*, 8 December 1984, p.42). Nonetheless, the experience taught the
Greek leadership, and presumably the Spanish and Portuguese, that 'to get what
you want in the EEC it is necessary to connect the unconnected and to threaten
the use of the veto' (ibid, pp.41-42). In this case, the notion that Spanish and
Portuguese memberships were linked to the resolution of the EC's existing
problems was reinforced by the unity established on tying expansion talks to the
settlement of the surplus wine problem.

The roles of Germany and France

Among the perceived outcomes of the process that began in Stuttgart was that

Germany's decision to act as 'paymaster' for the Iberian enlargement provided a guarantee for the linkages designed to solve the existent problems in the EC. Although, Germany was cast by the popular press and in academic circles as Spain's *'padrino'* in the negotiations process (while France was portrayed as the villain), Spanish officials learned a more complex lesson, one that reveals a deeper meaning behind the relationships among EC states. The elaborate measures designed to solve the Community's budgetary and agricultural problems had the potential for elevating Germany to the status of agenda setter within the EC. This would be cemented permanently if Germany were allowed to take charge of Spanish and Portuguese accession.

This was not a matter of merely absorbing information about economic aspects of EC widening. Rather it was accepting the terms of the cause and effect of states' actions on the structure of relationships within the EC. Through a purposeful participation in international dialogue, knowledge of the new relationships among issues of EC integration and expansion were transmitted to the Spanish leadership in the process of negotiations for Spanish entry. Linkages among issues reflected the normative relationships that constitute decision making in the Community. Fernando Morán explained in the Cortes:

> It is evident that the ingenuousness that we had in the final moments of the previous [Franco] regime of thinking that the obstacle [to EC membership] was exclusively political; that political homologization was going to suffice to obtain fair treatment in Europe. This has not happened, and it has not happened, in the first place, because the ideological motor of Europe has been diverted towards a Common Market dominated by interests - by the adjustment of interests - because...the life of the Community is a constant adjustment of interests... (*Diario de Sesiones del Congreso de los Diputados*, 6 June 1984, pp.5954-5955).

Thus, the extent to which the Spanish leadership accepted these relationships affected on the way they constructed their economic interests in the EC's institutional environment.

Just as German leadership in budgetary matters provided the normative framework for financial aspects of the Community's Iberian expansion, negotiations on those issues which were key to gaining French support followed the logic of French leadership. These issues could not be divorced from the relationship among issues proposed at Stuttgart and reconciled after the failed Athens summit. The debacle in the Greek capital merely brought into the open the issues that required resolution. They were subsequently solved, as was expected, under the leadership of the French at the Fontainebleau summit six months later (July 1984). In return for agreements on the settlement of the British contribution to the EC budget and terms for concluding disagreements over the content of the CAP, the French agreed to pursue a January 1, 1986 date for Spanish entry into the EC. Fontainebleau also reintroduced the subject of the Integrated Mediterranean Programs with an eye towards creating sufficient funds to finance this Mediterranean project (Morán, 1990, pp.206, 305-307). This clearly would appease the Greeks while doing so in the context of maintaining the health of EC finances.

In the realm of the CAP, Spain's fortunes rested firmly in French hands. In an intra-ministerial memo, the Spanish ambassador in France, Joan Reventós, argued to his superiors in Madrid that the Athens summit failure had the paradoxical effect of freeing the French government's hands because public opinion in France had come to see the EC process as stalled unless decisive action was taken. Given the preoccupation in both Paris and Madrid over resolving agricultural matters, Reventós advised Foreign Minister Morán: 'France continues to be the essential factor to which our strategy for gaining entry to the EEC should be directed.'[9] The Spanish Ministry of Agriculture acknowledged publicly that Spanish agriculture was a sort of 'picturesque hostage' in the:

> Strategy of change provoked by three internal Community facts: a) the rise in financial costs of the CAP, often to pay for the production of surpluses; b) the necessity to reequilibrate Community support for agriculture, with greater protection of Mediterranean agriculture and poorer and mountainous regions; c) the peculiar vision of agrarian policy of the more free trade oriented countries (*El País*, 30 August 1984, p.30).

Resolving the problems of the Common Agricultural Policy was central to Spain's entry into the EC because it was an issue that revolved around which country's vision of the CAP would become the dominant paradigm for future policy within the EC. Given the French government's multiple agricultural concerns, Spanish negotiators and the governments of EC members states played to French interests in inducing Paris to participate in upholding the norm of Community strength through issue-linkage. In this instance, it entailed linking French agricultural interests to the Spanish desire to gain EC membership, and the other EC states' interest to make sure this occurred at the lowest cost to the Community as a whole.

The question of North Africa

The Spanish willingness to accept EC imperatives is also illustrated by the way agricultural exports from the Maghreb countries were given priority in talks to include Spain in the Community. Spain's most competitive agricultural exports, citrus fruits and other Mediterranean crops, were in direct competition with exports from the North African countries of Algeria and Morocco. The European Community countries, led primarily by France, were insistent on maintaining advantages for Maghrebi agricultural exports at tariff levels lower than those enjoyed by Spain. The reason for this was the French concern for maintaining both economic and political stability in countries that had already flooded France (and the rest of Europe) with immigrants who were beginning to pose political problems at home. Roland Dumas, on the eve of being named French Foreign Minister in 1984 declared: 'The disruption of traditional channels of exchange with the Maghreb would provoke an uncontrollable chain of economic and social reactions which can carry with them the political destabilization of these countries' (*Información Comercial Española (Boletín)*, 25 April 1985, p.1469). The French traditionally enjoyed a privileged diplomatic presence in the Maghreb and were concerned that curtailing the agricultural advantages of that region in favor of Spain would jeopardize that role (Kramer, 1983).

Improved Spanish relations with France were important for unblocking difficult chapters throughout Spain's EC membership negotiations. As with many areas of Community politics, seemingly diverse matters were linked to a variety of issues regarding European integration. For example, Felipe González's May 1983 visit to Bonn, where he expressed understanding of the German position on deployment of the 'Euromissiles' (see Chapter Four), had ramifications for Spain's dealings with France regarding EC enlargement (MacDonald, 1988, p.82). The exchange of French goodwill towards Spanish membership in the Community for Spanish support of French positions in other areas worked in the other direction, with Spain making concessions during EC accession talks in exchange for France reversing its policy, for example, of harboring suspected Basque terrorists (ibid., pp.83-84). The institutionalization of French-Spanish cooperation both contributed to, and reflected, the larger process by which Spanish leaders accepted the norms of issue linkage that governed the process of European integration in its many facets.

As with the broader issues discussed at the Stuttgart summit, the issue involved in EC negotiations over Spain and Mediterranean agricultural exports was one of maintaining unity within the Community. As early as 1979 (two years following Spain's application to join the EC) there were hints that the French would advance Maghreb interests at the expense of short-term Spanish economic gain (Duchene, 1979). But French insistence only heightened awareness within the EC of maintaining good relations with North Africa and the rest of the Arab world. A study prepared on behalf the European Commission warned:

> The principle motivation for the EEC's Mediterranean policy at the outset were essentially political and strategic. the Mediterranean was seen as an EEC zone of influence of strategic importance on the exposed southern flank of the Atlantic Alliance where the Soviet Union had been increasing its naval presence.... The EEC's credibility and standing, particularly in the Arab world, depends on how it handles this aspect of the second enlargement (Taylor, 1980, pp.4-5).

By 1983 the issue of protecting traditional export advantages for the Maghreb countries had become codified within the EC. The European parliament, by a vote of 100 in favor to 68 opposed (with 10 abstentions) resolved that neither EC external relations nor the CAP should prejudice existing North African privileges. The resolution concluded: 'The politically desirable adhesion of Spain and Portugal [to the EC] must not prejudice commercial relations with the Mediterranean countries' (*Noticias Sobre la Communidad Económica Europea*, June 1983, pp.309-310). This vote nearly coincided with the Stuttgart summit.

The importance of new knowledge about the EC

Once again, the critical feature for understanding how knowledge functioned in changing the Spanish position is how the Spanish government accepted the logic of the EC despite the obvious negative effects this would have on the Spanish economy in general, and on Spanish agriculture in specific. The government was willing to make these concessions given its ideas about the importance of supporting European unity. The PSOE government had tied the long term future of Spain to increased European interdependence. It soon learned that this must be on EC terms which did not necessarily offer immediate benefits to Spain.[10] This is not to say that Spanish negotiators did not try to win the most favorable conditions for all sectors of the Spanish economy upon entering the EC. In fact, they did try. Rather, the government learned that Spanish membership must not challenge cohesion within the Community nor weaken the EC or its relations with third parties. If this resulted in short term economic dislocations in Spain, then that was the price to be paid.

The Spanish government came to understand that granting concessions on Mediterranean agricultural exports was one way of sowing goodwill with its North African neighbors from which Madrid perceived security threats. As I describe in Chapter Four, the Socialist government learned that the best way to improve relations with the Maghreb and deal with nascent military tensions was by renouncing a unilateral North African foreign policy and looking for European solutions. The compromises the EC asked Spain to make on economic matters, the Spaniards discovered, worked in this direction. Angel Viñas, one of Foreign Minister Fernando Morán's top advisors, wrote in 1984: 'The maintenance of the *status quo* in the region will not be easy and will imply, on the part of Spain, an active posture, not exempt of important economic costs, some of which have already materialized' (Viñas, 1984b, pp.96-97). These costs were directly related to the concessions Spain made on the time frame by which Spanish Mediterranean agricultural goods would be allowed free access to the EC.

As part of putting EC priorities first, the Spanish negotiators learned they would have to forfeit privileges enjoyed under Spain's 1970 Commercial Agreement with the EC. This would require compromising advantages Spain enjoyed under the 1970 accord although the Socialists had promised they would not be forced to take this step (*Estrategia Económica del PSOE*, 1980, p.74). But as Juan Antonio Payno points out:

> The EEC...relie[d] heavily on attacking the relevance of the Commercial Agreement with Spain of 1970, alleging that: (a) it was signed when the Spanish economy was weaker and (b) that its application is harmful for the EEC, because the reduction of tariffs applied under it (57 percent) is greater than applied by Spain (26 percent) (Payno, 1983, p.29).

As I have argued in this book, the process of creating new perceptions of economic interests required that the Socialist leadership adopt the EC's version of growth. The Community's economic paradigm prescribes a certain way of calculating economic costs and benefits of each EC policy. As if to underscore the links between the terms of Spanish and Portuguese entry and the solution of the Community's financial and agricultural problems, the March 1985 issue of the *Bulletin of the European Communities* juxtaposed the results of bargaining outcomes on the most sensitive issues with the resolution of the EC's problems under the heading 'Putting the Stuttgart and Fontainebleau Decisions Into Effect' (*Bulletin of the European Communities*, March 1985). What is evident to the reader of EC documentation was also clear to Spanish negotiators: Only through a combination of making bargaining concessions on the part of applicant countries and resolution of the Community's internal problems by current members would the southern expansion be possible. For Spain, this meant bowing to EC demands on agricultural exports, fishing rights, and social affairs (*Las Negociaciones Para la Adhesión a las Comunidades Europeas*, 1985; Alonso, 1985). The Spanish government first needed to accept the Community's notion of economic advancement before it could understand the long term gains in conceding on areas where Spain enjoyed advantages under the 1970 agreement.

Assessing economic interests and ideas about the EC

What the Socialists learned in the process of negotiating EC membership changed their perceptions of Spanish economic interests. Two trends can be observed: 1) The outcome of membership negotiations involved concessions regarding previously protected and/or competitive economic sectors; 2) Joining the EC precluded any possibility of instituting the domestic economic policies the PSOE promised prior to coming to power. Meanwhile, in changing its strategy for achieving economic growth and modernization, the government hoped to maintain its electoral hegemony by convincing domestic interest groups, party members, and the voting electorate that the new policies it advocated would benefit Spain at large.

The more Spain become integrated into the EC through the process of bargaining and negotiations over Spanish membership, the more Spanish leaders started assuming the interests of the EC as an institution. The Spanish leadership came to accept that the EC's priority of promoting the health of the Community took priority over the particular shot term economic needs of member states. The Socialist leadership conceded that economic dislocations would occur due to initial membership in the EC. Chief Spanish EC negotiator Manuel Marín argued that among the positive aspects of EC membership 'would be the modernization of Spanish society and an opportunity to make this society more open and competitive' (*Diario 16*, 21 November 1985). However, the process of learning about the realities of joining the EC forced the PSOE leadership to be more prudent about the kind of promises they could make concerning the benefits that the Spanish would accrue.

It is not necessary, nor is there space in this paper, to run through a complete list of economic concessions made as part of Spain's EC entry package.[11] Instead I will note a few highlights. Most Spanish agricultural products were subjected to a waiting period of ten years before being fully integrated into the common market (Story, 1995, p.43). Iron and Steel subsidies had to be eliminated by 1990, and restrictions on EC industrial imports were phased out over a two to seven year period (Tovias, 1995, pp.90-91). In addition, Spain was subjected to a waiting period before enjoying the benefits of free movement of labor in the EC, and also had to allow the importation of goods from non-EC countries at reduced tariff levels (ibid., pp.91-92). Especially humiliating was the barely averted trade war between the United States and the EC which erupted over American grain imparts to Spain after the USA objected to EC agricultural subsidies to Spain and Portugal included in the treaties of accession. Ultimately, Spain had to allow the American grain imports (Odell and Matzinger-Tchakerian, 1992). On another front, Spain's adoption of the EC's external tariffs meant a reduction in trade with Latin American countries with which Spain enjoyed positive cultural and political ties (Salmon, 1995, p.74).

One economic I alluded to earlier that would be hurt by EC membership was the Spanish fishing industry. Spain has the highest consumption of seafood in Europe and the largest fishing fleet. European Community negotiators were charged with the task of containing the powerful and competitive 'Spanish Armada,' while Spanish negotiators were under domestic pressure to protect the fishing sector. Despite these domestic imperatives, the Socialist government, in the end, bowed to pressure from EC states to reign in its fishing fleet. This became acutely apparent after a 1984 incident in which French warships fired on two Spanish fishing vessels in the Bay of Biscay. The response of the Spanish government was timid and created a precedent for concessions at EC talks. In a magazine interview, Foreign Minister Morán said:

...the law of the sea is developing in the direction of restricting the freedom to fish. The Spanish fleet is vary large, it now equals two-thirds of the entire Community fleet and this presents a problem because there is now an excess in vessels and a lack of fishing grounds. ...it is evident that the mentality of the [Spanish] fisherman needs to change in that he is now accustomed to a free ocean and has a tendency to act as he did before the present restrictive norms were established (*Interviu*, 28 March-3 April, 1984).

While the Spanish negotiators were able to brake the trend towards decreasing the size of Spanish catches in Community waters, as part of the agreements under which Spain joined the European Community the EC immediately assumed management of bilateral fishing treaties Spain had maintained with non-EC states. Furthermore, the EC won the right to represent Spain in multilateral fishing talks and during a seven year transition period the rights of Spanish companies to establish joint fishing enterprises in third countries would be gradually reduced. The introduction of the Value Added Tax, the cessation of state subsidies for fuel for fishing vessels, and the usurpation of administrative controls from fishing peak organizations to the Spanish government and the EC bureaucracy are other outcomes of entry negotiations where the PSOE government accepted the EC line (Oliver, 1985, pp.360-363). As with the Common Agricultural Plan, the Socialists accepted the following argument: that which promoted unity and cohesion in the EC would ultimately be best for Spain regardless of initial concessions. Despite the positive face Socialist government leaders tried to put on the outcomes of EC negotiations, fishing interests felt betrayed (Nogues, 1986, pp.101-102).

In the end, the Socialist government changed from protecting the narrow interests of Spain's huge fishing fleet to adopting the Community line that it was best to limit the size of the Spanish fleet in favor of strengthening the Common Fisheries Policy of the EC. Spain's leaders were convinced it was more in their long term interest to forge links of solidarity than to pursue immediate gains by unleashing Spanish ships on European waters. Interests changed to sowing harmony, and Spanish leaders learned that they could placate fears by accepting EC policy.[12]

Of course, Spain enjoyed a wide variety of both short and long term benefits from EC membership as well. As Kenneth Maxwell and Steven Spiegel observe:

Between 1986 and 1990 gross domestic product (GDP) grew at a rate of more than 4 percent per year, and GDP per capita rose from $6,000 to $12,600. Spain's economy shifted dramatically toward the EC through expanded trade and investment. Between 1985 and 1990 Spanish exports to the EC rose from 52 percent of total exports to 71 percent; concurrently, imports from the Community rose from 37 percent of total imports to 60 percent. EC participation in foreign direct investment also climbed from 40 percent of total foreign direct investment in the period 1980-1985 to 57 percent in 1990 (Maxwell and Spiegel, 1994, p.40).

In the long run, incorporation into the EC forced the government to practice a greater degree of fiscal discipline and exposed Spanish companies to competitive pressures with the result of forcing them to modernize. In addition, as I will discuss in Chapter Six, Spain has benefitted from a massive infusion of EC development funds under the rubric of the Community's cohesion policy.

With regards to the totality of EC negotiations, Spanish negotiators did not settle for entry at any price and did bargain hard so as to gain as much advantage as possible. But the interests of the Spanish leadership evolved towards delayed gratification, and the priority became to win EC membership with the knowledge that long term benefits would follow.[13] A leading PSOE theoretician and member of the Federal Executive of the PSOE argues that from the beginning the PSOE saw the EC as a challenge and that economic readjustments would be necessary. But it was more important to tie Spain's fortune to the European project because that, in the long run, would be more secure.[14] Spanish leaders became pragmatic, arguing that Spain could make its best case as a full member of the EC (*El País*, 6 December 1984, p.53). Indeed, the short run costs of EC membership were quite severe. As Alfred Tovias observes: 'Between 1985 and 1987 the trade deficit with the Community increased four-fold. The same pattern repeated itself afterwards...Since overall Spanish protection remained very high by OECD standards, the impact of eliminating tariffs towards selected groups of countries was tremendous' (Tovias, 1995, p.93). In addition, while Spain's GDP rose by 4.5 percent in the period between 1986 and 1990, unemployment was at its highest level since Franquism (18.6 per cent) and inflation rates remained high (Maxwell and Spiegel, 1994, p.47). Finally, despite modernization of much of the Spanish economy, a wide variety of companies either were forced out of business due to lack of competitiveness, or were acquired by foreign firms.

The domestic context

If the long term goals of the Socialist Party remained constant through the period of negotiations for EC membership, the means by which domestic economic justice would be delivered in Spain were altered substantially as international interdependence became more a reality. Among the lessons learned by the PSOE government was that promoting the economic viability of the EC actually can be conducive to creating the proper climate for the transformation of domestic society. European Community membership for Spain required that the Spanish government jeopardize traditionally protected sectors of the economy. While these sectors would suffer in the short run, the Spanish economy as a whole would benefit from EC entry.

Given that one of the Socialists' goals was to dismantle the structures by which certain privileged sectors controlled the economy under Franco, the relevance of the workerist/Marxist rhetoric that the PSOE had championed since its days of clandestinity no longer conformed with the party leadership's new perception of European economic realities.[15] The Socialists learned that to modernize the economy they could not reconfigure economic structures completely nor dispense with those economic classes that propelled the Spanish economy. Socialist economic policies turned towards neoconservative principles, with an emphasis on 'stern monetary controls, sales of profitable state-owned assets, lowered taxes, controlled wages, [and] incentives for investment' (*The Economist*, 4 January 1986, p.35). A former economist at the Banco de España says that the Socialist government learned from the failures of the French Socialist experiment and the basic lesson was that a country's economy, to be successful, must be appropriate to its surroundings.[16]

The previous centrist UCD government began to move in this direction and was aided by its insulation from interest group pressures. The consensus surrounding the democratic transition permitted successive Spanish governments (including the Socialist government) a degree of autonomy from traditional organized interests (Bermeo and García-Durán, 1992). For the UCD government, this implied freedom from pressure from entrenched business interests (Armero, 1989, pp.167-169). For the Socialist government, this meant the ability to disregard labor union demands for compensation for economic dislocation (Bermeo and García-Durán, 1992, pp.62-63). At the same time, the PSOE government was forced to pursue a more aggressive reconversion of the Spanish economy to reward the population for suffering short-term economic dislocations. The emergent middle class nature of the Spanish electorate enabled the Socialists to pursue an economic agenda consummate with EC priorities.

Let us take a moment to assess the PSOE's electoral strategy, since it has been the subject of some debate. Analysts of Spanish politics have described the strategy of the PSOE as unabashedly electoral by design. They have seen the actions of the PSOE in the democratic period as motivated by a tactic to create a parliamentary majority by capturing the electoral center. Donald Share quotes Felipe González to make this point: 'There can be no democratic social transformation without a majority. And in order to obtain a majority it is essential to represent a much wider spectrum than originally planned' (Share, 1986, p.183). However, unlike proponents of electoral motivations in PSOE politics, I maintain that the Socialist leadership did not merely seek to *represent* a wider spectrum of the Spanish electorate, but to *create* one. In other words, the Socialist Party's new electoral strategy was more an *outcome* of the agenda established by EC membership, rather than its cause. This is especially true, given that the PSOE's economic interests had been altered so dramatically in such a short period of time. The terms by which Spain entered the EC were precisely those that did not immediately redress disequilibria in the Spanish economy, but

96

prepared it for long term modernization and growth. Closer ties to Europe and increased international obligations could contribute to revolutionary changes in Spanish society which would make social democratic electoral ends easier to achieve. Socialist leaders shifted their emphasis from stressing the ultimate economic rewards to underscoring the means by which these rewards could be achieved.

Naturally, PSOE leaders hoped that this would enable them to forge a long term electoral majority. However, the impetus for change did not come from need to appeal to the electorate as presently constituted. Rather, the initiative for such a drastic overhaul of the Spanish economy came from the government and its desire to join Europe.[17] Because this would entail short run dislocations, PSOE leaders gambled - just as they gambled on the NATO issue - that they would be able to convince the people that the government's foreign economic policies were correct.[18] In essence, many things the government did it did because the main leaders thought that they were the only ones who knew the truth. This was a conviction that dated from the 1970s and continued to inform members of the Socialist government in their negotiations to secure Spanish membership in the EC.

On a related theme, the PSOE saw EC membership as a way to legitimize itself as a party of state and the only viable ruling alternative in the face of a political right still identified with the Franco regime, and a political left in disarray. The internal confusion within parties of the right and left allowed the PSOE to assemble a majority government following the 1982 elections (Penniman and Mujal-Leon, 1985; Gunther, Sani, and Shabad, 1986; Gunther, 1987; Pollack and Hunter, 1987a). Nonetheless, the PSOE needed to solidify its voter base and, more importantly, demonstrate that it was capable of competent rule after the confusion that characterized the last years of the UCD government. As Nancy Bermeo and José García-Durán point out: 'The many Spaniards who turned away from the UCD and voted Socialist in 1982 did so not because their personal ideology had shifted leftward, but because they had been alienated by the infighting and indecision of the UCD' (Bermeo and García-Durán, 1992, pp.53-54).[19] Membership in the Community did go a long way in solidifying this catch-all position in part because of the overwhelming popular support for EC entry. Despite objections that the treaty as negotiated would harm various sectors of the Spanish economy, every political party supported the treaty with the vote to approve in the Spanish Parliament being unanimous, 309 votes in favor and none opposed (*El País*, 27 June 1985). This attests to the eagerness of all factions to become part of Europe. The PSOE government took advantage of the desire to tie Spanish democracy to the EC to win this type of approval. The government knew that even with its objections, the strong desire on the part of the opposition parties to secure EC membership would force them to approve the government's proposal thus giving the PSOE government a degree of approval and legitimacy it needed to become a party of state.

If the PSOE leadership's perceptions of what was in Spain's best economic interests underwent a noticeable transformation, it would seem that its ideas about European integration were unchanged. Indeed, the Socialists continued to put their faith in the benefits EC membership would hold for Spain. This is because they persisted in seeing Europe as an antidote for traditional Spanish ills. The image of Europe as the counterpoint to Spanish exceptionalism persevered as a guiding principle. The rhetoric of the government reflected this mythologizing of Europe in Spanish eyes. Upon concluding negotiations to enter the EC, the government issued a statement that read in part:

> The integration of Spain into community Europe, supported from the start by all political forces and sectors of society, supposes the age-old aspiration of all Spaniards, which successive governments born under our democratic experience have pledged to undertake. Such a broad consensus which has formed around an objective of national character has been, in the Government's judgement, a fundamental element in achieving this success (*El País*, 3 April 1985).

This glowing picture of Europe no doubt expresses a continuing positive image of Europe.

However, the more Spanish leaders participated in the process of uniting Europe through the EC, the more their ideas reflected normative relationships within European institutions. Perhaps most important was the identification of Spanish interests with the idea of European unity. What emerged from the failed Athens summit was the new idea that what was most important was the reaching of unity of action. This became the touchstone of the EC in almost a fanatic sense. But it was accepted whole heartedly by the Spanish leadership.[20] Unity within the EC meant more than simply deciding on a common course of action. It meant (and continues to mean) finding solutions to member state demands through trade-offs designed to strengthen the Community's economic viability. In calling on the *Cortes* to approve the treaty of accession to the EC, Fernando Morán argued:

> Joining the Community is not a calculus of duties and privileges, adhering to a positive or negative result calibrated this very moment, 25 June 1985. Joining the Communities is to be inscribed within a process of creation of an economic and eventually political system in Europe, doing so through the instruments of existing institutions, accepting the rules of derived and progressive law that are increasingly intense, based on ideas, attitudes and an international position in all areas, not only in those established in the economic and social issues in the [EC's] commercial treaties (*Diario de Sesiones del Congreso de los Diputados*, 25 June 1985, p.10187).

It is not necessary that member states reject perceptions of particular national interests in favor of some 'Community interest.' Rather, it requires that states perceive that promoting the strength of the Community translates into boosts for each state's national interest. Knowledge of the necessity and 'reality' of issue linkage then becomes the currency for forging cooperation on building the EC.

Summary

Throughout the 1970s and 1980s the leadership of the Spanish Socialist Party subscribed to the notion that membership in the European Community would be a positive development for Spain. By tying Spain to the engine of the EC, the argument went, the country's economic backwardness would be overcome and Spain would complete the process by which it was socialized by European political and cultural values. This view was reinforced by European countries which had treated Franquist Spain as a pariah state and refused to grant full EC status to Spain until democracy was restored.

However, the precise way in which the Community would secure perceived economic goals was marked by uncertainty. During the immediate post-Franco period, PSOE economic policy proposals advocated traditional socialist solutions and an array of redistributive measures. These positions were softened during the process of democratic transition. When confronted with the task of negotiating entry into the EC, this uncertainty, combined with the Socialists' continued favorable image of the Community, made government leaders susceptible to the arguments of European leaders as to how Spanish membership in the Community should be undertaken.[21]

The arguments used by European leaders appealed to the Spaniards' positive ideas about the EC. Among their claims was that Spain could benefit most from Community membership only if unity within the EC was maintained and the Community continued to be economically strong. Therefore, the terms under which Spain joined the EC should strengthen the Community for Spain to reap long term gains. This process of learning about the realities of life within the EC helped define more clearly for the Spanish leadership their long term economic interests. The idea of Europe as something overwhelmingly positive gave way to what Foreign Minister Fernando Morán calls the process of 'making an ideology out of pragmatism' (Morán, 1990, p.138).

The terms by which Spain joined the European Community were not at all satisfactory to many segments of the Spanish population. The PSOE government had to go a long way in convincing some segments of the Spanish population that EC membership would have positive effects. It had to rely on the generally positive image of the Community held by the vast majority of the Spanish electorate to sell disaffected circles on the beneficial effects EC membership would have on Spain writ large. However, this project was bolstered by the direction the EC took towards the overall economic health of the Community and promises of greater economic growth for the entire twelve country organization. In the next chapter I will explore how this project has progressed in the first decade of Spanish membership.

Notes

1   Because this chapter deals with events from the late 1970s through the mid 1980s, I shall use the term 'European Community' (EC) to denote the organization currently known as the European Union (EU).

2   The negotiations for Spanish entry to the Community lasted from 1977, when the UCD government originally applied for EC membership, until the summer of 1985. The most controversial and sensitive areas were not resolved until the last six months of membership talks. These areas included fishing, certain agricultural sectors (including fruits and vegetables, olive oil, and wine), and social policy. On the negotiations process, see (*Las Negociaciones Para la Adhesión de España a las Comunidades Europeas*, 1985; Alonso, 1985).

3   Indeed, the PSOE defined itself as a 'Marxist' party for the first time at the 1976 Congress (Holman, 1996, p.84). See also Guerra, 1978, p.116.

4   According to Richard Gillespie, the debate actually was not waged over ideological issues but over party discipline (Gillespie, 1989, pp.337-356).

5   On the terms of the 1970 association treaty between Spain and the EC, see Maxwell and Spiegel, 1994, p.38.

6   At the time Spain joined the EC, Spain had the third largest fishing fleet in the world. By contrast, none of the EC states were among the top ten fishing countries in the world (Oliver, 1985, pp.357-358). See also Maxwell and Spiegel, 1994, p.39.

7   Over the period from August 1990 to July 1991 I conducted over three dozen interviews with Spanish political and economic elites. One of the questions I asked members of the Socialist Party or Spanish government was: What role did the example of the failure of the French socialist economic experiment under President François Mitterrand play in influencing the economic policy choices of the Spanish Socialist government? Of eleven interviewees who responded directly to this question, only three said that the PSOE had decided not to follow a

classical socialist economic policy even before Mitterrand came to power. The other nine maintained that Mitterrand's failure either had a large demonstration effect on the PSOE or, at least, confirmed the PSOE's hunch that a socialist economic plan would be a disaster.

8   Personal interview. Another former senior official told me that during the period of negotiations there was a continuous process of recalculating the costs and benefits of EC membership. He went on to say that the give and take of the talks was, in itself, seen as a positive phenomenon. Personal interview. In addition, a PSOE parliamentarian claims that the government could not possibly have anticipated the costs and benefits of EC membership.

9   This information was supplied in an internal memorandum from Joan Reventós, Spanish Ambassador to France, to Spanish Foreign Minister Fernando Morán (12 December 1983, p.5).

10   Concerning agricultural exports, one Spanish negotiator in EC membership talks commented: '[I] have tried to point out...that the coupling of Spanish and Community agriculture is global, economically profitable, and strengthens the Green Europe, with sub-sectoral problems which must not obscure the perspective of the whole...' (Botella, 1984).

11   Although the Socialist government likes to defend the agreement it signed for entry into the EC, less partisan voices take a more objective position. One senior official at the Banco de España told me that the enthusiasm for Europe had its drawbacks: 'When you accept European integration whole heartedly, you accept a lot of negative things along the way. The outcome of the EC entry talks were not all that favorable for Spain. But there wasn't a lot of discussion on Spain joining the EC; it was pretty much agreed to all around.'

12   At home, this policy was sold to the disgruntled fishing regions as one which would modernize the Spanish fishing industry. In fact, the EC's Common Fisheries Policy provided insufficient aid and guidelines to modernize the Spanish fishing industry, forcing the Spanish government to provide additional funding and support to bring the sector up to competitive standards (Jaen, 1989, pp.225-228).

13   One former economic advisor to the Socialist government stated in an interview for this project that the leadership's enthusiasm for European integration has blinded them to the costs and benefits of joining Europe.

14   This information was related in a personal interview.

15   This information was related in an interview with a confidant of President Felipe González.

16   Personal interview.

17   In an interview conducted for this project, a former PSOE government minister asked rhetorically, in the case that the pro-European enthusiasm of the PSOE leadership had not overlapped with the sentiments of Spain's large center vote, what would the PSOE have done: modified its position to capture the center vote, or maintained its pro-Europeanism? In this most extreme case, the former minister, speaking for himself, but as a knowledgeable member of the PSOE leadership, thinks that the PSOE would have pursued the latter path. That is, it would have maintained its pro-European agenda and not have gone after the center vote. Quite simply, the pull of Europe was the overriding factor.

18   A former PSOE government official related in an interview for this project that the PSOE did not make economic changes to get votes. Rather, it got votes by making successful economic changes. Indeed, the PSOE undertook plenty of very *unpopular* economic policies (like closing factories, etc.) which certainly did *not* win it votes. During the 1986-89 legislative period, however, the PSOE's strategy was much more designed to win votes, once economic modernization was well underway.

19   A worker voiced these sentiments, in what typified the attitudes faced by the PSOE government: 'A lot of people liked having a center-right government. But the [UCD] government did not do anything, so we had to have a change. I did not vote Socialist because I wanted Socialism' (Kurlansky, 1983, p.30).

20   Speaking at the College of Europe in Bruges, Belgium on October 10, 1985, Felipe González declared: 'If we wish to advance the road to political integration, it is important first to overcome the conflict between national and EC interests. We cannot support those who claim that nationalism is realistic, and integration merely idealism' (*Europe*, January-February 1986, p.48).

21   One top Spanish economic official, Luís Angel Rojo, noted: 'Europe today is not an ideal model, but still, it has a lot to teach us; and if we learn quickly and think on our own account, perhaps we will have some things to contribute to the European dialog' (*Cambio 16*, 8 April 1985, p.23).

6 Spain's European policy after 1986

In this chapter I offer a discussion of Spain's European policy beyond the momentous events of the early and mid 1980s.[1] I do this to determine if the unfolding of Spanish foreign policy subsequent to 1986 - the year Spain entered the EC, and approved NATO membership in a national referendum - conform to the theoretical framework I offer throughout the rest of this study. Some explanations of Spanish foreign policy in the immediate post-Franco period focus on the nature of democratic transition and consolidation (see Chapter Two). These theories would predict that once democracy was consolidated in Spain, Spanish foreign policy would take on a different shape. Instead, I argue that Spain's European policy is formed more by the conceptualization of European integration at the level of European institutions. Therefore, the theoretical construct that informs this book anticipates that Spanish foreign policy will be shaped less by developments in Spain's domestic politics and more by the ongoing process of European integration itself.

Review of the Spanish case in the early and mid 1980s

Spain's resolution of the contentious NATO issue and entry into the European Community, both occurring in early 1986, represented a turning point in Spanish politics. Spanish leaders successfully discarded the old idea that 'Spain is different' from the rest of Europe and shepherded Spain into its 'rightful place' in European affairs.[2] As Esther Barbé points out, Spain took a more realistic view of European institutions 'once it had overcome "the Europeanist illusion" that came with the homogenization of the "isolated country" with its European neighbors' (Barbé, 1995, p.114). This meant a retreat from the Socialists' claims of the negative security effects of membership in NATO, and a reformulation of perceptions of what was in Spain's economic interests in the process of EC integration.

During the period in question, the linkages between Spain's continued membership in NATO and its proposed entry into the EC, while not formal, served to focus the minds of Spanish leaders on the possible harmful effects of jeopardizing European unity (Mujal-Leon, 1986, p.229). Similarly, the need to strengthen the economic health of the European Community required Spanish leaders to moderate their demands and adopt a broader conception of long term economic interests. In both these instances, Spanish leaders were forced to question old assumptions and adopt new conceptions of what Europe means, what their claims to what specific foreign policies imply, and what Spain's national interests should be.

As the changes in Socialist foreign policy positions up to 1986 show, the PSOE governing elite adapted its thinking about foreign affairs through a process of learning about European political realities as conceptualized by their European counterparts. One interesting feature is the degree to which Socialist leaders were willing to acknowledge that this learning took place. In a 1987 interview Felipe González admitted:

> Facing society [the party] has announced changes of position....At times it is said that this implies abandoning utopian ideas or positions of principle. I think that here there has been a difficult process of learning for everyone and education for everyone....The transition from a dictatorship, which left a large accumulation of ideology, to a position that is the position of the European Left in its entirety while maintaining the peculiarities that every country has, has been undertaken in Spain in a very rapid fashion and led by the Socialist Party (Calvo Hernando, 1987, pp.181-182).

However, it is important to note that European international relations equally were altered by the absorption of Spain into the mainstream of continental affairs. Therefore, we should understand this learning process not as a one-way street from the core to the periphery, but as a process by which European political reality was fundamentally altered by all parties involved.

Because I adopt a position in which political reality is viewed as socially constructed, the type of learning and assimilation of knowledge I describe does not imply that Spanish leaders necessarily learned the 'right' lessons about how the world works.[3] Nor did they simply discard simplistic ideas about politics in favor of more complex ones. As Jack Levy writes:

> A more complex world view does not always lead to a superior understanding of the world or to a better sense of how to advance one's own interests, and a better understanding of the world does not always require a sophisticated cognitive conception. One can be complex but wrong, or simple but right (Levy, 1992, p.8).

In other words, Spanish leaders lost confidence in the knowledge base that supported their world view and adopted the prevailing notions accepted among Western European elites of cause-and-effect relationships among specific policies. They learned what was accepted political reality as it was constructed by the leaders of Western European political society.

Perhaps more than at any other time in Spain's history over the last five hundred years, then, Spanish foreign policy in the early 1980s was focused primarily on relations with the rest of Europe. The advent of democracy in Spain made European countries more willing to extend full membership and privileges in European institutions. Likewise, increased ties with these institutions, and with European leaders, helped the Socialist government in Spain to discard ideas framed through the experience of political life under dictatorship and adapt interest perceptions to European norms. In defense matters, this meant switching to support of Spanish membership in NATO, while in economic matters this meant accepting the logic of European integration established by leading EC states. By enduring as a consolidated democracy and by becoming established members of the EC and NATO, Spain has emerged as a full partner in discussions of the future of European integration (Pérez-Díaz, 1990, p.37). However, as I will discuss in the concluding chapter to this book, a country need not be a 'full member' of international society to have an effect on it.

Spain's European policy since 1986

After having established democracy, resolved the debate over the Atlantic Alliance, and achieved membership in the European Community, Spain's leaders since 1986 view European integration from the vantage point of full-fledged members of NATO and the EU. They have come to see that the process of European integration has intrinsic values of its own beyond serving as an anchor for Spanish democracy. Spain was fully in favor of the Single European Act, the single market program embodied in the 'Project 1992,' and the Maastricht Treaty.[4] Now, Spanish leaders are attempting to ensure that what constitutes the 'community's interests' benefit the less developed economies in the European Union, as well as leading to prosperity throughout Europe. In the realm of security, the Spanish government has acted to maintain unity of action among European states within Western defense institutions, and has been an active player in the search for a formula for post-Cold War security in Europe.

The Spanish experience of membership in European institutions has fulfilled the Socialists' idea of what it is like to be 'normal' members of Europe. Richard Gillespie has pointed out:

> As European integration deepened, it became even more crucial than in the past for Spain to place itself among the 'core' European countries in

order to avoid the danger of 're-peripherization' in the event of the moves towards European convergence breaking down and a 'two-track' Europe resulting (Gillespie, 1995b, p.198).

Unlike Greece, for example, Spain has enjoyed a degree of credibility while attempting to forge a community interest in economic and defense related matters. While important segments of Greece's political elite - most notably, members of the socialist party PASOK - were unsure or openly doubtful of the supposed benefits that membership in European institutions would bring, opposition to Europeanization within Spanish elite circles has been virtually non-existent.[5] Susannah Verney has observed that Spain and Greece differ in their paths of economic development and economic institutions, their different routes to democratic transition and consolidation, and their distinct histories of relations with the rest of Europe.[6] Drawing on Verney's observation, Berta Álvarez-Miranda argues that these structural and attitudinal differences have rendered Spain more receptive to the processes of European integration (Álvarez-Miranda, 1995). Thus, unlike Greece, Spain has enjoyed a degree of credibility while attempting to forge a community interest.

This affirmation of European unity has won support for Spain by the other members of NATO and the EU. Countries like Greece that come across looking petty and self-interested in difficult areas of European security or when making demands in EU negotiations find that the institutions of European integration are ill-suited to parochialism. In addition, other states are not predisposed towards configuring European institutions to cater to narrow demands. Spanish concerns, by contrast, *are* taken seriously by other NATO and EU members because they are perceived to promote the common good. Thus, when institution-building within Europe takes place, the common vision advanced by Spanish leaders largely is built into the design of these institutions.

The Socialist government that was in power in Spain from 1982 to 1996 was unwavering in its support for European integration. It understood Spanish history as revealing one indisputable fact: Whenever Spain has been isolated from the rest of Europe it has experienced authoritarian governments and has fallen behind Europe in economic modernization. The solution, then, is to hitch Spain to the 'train of Europe.'

Yet broad goals must be substantiated through specific strategies. The abstract 'idea of Europe' has existed in many guises throughout history. The means chosen to achieve European integration reflect changed knowledge shared among European leaders about how best to achieve unification while serving the interests of European states. In instances where this knowledge is institutionalized, interests converge and the idea of European integration is advanced. Spanish leaders thus learned an interesting lesson on the eve of joining the EC in 1986: Because the Single European Act was devised in part to accommodate the southern enlargement of the EC, Spain's own national interests (and those of every EC state) depended on maintaining the health of the Community as a whole. The Single European Act (SEA) and the final stages of Spanish and Portuguese EC membership were negotiated simultaneously. This principle of linking national interests to community interests has continued through the Project 1992 and the drive towards fulfilling the elements of the Maastricht Treaty (Ortega, 1994, pp.151-154). In the realm of security policy, this has meant Spanish support for a panoply of European defense institutions and military actions. In most areas discussed of European economic integration, solutions to issues of Spanish concern exist within a larger EU context.

Spain and European security relations since 1986

In the post-1986 period, Spain's Socialist government sought a greater role in shaping European politics. The government's foreign policy was a reflection of its leaders' political maturation and self-conscious desire to make Spain a legitimate partner in the process of European integration. This is not to say that Spanish leaders resolved every question regarding European political integration. Rather, they came to see themselves as full partners in the process and not students under the tutelage of the established European democracies. Spain's foreign policy also has been a function of the dynamics of a European integration process which has been characterized by rapid change. As the intense ideological debate that erupted from Spain's entry into NATO in May 1982 illustrates, Spanish membership in Western defense institutions has been much more than a simple matter of participation in a series of military coalitions. In the process of adopting the European point of view on NATO, the Socialist government leadership toned down its anti-American rhetoric and sought to participate in the construction of a new European security space.

This is important for explaining post-1986 Spanish defense policy. No longer did the government portray NATO as an instrument of the United States. - a bully which had legitimated Franquist rule. Instead, membership in NATO was an exercise in promoting the maintenance of European peace. In a speech at Harvard University in 1988 Felipe González proclaimed:

> And from this [the conviction that Spain should end its tradition of isolationism] arises our intention to share with the other Europeans not only values and projects of economic integration and political cooperation, but also our obligations to collective security. This is what explains why Spain, after more than a century of seclusion from all types of alliances, has approved by popular referendum - the sole case up to now - the continued membership in the Atlantic Alliance and has expressed its disposition to participate in the new phase of the Western European Union. All of this reflects a clear commitment to solidarity in European and Western defense...(González, 1988).

As González's remarks indicate, the adoption of a European point of view has had repercussions for Spanish foreign policy ideas in general, and about security policy in specific. Whereas the government previously construed Spanish security in a narrow sense, it has come to accept the logic of collective security that is integral to the Western defense community.

This is extremely relevant to European security in the post-Cold War era. In sharp contrast to the bipolar conflict, Spain is central to the emerging security issues in post-Cold War Europe. The demands for autonomy by Spain's distinct linguistic and cultural regions, Spanish vulnerability to instability in North Africa, the rise in activity by right wing extremist groups and racist thugs, and penetration by international drug traffickers are examples of security threats to Spain that parallel larger dangers to European security. Thus, Spain's traditional security concerns now resonate in Europe's new-found preoccupation with instability in the Third World in general, and along the shores of the Mediterranean in specific.

Spain's eagerness to participate in Western and European security arrangements can be seen in a variety of areas. In addition to the Spanish government's continued cooperation with the United States and NATO, it also has taken steps to promote the uniquely European component of common Atlantic defense. This is in accord with the government's consistent enthusiasm for European integration writ large. A major step Spain took in this direction occurred in 1988 when it joined the Western European Union (WEU). Initially, Spain raised eyebrows with other WEU states when it applied for membership in the organization but declared that it would prefer to act militarily only in areas of Spain's own national interest, and insisted that nuclear weapons not be installed on Spanish soil. When Spanish leaders softened their demands and accepted the Hague Platform, the Rome Declaration, and the Brussels Treaty, Spain was granted WEU membership on 14 November 1988 (Rodrigo, 1992, pp.109-110). Although the WEU is still an organization with very little meaning outside NATO, the Spanish leadership shares with the French government, among others, the desire to give the WEU more independence from NATO and more coordination with the European Community (M. Clarke, 1991, pp.184-185). This is especially important, given the Spanish government's interest in expanding the scope of the EU's economic and political union to include the creation of a unified EU foreign policy.

In addition, increasingly Spain has fulfilled its obligations militarily in Europe. In 1992 the Spanish government approved a new statement on defense policy known as the 'Directiva de Defensa Nacional' (DDN). Fernando Rodrigo observes: 'The new DDN explains that the security of Spain is not only related to the defense of territory; it speaks also of the importance for Spain of the European strategic landscape and of other world crises that could affect its security' (Rodrigo 1995b, p.163). Thus, while the Socialist government in the 1980s made sure that the United States agreed not to station nuclear weapons on

Spanish soil and insisted that the USA remove its Air Force Wing 401 from the Torrejón air base, Spain remains essential to NATO providing air and sea defenses to the vital Western Mediterranean which are crucial for European security (Maxwell and Spiegel, 1994, p.56).

The clearest expression of the change in Spanish security policy and attitudes towards collective security was Spain's support for the allied coalition effort in the 1990-91 Persian Gulf crisis and war. The Spanish government pledged two corvettes and one frigate from the Spanish Navy to assist in the embargo against Iraq. Speaking before the *Cortes*, President González defended his decision to deploy these ships, and grant permission to the United States to use its air bases in Spain as a staging point for troop deployment:

> I want to say that the Government has...taken, the decision to send the frigate and the two corvettes, as much as the decision to facilitate the deployment of troops of the United States to the Persian Gulf countries, with the full liberty, responsibility, and conviction that is our obligation in defense of our interests as a country, in defense of our interests in accord with our European vocation, and in defense of our interests as members of the international community (*Sesión Informativa Sobre el Conflicto del Golfo Pérsico*, 1990, p.17).

During the war, American long-range bombers also relied heavily on the United States air base at Morón de la Frontera as a principle staging area for bombing raids on Iraq. The Spanish government's decision to support the allied war effort provoked a great deal of angry response in Spain and protest over the sending of Spanish forces to the first overseas military adventure in which Spain has participated since the Spanish-American War.[7] What is remarkable, however, is that the level of protest was far more muted than in other European states like France, Belgium, and even Germany, which sent no combat troops at all.

Felipe González defended his decision to assist in the preparations for war by arguing that it served Spanish interests of cementing Spain's place in Europe:

> We think that [the decision] is coherent with our political project, not only with our project to create an economic Europe or a Europe with an interior market, but a Europe that is politically united and, therefore, with the capacity to make decisions in the realm of foreign policy and security policy and, thus, the decision is coherent with our effort to add our voice to the other Community countries (*Sesión Informativa Sobre el Conflicto del Golfo Pérsico*, 1990, p.20).

Similar to the way that González defended his decision to support continued Spanish membership in NATO, his analysis of the Gulf War situation was framed by the wider process of European integration in its many aspects. The difference is that the reversal on NATO in the early 1980s was prompted by the urging of other European leaders, whereas González's decision to pledge Spanish support for action against Iraq was simultaneous with the actions of other Western countries, and complementary to them.

Following its successful participation in the Gulf War effort, the Spanish government attempted to assume a leadership role in the resolution of the war in the former Yugoslav republics. The search for solutions based on a common European response was reflected in Spain's backing of the ill-fated safe haven concept for Bosnian Muslim refugees.[8] Working with other European leaders and with the United Nations, the Spanish government was optimistic that a unified European response could be formulated. Yet despite the common idea that the Balkan war threatened the norms of national self-determination, the Europeans - including the Spanish government - for the most part found the search for consensual understanding on how to end the war difficult. Indeed, many aspects of the resolution of the Balkans conflict to date have been engineered not by the European Union, but by NATO under the leadership of the United States, a country with which the PSOE had a difficult relationship during the initial post-Franco era in Spain.[9]

The Balkan tragedy alerted Europeans to the types of security threats they face in a post-Cold War world. While the superpower nuclear threat has faded, problems of ethnic nationalism, regional instability, and uncontrolled migration have risen to the fore. Many of these problems reside in countries on Europe's borders. The theme of security along Europe's periphery has taken on added significance with the increased flow of economic refugees streaming into Europe. For Spain, the point of reference is North Africa, specifically, the countries of northwest Africa that comprise what is known as the Maghreb. Miguel Angel Moratinos, Spain's Foreign Ministry Director for North African Affairs commented: 'To create prosperity and stability in the Maghreb is to assure peace and security in Spain. To permit instability and underdevelopment in North Africa is to invest in crises and conflicts that, whether we like it or not, will be exported here' (The New York Times, 20 March 1991, p.A13). In 1992, the Spanish government released a report on security in Africa and the Middle East and concluded that 'the Maghreb today is a time bomb that Europe is able to deactivate' (López García and Nuñez Villaverde, 1994, p.141).

Spain has been instrumental in initiating a Mediterranean policy for the EU. In some sense this is ironic since early PSOE statements on Mediterranean policy in general, and the Maghreb in specific, were informed by the party's 'Third Worldist' tendencies which characterized PSOE foreign policy theory in the immediate post-Franco era. Based on its Third Worldist philosophy, the PSOE government initially set out to undertake a unilateral policy towards its southern Mediterranean neighbors. Over time, however, Spain has formulated its Mediterranean policy within the framework of European institutions. Thus, the lead that Spain currently has taken demonstrates accumulated learning on Spain's part, and also shows the degree to which Spain has internalized European norms so that it actually champions them (Tovias, 1995, p.103). As Andrés Ortega points out: 'Many problems that used to be bilateral now have a European Union dimension. ...In its approach to the Maghreb, Spain needs the European Union as a force and means multiplier' (Ortega, 1995, p.44).

Regarding the Europe's Mediterranean policy in specific, after establishment of the EC's Global Mediterranean Policy (GMP) in 1972, talks between southern EU states and North African countries remained dormant until southern EU states placed them on the agenda in the mid-1990s. At the July 1995 Cannes summit of the European Council, Helmut Kohl and Felipe González were instrumental in developing a new package of increased economic aid for both Eastern Europe and the Mediterranean region. This is increasingly important for European security in light of the rise of Islamic fundamentalism in the Maghreb. The December 1991 electoral victory of the Islamic Salvation Front in Algeria and the subsequent nullification of the elections by the Algerian military focused the minds of Europeans on instability in the region (Ortega, 1995, pp.36-37).

Spain's traditional 'special relationship' with the Arab world allows it to pursue a leadership role in this effort.[10] Among the most important institutional spaces championed by Spain to coordinate a European response to instability in the entire Mediterranean region is the Conference on Security and Cooperation in the Mediterranean (CSCM). The CSCM was formalized in 1991 by France, Italy, Spain, and Portugal after the so-called four-plus-five talks were initiated between the aforementioned European countries and five North African states (Badini, 1995, pp.111-112; Rodrigo, 1992, p.113). The CSCM, which was patterned after the Conference on Security and Cooperation in Europe (CSCE), would operate in a complementary fashion to, but independently of, the European Union.[11] After the creation of the CSCM, the Western European Union carried out an ongoing dialogue in Brussels with ambassadors from the Maghreb states, but these talks did not yield meaningful policies beyond institutionalizing such confidence building measures as the talks themselves (Casanova Fernández, 1993, p.46).

The EU experienced a change of mood beginning in 1994 and extending through 1996 when Greece, France, Spain, and Italy held the rotating presidency of the European Council in near succession (Germany held the Council presidency during the second half of 1994 between the Greek and French presidencies). At the June 1994 Corfu summit Greece proposed a conference on Mediterranean issues that would be held during the Spanish presidency of the European Council. On 19 October 1994, the European Commission proposed an economic and security plan for the Mediterranean to lay the groundwork for the EU Conference on the Mediterranean, held in Barcelona 27-28 November 1995. The Barcelona Conference produced an aid package that includes 4.7 billion ECU ($6 billion) in assistance to twelve non-EU Mediterranean states between 1996 and 1999, and also guarantees the gradual lifting of trade barriers on selected products culminating in a regional free trade area by the year 2010 (*The Economist*, 2 December 1995, pp.49-50; *El País* International Edition, 27 November 1995, pp.4-5).

While the EU's Mediterranean policy is still a work in progress, it is an indication that the European Union is seeking to provide an institutional context to deal with pressing post-Cold War security concerns. Spanish participation in these efforts marks the culmination of the transformation from Spain's unilateral policy towards the Mediterranean to its acceptance of the EU as the proper forum to create stability in the region. This is important as regional instability in the Mediterranean constitutes a significant threat to European security. NATO and the WEU were created to deal with superpower related defense matters and have not yet devised a strategy for dealing with 'out of area' conflicts. Spanish leaders have exhibited a degree of foresight in recognizing that Europe's security depends on a coordinated effort to confront diffuse threats which affect all European states regardless of their proximity to zones of regional instability.

Finally, perhaps the most telling indication of changed attitudes in Spain about Western security institutions was the ascension of Spain's Socialist Foreign Minister Javier Solana to the position of NATO Secretary General in December of 1995. Solana was one of the members of the Socialist government in Spain that was most opposed to Spanish membership in NATO in the early 1980s. His selection as NATO chief coincided with the decision by the Spanish government to incorporate Spain fully into the alliance's Military Committee, leaving the country out of only NATO's Integrated Military Command Structure (*El País*, International Edition, 11 December 1995, pp.1-3). Solana himself was honest about his radically changed views about NATO: 'Those who are not extremely conservative, and I am not, must be ready to change with the times' (*The Economist*, 9 December 1995, p.51). This is a stunning admission among the leaders of a political party that only a decade earlier accepted membership in NATO only grudgingly.

What the brief review of Spain's security policy in Europe presented here illustrates is the fact that Spanish leaders are eager to work within the institutions that coordinate European security. Within NATO, Spain has played an active role, as exemplified in the Persian Gulf crisis and the war in the Balkans. Within the European Union, Spain has worked with its partners to adopt a policy towards the Maghreb that furthers the EU's interests in the region, become a member of the WEU, and acted in favor of nascent organizations such as the joint 'Eurocorps'. This is far different from the dubious attitude Spaniards took towards Western security institutions in the immediate post-Franco era.

Spain and European economic integration since 1986

Negotiations for Spanish membership in the European Community during the 1980s came at a time when the EC itself was facing uncertainties. The act of incorporating Spain into the Community became an occasion for undertaking fundamental change of the EC. Gian Paolo Papa - the Director of the EC Commission in Spain - declared that the remedy to the errors of the past would come:

> Only via the multiplier effect that is created through actions undertaken not at a national level but at a European level....In order for this conception to be established only one condition is necessary: that a significant group of entities, a sufficient number of people in socioeconomic and political circles identify clearly with the common European interest. This is the task that Spain can and must contribute with its membership in the Community....Membership is not only an exercise in accounting. It deals with jointly defining the future of the Community, and the integration of Spain represents, above all, the possibility to participate in this common reflection (Papa, 1985, p.64).

Thus, Spanish entry into the EC transformed the reality of European integration, just as it was transformed during the first enlargement of the EEC, and just as it has been transformed by the momentous changes that characterized the EC in the period since Spain became a member.

As with Spanish relations with NATO since 1986, Spain's membership in the EU has been marked by continuity with the principles that were codified by Spanish accession to the Community. Having shed the last of its pretensions of being a party of the masses, the PSOE worked towards deepening the economic modernization that has accompanied EC membership. The first test of Spain's commitment to cooperation in forging closer links among the member states of the European Community was the negotiation of the Single European Act (SEA) in 1986. Spain, Greece, Portugal, and Ireland were concerned that as the EC moved forward, funds would be allocated for development in these less developed states (Garrett, 1992, pp.544-545). However, the Spanish government did not press these demands so as to derail the completion of the internal market as envisioned by other Community members. Rather, it engaged in the type of confidence building that characterized negotiations for Spanish membership in the early 1980s, and has become a leader in the search for solutions to Community problems. This pattern was continued through the creation of the Single Market in 1992 and the signing of the Treaty of European Union (TEU) in Maastricht.

Space limitations do not permit a full review of Spanish experiences in all facets of European economic integration. However, two issue areas provide a picture of how Spain has fit into the process of European economic integration. The first is economic and monetary union (EMU), and the second is the European Union's cohesion policy. These two policy areas are representative of the way that Spain has internalized European norms at the same time as it has emerged as a player in the ongoing debate over how these norms should be translated into policy.

Economic and monetary union benefits less developed EU countries like Spain. Even with all barriers to the free movement of goods, services, capital, and labor removed, the absence of a single currency and European central bank makes economic development difficult in regions of the EU that rely heavily on foreign investment to fuel their economies.[12] The Spanish peseta was introduced into the European Monetary System (EMS) during the summer of 1989 and was timed to coincide with Spain's presidency of the rotating European Council which culminated at the Madrid Summit. Countries like Germany were in favor of all EC currencies tied to a narrow exchange rate band, but also were willing to wait for Spanish interest and inflation rates to fall before asking Spain to tie the peseta to a narrow fluctuation rate required by the EMS (De la Dehesa, 1988b). In addition, most EC states were eager to commit Great Britain to joining the EMS, and the peseta's entry into the exchange rate system would put pressure on London (*ABC*, 22 June 1989, p.39). Indeed, there is some evidence that German leaders bargained with the Spanish in return for the peseta's early entry into the EMS so as to put increased pressure on British Prime Minister Margaret Thatcher.[13] González was eager to serve as an effective host in Madrid and had his own agenda which included passage of the so-called Social Charter, something to which the British were opposed (*El País*, 25 June 1989, pp.16-19; *ABC*, 26 June 1989, pp.73-80). In exchange for strong German support of the Social Charter González agreed to place the peseta prematurely within the EMS.[14]

The decision by the Spanish government to insert the peseta into the EMS in the summer of 1989 was largely a political move. Prime Minister González wanted to demonstrate that Spain was committed to complete economic integration in the EC. However, the decision also advanced Spanish economic strategy. The fixed exchange rates permitted the government to pursue an unconventional 'policy-mix' by relying on the 'imported credibility' the deutschemark afforded through the European Monetary System (Pérez, 1994). As long as the deutschemark lent credibility to the peseta through the EMS, Spanish economic policy makers were free to pursue policies that encouraged foreign investment and allowed the government to engage in social welfare spending while holding the line on wage increases.

However, this economic strategy had pernicious effects on the EMS. By September of 1992 the six per cent fluctuation rate established for the peseta in 1989 and the Spanish government's economic 'policy mix' contributed in part to what has become known as the EMS Crisis of 1992-93. During the crisis the peseta came under heavy fire in financial markets and the Spanish government was forced to undertake three devaluations of the peseta resulting in a 19 per cent drop in the value of the currency instead of withdrawing from the EMS entirely (*La Vanguardia*, 17 September 1993, p.58). The government was then forced to seek a wider berth for the peseta within the EMS, asking for, and receiving, a 15 per cent fluctuation rate, as opposed to removing the peseta from the EMS altogether.[15] Yet, unlike leaders in London and Rome, Spain's government refused to withdraw the peseta from the EMS, preferring the ignominy of three devaluations and the currency's loss of 19 per cent of its value against the deutschemark in little over half a year.[16]

During the Spanish presidency of the European Council (July-December 1995) monetary union was again on the agenda. The Reflection Group on the 1996 Intergovernmental Conference (chaired by Spanish Secretary of State for EU Affairs Carlos Westendorp) affirmed its unanimous consensus to work towards a single currency by the time frame agreed to in the amended Maastricht Treaty. Specifically, EU Economy and Finance ministers decided at their meeting in Valencia (29 September - 1 October 1995) that a first group of EU states should be in a position to adopt the new currency by 1 January 1999. The European Central Bank is also to be operational on that date. The single currency is then to be in circulation in all EU states no later that 31 December 2001, with a six month transition period in which the single currency will circulate alongside existing currencies. National currencies would then disappear by 1 July 2002. The will of Spanish economic policy makers to comply with the convergence criteria was revealed on the verge of the Madrid summit in 1995 when the Governor of the Banco de España Luis Ángel Rojo declared that Spain plausibly could be ready for the single currency by 1999 from an economic standpoint, although politically this would be difficult (*El País* International Edition, 27 November 1995, p.23).

The expected difficulties faced by EU member states in meeting the requirements for participating in the single currency has been the source of domestic political tension in various EU states. This was most notable in France during the weeks prior to the Madrid summit. Faced with a bloated public deficit, the French government proposed changes in the pension plan for state employees, leading to a mass walk-out by public sector labor unions, government bureaucrats, and their sympathizers (*The New York Times*, 8 December 1995, p.A1). The French government's decision to force a showdown with state employees in order to trim the budget was tied directly to the requirements for EMU (Dillingham, 1996). The Spanish government wished to avoid the same fate as France. 'In April 1992 the government presented its economic agenda, entitled *Programa de Convergencia 1992-96*, which laid out its plans for attaining the Maastricht criteria' (Maxwell Steven Spiegel, 1994, p.51). This plan ran into problems, and Spain's Minster of Economy, Pedro Solbes, warned in late 1995 that the overheated Spanish economy - brought about in part by government spending - was straining the public deficit and forcing the Banco de España to keep interest rates high to avoid inflation. Solbes hinted that public spending would have to be cut significantly if Spain was to get on track for monetary union by 1999 (*El País* International Edition, 23 December 1995, p.23).

Most observers do not expect Spain to fulfil the convergence criteria by 1999. However, Spain's economic leadership claims that there is still the possibility of being ready for the single currency by the deadline and is making efforts to do so. In a series of appearances before parliamentary commissions and in public fora, Banco de España Governor Rojo argued that Spain can be ready for the single currency by 1999, but only if it takes measures to meet the convergence criteria, most notably, the reduction of the public deficit (*El País* International Edition, 27 November 1995, p.23). Rojo was realistic in his public pronouncements, however, and acknowledged that meeting the convergence criteria by 1999 would impose short term hardships on the Spanish economy.

The question, then, is if the Spanish government is willing to suffer domestic political tensions, along the lines of those experienced in France, in the name of monetary union. Part of Rojo's concern at the end of 1995 was based on the fact that the Socialist government of Felipe González was under intense fire over charges of corruption and was not expected to fare well in the anticipated elections expected for March of 1996. Ironically, this uncertainty may have had a catalytic effect on Spain's policy towards EMU. González may have calculated that he had nothing to lose by advancing a program of austerity given that polls already showed he was likely to lose the upcoming elections. Furthermore, the main opposition party, the Partido Popular, after emerging victorious in the 1996 elections, found itself in a similar situation as the Chirac government in France. That is, it could use its electoral mandate early in its administration to cut government spending to meet the convergence criteria for EMU.

This willingness of Spain's leaders to submit the Spanish economy to short term dislocations in expectation of long term benefits is significant given that low unemployment rates are not among the convergence criteria for EMU. Indeed, fulfillment of the convergence criteria not only would not necessarily lower Spanish unemployment rates, but probably would sustain high joblessness. Spanish leaders' greatest fear, then, is of the 'two-speed' Europe that would delay the benefits of EMU for the weak currency members of the EU while still trying to comply with the convergence criteria. Having tied its fortunes to the philosophy of currency stability, Spain's leaders need to make sure that Spain is ready to reap the benefits of monetary union. In the short run, Spain will face its fair share of economic dislocations caused by meeting the convergence criteria. In the long run, Spanish leaders (on both the left and right) accept the logic that a single currency will lead to greater economic growth by lowering transaction costs and making capital more mobile.[17] In 1994, in a public show of confidence in the logic of monetary integration, Spanish decision makers indicated that they would not veto a decision to issue the single currency even if Spain were not in the group of states that met the convergence criteria (*El País*, 6 June 1994, p.51). Spain's current government leaders likely will stick to that commitment.

The other area that demonstrates Spanish adherence to European Union norms is the EU's 'cohesion policy'. This is the set of policies by which funds are made available to foster development in the least prosperous regions of the Union. Although even the wealthiest EU states contain regions qualified for cohesion policy funds, the great bulk of these funds have been directed to the four least developed member states of the Union, the so-called 'poor four' of Greece, Ireland, Portugal, and Spain. It is in these countries that the beneficial effects of EU membership have not completely taken hold.[18] Thus, cohesion policy is an especially pressing concern for Spanish leaders.

Funds for regional development exist in two forms that operate in distinct fashions. Structural Funds are designed to assist all economically backwards areas of the European Union. There are a variety of types of funds available dealing with agriculture, regional infrastructure, industrial policy, etc. The most important element of the Structural Funds is the European Regional Development Fund (ERDF). Because the Structural Funds are destined for regions of the European Union - as opposed to member states - the administration of the funds has led to a proliferation of interlocutors and claimants. This has occurred much to the chagrin of states such as Spain, which fear that the multiplication of channels by which Structural Funds are distributed has made the program inefficient and unwieldy (G. Marks, 1996; Ruiz-Navarro Pinar, 1991). The newer Cohesion Funds are designed to aid not specific regions of the EU, but the four poorest EU states, whose GNP per capita is below 90 per cent of the Union's average. The types of programs to be funded are restricted to domestic infrastructure, and projects for environmental recovery around zones of industrial and agricultural development.

Spanish leaders have subscribed to the idea of fashioning a common interest of cohesion, and argue that development funds are necessary if Spain is to achieve the convergence criteria necessary to go forward with the EU's proposed economic and monetary union. European Union funds, in fact, have been instrumental in promoting economic growth in poorer areas of the EU. Still, Spanish leaders remain worried by the Union's financing arrangements which offset the positive effect of Structural and Cohesion Fund transfers. In effect, the result of the Value Added Tax (VAT) and high levels of consumer spending in less wealthy EU states has been such that Spanish leaders fear Spain will become a net contributor to the EC's budget (Biehl, 1992, p.57).

Thus, Spain has lobbied within the EU for an overhaul of budgetary and financial accounting. For example, in 1990 when the European General Affairs Council was enmeshed in one of the semi-regular disputes over EC finances, the Spanish government was intent on making sure there would be adequate funds:

> ...to compensate the poorer member-states for the adverse effects of greater integration. Once the formal negotiations began, Spanish demands became more open and comprehensive, culminating in May 1991 in a proposal that the Community develop a financial mechanism along the lines of the German Finanzausgleich (Ludlow, 1992, pp.76-77).

In this, Prime Minister González not only was proposing the design for a possible

EC compensation fund, but was also appealing to the sensibilities of the Community's wealthiest member.[19]

An effort was made by EC member states to resolve the issue at the European Council's Maastricht Summit in December of 1991. In April of the previous year, during a meeting between Spanish Prime Minister Felipe González and German Chancellor Helmut Kohl on Lanzarote in the Spanish Canary Islands:

> ...the Spanish host took advantage of the occasion to sound out his guest over the latter's willingness to accept the creation of a sort of inter-state compensation fund to augment the current structural funds as a means of deepening the economic and monetary union of the Twelve and to assist the poorer members of the EC to improve, for example, their domestic infrastructure (*El País*, 29 April 1991, p.20).

However the matter was not resolved later in Maastricht as EC members were unable to arrive at a satisfactory solution over the objection by some that such a solution, in conjunction with establishing strict criteria for participation in monetary union, would lead to the much feared 'two-speed' Europe. The new Cohesion Funds proposed by Spain are designed, in part, to make up for the regressive way that EU states are charged to finance the Union's budget.

The issue came to a head at the December 1992 Edinburgh Summit (*The Times* [London], 14 December 1992, p.7a). Spain's Prime Minister was portrayed as the chief spokesman of the poor four. His demands were threefold: Revision of the Structural Funds, modifications in the EU's system of financing its budget, and creation of the new Cohesion Funds. 'González accuse[d] Britain of "stealing" Spain's money by scaling down plans by Jacques Delors...to increase the EC budget by 37% by 1999' (*The Sunday Times* [London], 6 December 1992, p.1/2c). At issue were the regional development funds. González demanded 'a sharp increase in the community budget [ceiling] - from the equivalent of 1.20 percent of the community's total gross national product...to 1.32 percent by 1999' (*The New York Times*, 13 December 1992, p.26). Although a compromise was reached in which González did not get everything he wanted for Spain, the issue became a *cause célèbre* and the Spanish leader did make sure the attention of every EU leader was focused on the matter. As a result of this debate, 15 billion ECU were set aside for the new Cohesion Funds between 1993 and 1999 of which 8 billion ECU are earmarked for Spain (Maxwell and Spiegel, 1994, p.41). In addition, 'the objective of social and economic cohesion became the subject of a special protocol as well as of specific provisions in the [Maastricht] Treaty' (Constas, 1995, p.142).

As one senior foreign policy advisor to former Spanish Prime Minister González has pointed out, regional development funds are a good example of how individual EU states can both protect their individual interests and create community interests.[20] On the surface, Spanish policy in the realm of cohesion may come across as purely parochial. But Spanish leaders are uncomfortable giving that impression, and would prefer that their efforts be seen as congruent with EU norms of equalizing standards of living throughout the Union. They point our that with few exceptions, most EU states benefit in one way or another from cohesion policy, especially the Structural Funds that are earmarked not necessarily for the poorest member states, but for underdeveloped regions. In this respect, just to take two states as examples, wealthy Germany can obtain funds for the new eastern *länder*, and the United Kingdom can offset the deficit it incurs through the Common Agricultural Policy with funds for urban renewal and industrial revitalization. In addition, Spanish leaders like to point out that improved economic conditions in poorer areas can benefit economies that do business with these regions, thus boosting economic performance throughout the EU.

In sum, Spain's experience of membership in the European Union has been one of fitting into established EU norms and, when possible, demonstrating that Spanish interests and the Union's interests as a whole overlap. This is a reflection of the lessons Spanish leaders learned when negotiating membership in the EC. From the Stuttgart summit forward, the understanding shared among European leaders was that individual member states of the European Community would benefit only if the economic health of the EC is maintained. As the European Community was transformed into the European Union by means of the Maastricht Treaty, this principle has been maintained. And as Spain has become one of the more important players in the process of European integration, its leaders have demonstrated that the future economic well-being of both Spain and the EU are intertwined. At times it may appear that Spanish leaders press their case rather forcefully. But as the examples of EMU and cohesion policy show, they understand that Spanish economic gains are impossible unless they are tied to the long term aims of European integration.

Leadership change in Spain and the future of European policy

It would appear from much of the material presented in this book that a great deal of European integration depends on the individual leaders of the member states and their advisors. Indeed, Spain's European vocation was advanced vigorously by former Prime Minister Felipe González. Elected to office in 1982, González forged ties with other European leaders, allowing him to play a large role as one of the chief agents of change in the process of European integration. Yet, while it is true that González was the central figure in Spanish politics for more than a decade, most members of Spain's political parties also share his *Euroenthusiasm* (Álvarez-Miranda, 1995). As we saw in Chapter Two of this book, the 'idea of Europe' holds a privileged position in the foreign policy thinking of Spain's political class. Thus, it is safe to assume that González's successors will continue following the general parameters of Spain's European policy established during the Socialist era.

On 5 May 1996 José María Aznar was sworn in as Prime Minister of Spain, ending over 13 years of Socialist Party rule.[21] The new prime minister is a rather serious man who emerged from Spain's emergent technocratic class. A former tax inspector and leader of the autonomous community of Castille-León, Aznar now has before him the tasks of maintaining the trend towards increasing Spanish participation in European foreign and security affairs, getting Spain to meet the four convergence criteria for EMU, and continuing former prime minister Felipe González's efforts to institutionalize EU cohesion policy.

Despite Aznar's lack of experience in foreign affairs and his more low-key style than his predecessor, it is unlikely that there will be any significant deviation in the European policy of Spain's new conservative coalition government. This is true for both the security and economic aspects of Spain's European policy. The new government likely will seek to explore the construction of a European foreign and security policy while remaining engaged in the Atlantic Alliance. In addition, the new prime minister is committed to constructive engagement in the Mediterranean to promote stability in the region and ease anti-immigrant tensions in some EU member states. With regards to the EU's agenda of economic and monetary union, Aznar now has the opportunity to push towards fulfillment of the convergence criteria in Spain. At the end of his tenure in office, Felipe González began to hint that he would impose measures designed to help Spain fulfil the convergence criteria. González may have calculated that he had nothing to lose by advancing a program of austerity given that polls already showed he was likely to lose the upcoming elections. The victorious Aznar administration may find itself in a similar situation as the Chirac government in France. That is, Aznar can use his electoral mandate to cut government spending to meet the convergence criteria for EMU. However, as the French example shows, this likely will provoke a degree public opposition. Therefore, Aznar must make clear that the short term dislocations caused by spending cutbacks will yield long term gains. Finally, in the area of cohesion policy, Aznar may be able to play upon the goodwill he enjoys among his EU colleagues since he is not tagged with the reputation of chief plaintiff for the 'poor four' as was González. However, Aznar, like González before him, can be expected to invoke the norms of economic and social cohesion enshrined in the integration process as he stresses Spain's case. The point of this discussion is that the change of government in Spain likely will not alter the European path charted by Felipe González and 13 years of Socialist Party rule. There is near unanimous consensus in Spain that there is a seat for Spain on the train of European integration and that Spain can play a constructive role determining the direction of integration while defending Spanish interests.

Summary

In sum, Spain's post-1986 experiences reinforce the conclusions drawn from the NATO and EC cases explored in Chapters Four and Five of this book. That is, Spain's policies towards European integration reflect the way Spanish leaders have come to agree with their European counterparts' understanding of the mechanics of integration. The norms of European integration hold that states should forego short term gains in favor of policies that best serve their common long term interests. Spanish leaders believe in the idea of European unification in its broadest sense, and therefore have internalized these norms. Recent events also demonstrate that Spain is a partner in the construction to solutions of European integration, and not a weak policy-taker (Gillespie, 1995b, p.200). The evidence shows that norms of European integration are constructed such that all states can play a role in deciding the shape of the new Europe. This confirms the argument that, even as a candidate for membership in European institutions, Spain was never 'forced' to make decisions against its will but, instead, was engaged in a larger process of socially constructing the reality of European integration.

The findings discussed in this chapter should put to rest arguments about 'Spanish exceptionalism' in Europe. In the immediate post-Franco era, observers both within and outside Spain feared that the legacy of isolationism established before and during the Franco dictatorship would make it difficult for Spain to become a regular member of Europe. However, as we have seen, Spain has inserted itself with little difficulty into the institutions that normalize European security and that shape European economic integration. To some degree this can be attributed to Spain's size. A country with nearly 40 million inhabitants and an economy that ranks among the ten largest in the world cannot remain on the periphery of European affairs forever.

Yet structural characteristics alone do not tell the whole story. Spanish leaders across the political spectrum have idealized the concept of Europe as the proper setting in which to anchor Spain's post-Franco democracy. In the early and mid 1980s this idea made Spanish leaders receptive to the logic of European political realities. In the period since Spain entered NATO and the EC, the Spanish government continued to demonstrate its commitment to fulfilling both the dream of the founders of the post-World War II integrationist movement, and the policy agenda of Europe's current political engineers. As we shall see in the next two chapters, the Spanish experience serves as a model for understanding the European policies of the formerly communist countries of Central and Eastern Europe and as a test case for theorizing about the nature of European integration. This chapter has established that Spain does not constitute an exceptional case and therefore allows us to use Spain as a template for additional empirical and theoretical inquiry.

Notes

1   Portions of this chapter are adapted from Michael Marks, 'Moving at Different Speeds: Spain and Greece in the European Union', in Katzenstein, Peter J. (ed.) (forthcoming), *Tamed Power: Germany in Europe*, Cornell University Press: Ithaca, NY.

2   The title of the memoirs of former Foreign Minister Fernando Morán - *España en Su Sitio* (Morán, 1990) - translates as 'Spain in its Place'.

3   As I detail in Chapter Three, by 'knowledge' I mean shared understandings of subjective reality. This does not imply that there is such thing as 'right' or 'wrong' knowledge or lessons. For a theoretical discussion of this point, see Sandholtz, 1993, p.11.

4   In October 1992 the Spanish parliament approved the Maastricht Treaty with only three votes opposed, while other European countries delayed action on ratifying the treaty (Maxwell and Spiegel, 1994, p.42).

5   I would like to thanks Nikiforos Diamandouros for his insights on this subject.

6   Susannah Verney, unpublished manuscript.

7   Spanish forces were involved in skirmishes in Morocco and the Spanish Sahara during the twentieth century, but these regions were considered part of metropolitan Spain. The novelty of Spanish troops sent overseas was not lost on the author of this book. I arrived in Spain shortly after the Iraqi invasion of Kuwait. The subsequent voyage of Spanish ships to the Red Sea was covered extensively on Spanish television, replete with images in Spain of weeping mothers of the Spanish sailors. Spanish regulars have not seen combat since the Spanish Civil War.

8   I want to thank Peter Katzenstein for bringing this to my attention and for his advice on this topic.

9   Commenting on the American contribution to solving the Balkans war, NATO Secretary General and former Spanish Defense Minister Javier Solana observed: 'When the USA and Europe have worked together is when the best results have been obtained; this is a good lesson to learn' (*El País* International Edition, 11 December 1995, p.2).

10   Kenneth Maxwell and Steven Spiegel point out that Spain's decision to recognize Israel in 1986 represented the culmination of the PSOE's rejection of its 'Third Worldist' tendencies (Maxwell and Spiegel, 1994, pp.54-55). Still, Spanish leaders attempted to maintain their positive ties to the Arab World.

11   The Conference on Security and Cooperation in the Mediterranean was first proposed by Italian Foreign Minister Gianni De Michelis, and supported by Spain, at a meeting of EC foreign ministers on Mallorca in September 1990 (Olmo, 1991; Yesilada, 1995).

12   The benefits from currency unification are many, ranging from reducing currency transaction costs, to creating economies of scale, to reinforcing quality competition over price competition, etc. (Welfens, 1991, p.40).

13   This assertion is based on interviews conducted in Spain with economists, an official of the European Commission in Spain, and Spanish government officials.

14   Whether or not the Peseta's insertion into the EMS in 1989 was premature is debatable.   Conversations conducted with Spanish economists indicate they felt the move was undertaken in haste and only for political motives. Sources within the Spanish government, however, dispute that assertion and argue that the decision was consummate with the government's economic agenda.

15   Even with the 15 per cent fluctuation band, the peseta was again devalued, on 6 March 1995, by 7 per cent.

16   *The New York Times* reported: 'Government officials insisted that unlike Britain and Italy, Spain was committed to remaining within the monetary system and regarded the fiscal discipline needed to remain there as an essential tool of economic policy. Spain would want any changes in exchange rate levels to amount to a comprehensive realignment aimed at guaranteeing future stability' (*The New York Times*, 5 November 1992, p.D2). This view was supported by a senior official in the Banco de España in an interview conducted for this project.

17   Spanish economist Emilio Ontiveros pointed out in an interview three advantages of devaluation of the peseta over withdrawal from the EMS: 1) It shows Spanish respect for the Maastricht Treaty, 2) It enhances the credibility of the Spanish economy, 3) It allows Spain access to information made available through the EMS.

18   As Keith Salmon points out, even after a decade of EU membership, Spain continues to have one of the least competitive economies among OECD states given the remaining inefficiencies inherent in Spanish economic structures (Salmon, 1995).

19   Jeffrey Anderson has argued that the creation of the Cohesion Funds and an overhaul of EU budgetary practices represented a compromise between Spain and Germany under which Germany agreed to some of Spain's demands in return for Spanish agreement not to veto EMU as spelled out in the Maastricht Treaty (Anderson, 1995, p.142).

20   These observations were made in an interview with Carlos Alonso Zaldívar, Director of the Department of Studies, part of the cabinet of former Spanish Prime Minister Felipe González.

21   Aznar's Popular Party fell short of an absolute majority in the 3 March 1995 parliamentary elections, forcing the conservative leader to forge a center-right coalition government with regional parties from Catalonia, the Basque region, and the Canary Islands.

7 Comparative perspective

In this book I have had two purposes thus far: to explain changes in Spanish policy towards the European Community and NATO, and to develop a theoretical framework for understanding similar instances of foreign policy creation under circumstances comparable to those found in Spain. The empirical material on Spain helps establish the usefulness of the framework of analysis elaborated in Chapter Three. It constitutes what Harry Eckstein calls a 'plausibility probe', that is, preliminary research to determine the validity of a given line of research to determine if more study is warranted (Eckstein, 1975, pp.108-109). However, in order to further validate this framework it is necessary to conduct additional preliminary case studies to supplement the Spanish example. In this chapter I shall offer a research agenda for gauging the generalizability of the theoretical construct developed in this book beyond the Spanish case. In addition, I shall review the foreign policy experiences of a group of new European democracies to test the applicability of this book's propositions. Space limitations do not permit a full examination of these countries' foreign policy experiences. Rather, the empirical review is offered for suggestive purposes to offer a preliminary test of the conclusions drawn from the Spanish case.

Research agenda

The best candidates for initial comparison with Spain are the other two Southern European countries that consolidated democracy in the 1980s. Greece and Portugal, like Spain, were authoritarian states that returned to democracy in the period 1974-77. All three countries were governed during all or part of their democratic transition periods by socialist parties with close ties to fraternal parties in the rest of Europe. In addition, the governments of all three countries have paid particular attention to relations with the EC and NATO in the 1980s. Given these similarities, comparisons among Greece, Portugal, and Spain are considered valid and have been undertaken to explore various aspects of their post-dictatorship political experiences (Kohler, 1982; Pridham, 1984, 1990; Williams, 1984; Lijphart, et.al., 1988).

The formerly communist states of Central and Eastern Europe (CEEC)[1], which currently are trying to consolidate democracy, also serve as good cases with which to undertake a preliminary comparative study with Spain. In the wake of the demise of the bipolar Cold War system, the leaders of the formerly communist states must arrive at new conceptions of economic and security interests. They are doing so during a period of uncertainty, when old ideas about politics are in flux (Larrabee, 1992, pp.130-171). Naturally, the formerly communist countries of the Soviet bloc face far more obstacles in integrating with the West than did the Southern European countries that emerged from dictatorship during the 1970s. The CEEC had little to no experience with market economies during the Cold War era, were ruled by communist parties that exerted totalitarian control unlike the authoritarian governments of Southern Europe, and in most cases had scant pre-war democratic experiences. However, the CEEC have made remarkable strides in integrating with the West. By the end of the first two or three years following the collapse of communism many former Soviet bloc states conducted as much 50 per cent of their trade with the West (Galinos, 1994, p.21), and most of the CEEC have entered into security agreements with NATO by participating in the Partnership for Peace initiative. Furthermore, the rapidity with which the CEEC turned to Western and European institutions reflects an ability to take advantage of political opportunities and conduct innovative foreign policies. Thus, while there are notable facets of the politics of Central and Eastern Europe which makes comparison with Southern Europe not entirely comparable, there are enough significant similarities to warrant investigation of the European foreign policies of these two regions.

My argument about Spain and other new European democracies is that homologization of norms between these states and Western Europe involves the transmission of consensual knowledge about the nature of international politics. However, one must first ask why knowledge is shared by some countries but not by others. The Spanish case suggests three factors at play: First, uncertainty can create situations in which leaders focus outward towards the international arena, and may be influenced by knowledge that reduces or minimizes tensions caused by this uncertainty. In the second place, preexisting ideas predispose some national leaders, but not others, towards sharing knowledge with the rest of the European community. The nature and durability of ideas will no doubt shape the degree to which states' leaders are receptive to new knowledge. The third reason new knowledge is accepted by the leaders of former authoritarian or totalitarian states is that close ties with Western European counterparts may be established early in the new political era.

The uncertainty factor is an important concept in understanding foreign policy in new democracies as the Spanish case has illustrated. According to Peter Haas, 'poorly understood conditions may create enough turbulence that established operating procedures may break down' (P. Haas, 1992, p.14). Uncertainty may be fueled by factors relating to newness of democracy or elites, tentative steps toward joining international organizations, or fundamental international systemic change. As I explain in Chapter Three, uncertainty also can be a function of tension among leaders' ideas about the world, knowledge based claims, and interest perceptions during periods of change. This was clear in Spain as the Socialist government attempted to reconcile its pro-European enthusiasm with its claims of national economic and security interests (Armero, 1989, p.153).

The existence of ideas that predispose leaders towards participation in the sharing and construction of political knowledge is the second important aspect that we should keep in mind as we expand the empirical research beyond the Spanish case. The material on Spain presented in this book suggests that what accompanies the adoption of European norms, and is absent when adoption does not occur, is the introduction of new knowledge to new democracies when old ideas no longer serve viable as policy aids, or when the relationship between old ideas and interests is in flux. The demise of dictatorial or authoritarian regimes almost always leaves an opening for political experimentation as old ideas are discredited or discarded.

The third important factor which should guide our investigation of additional cases is the transmission of knowledge among international elites. The more closely governmental leaders participate in the construction of European political reality (acquire new knowledge), the more likely their interest perceptions and political ideas change in the direction of established European norms. This is not to say that mere contact with other countries leads to adoption of international norms. Rather, when leaders of new democracies actively participate in the construction of shared European political reality - as opposed to pursuing nationalist and/or isolationist policies in accord with pressures from internal sources or policies of other regional systems - the construction of political ideas and interests are defined in these terms.

Using the Spanish case as a guide, in a preliminary review of the other new democracies of Southern, Central, and Eastern Europe I expect to find the following: Where a common set of knowledge based claims are shared with Western European states, leaders in former authoritarian and totalitarian countries will pursue paths convergent with the normative precepts of the rest of democratic Europe; where these claims are not shared, policy paths will diverge.[2] The ideas that guide foreign policy in these new democracies are a combination of perceptions of past practices, and leaders' sense of national identity and historical memory. As in the case of Spain, what constitutes the 'idea of Europe' is fundamentally an empirical question, and research on the European foreign policy of other new European democracies must begin with an examination of the origins of foreign policy ideas. The findings in this chapter should be treated as preliminary in nature. My goal is not to offer definitive conclusions about policy formation in these countries, but simply to determine whether or not research based on the categories of ideas and knowledge is a fruitful strategy for explaining foreign policy change in states that resemble the Spanish case.

The foreign policies of new European democracies

Southern European countries

Greece, Portugal and Spain all made the transition to democracy in the critical years between 1974 and 1977. The circumstances surrounding the collapse of the dictatorial regimes were different for each of these three countries. In Portugal, a group of left leaning junior military officers exasperated by the colonial wars in Angola and Mozambique overthrew the remnants of the Salazar regime in 1974.[3] A series of short-lived unstable governments followed in the wake of the 'Carnation Revolution' before a Western style democracy was established. In Greece, the junta known as the Colonels' Regime voluntarily relinquished power in 1974 after launching an unsuccessful military campaign to liberate northern Cyprus from Turkish troops which had invaded the island earlier that year. Given the brevity of the Colonels' Regime (1967-74), Greek democrats were able to draw on their pre-junta experiences and restore legitimate government with little difficulty. Spain's dictatorship died along with its leader, Francisco Franco, in 1975. Franco's hand-picked successor, King Juan Carlos I (grandson of the last king of Spain, who abdicated in 1931) did not deliver on his promise to the dictator to continue Franco's brand of authoritarian rule. Instead he presided over the dismantling of the Franquist state and the writing of a new democratic constitution which was ratified in 1978.

Despite the differences in regime transition, the new Southern European democracies shared an important similarity in the area of foreign policy. Each of these countries was isolated from the rest of Europe during the authoritarian eras, and therefore many of their leaders saw the end of dictatorship as an opportunity to engineer a return to the European mainstream. The question, then, is to what extent did uncertainty, ideas, and international linkages play a role in the formation of European policies in each of these countries? We know that in the case of Spain there was relative unanimity among political elites that membership in European institutions would provide a solution to perennial political and economic backwardness. However, different interpretations of Spain's recent history produced antagonisms in the realm of security, and NATO in specific. Once the linkages between economic and security integration in Europe were made manifest, Spain emerged as a strong supporter of the integration process in its many facets.

In Portugal, the absence of a dominant group of leaders in the early years of democratic transition led to a greater initial sense of uncertainty about foreign policy matters (Eisfeld, 1990, pp.85-86, 90-91). Having just extricated themselves from the colonial wars in Africa, Portugal's political elite engaged in a fractious debate about the country's place in the world. Although Portugal had been a member of NATO, various factions of Portugal's post-revolutionary elite advocated a variety of foreign policy orientations, including alliance with the Warsaw Pact (Manuel, 1996, p.70). This debate worried foreign observers (including American Ambassador Frank Carlucci) who feared that Portugal might reject its membership in NATO and land in the Soviet camp. Although these fears subsided after the more leftist elements of the provisional government were marginalized as Portuguese democracy took hold, the uncertainty of Portugal's leaders produced an initially hesitant foreign policy. Indeed, the constitution drawn up after the revolution hinted at an isolationist Portuguese foreign policy and contained technical elements that would have to be changed if Portugal was to join the European Community (de Pitta e Cunha, 1983).

After these initial ambivalent steps, the majority of Portugal's democratic leaders favored closer ties to the rest of Europe. The eagerness of these leaders to make their country 'part of Europe' stems from ideas about overcoming the ills associated with past centuries of isolation. In the past, both Spain and Portugal have explored extra-European orientations to make up for being excluded from continental prosperity. In the case of Spain this meant pursuing a 'special relationship' with Latin America and the Arab world, whereas for Portugal this meant maintaining the remnants of the Portuguese overseas empire in Angola and Mozambique (Bruneau, 1977; Gama, 1990). The idea of Europe as a substitution for these extra-European orientations has shaped the desire to share in the construction of a new economic space under the auspices of European economic integration. As with Spain, Portugal's entry into the EC was framed within a symbolic context that was broader than pure economics (Robinson, 1979, p.272). As Kevin Featherstone writes: 'A common theme is of [EC] accession presenting "a grand challenge" - and one accepted by the whole population - whilst European unity itself was a "vast and profound" objective' (Featherstone, 1988, pp.294-295). Nancy Bermeo observes that even during the Salazar dictatorship, Portuguese governmental elites recognized the futility of pursuing an *ultramar* (overseas) orientation if economic modernization were to take place. Therefore, the 'Europeanist' direction was established during the authoritarian period when the failed 'Africanist' policy became obvious, and was merely accelerated in the democratic era (Bermeo, 1988). This highlights the degree to which ideas shape goals. Given that the economic benefits Portugal would gain through EC membership were not much greater than those it enjoyed in the European Free Trade Association (EFTA) economic considerations became secondary to the symbolic elements of being recognized by the EC as a consolidated democracy.

The last critical element for understanding how Portugal's initial post-revolutionary chaos was replaced by a stable Western and European orientation is the relationship between Portuguese and international elites. The leaders of the Portuguese Socialist Party (PS), especially, placed political importance on European integration with an emphasis on using membership in the EC to cement Portuguese democracy into place (Cravinho, 1983). Mario Soares, the founder and leader of the PS, was a central figure in the Socialist International and was on friendly terms with most important European leaders. Thus, as Jonathan Story explains,

'international influences played a determining role in the revolution which transformed Portugal from a corporate and colonial state to a nation state' (Story, 1976, p.420). Western statesmen felt they needed to take a stand against radical elements in Portugal's transitional governments that challenged the ability of European politics to deal with economic downturn and the subsequent lack of confidence in the system (Maxwell, 1976).

Employing the theoretical framework developed in this book, Paul Christopher Manuel puts all these elements together. Manuel has traced out the evolution of Portuguese ideas, interests, and foreign policy knowledge claims over a period encompassing the collapse of the Salazar/Caetano dictatorship and the democratic transition and consolidation. Manuel explains how competing ideas about Portugal's place in the world and claims about the nature of international relations had to be reconciled with Portugal's very obvious interests of surviving as a small economy in the world market and securing Portuguese security in the face of long-standing alliances with the United States and Great Britain (Manuel, 1996). The process by which Portuguese learning took place was influenced in large part by the defeat of leaders with a particularistic vision of Portuguese foreign policy, and the rise of a class of political elite with longstanding ties to the international community (ibid).

As in the case of Portugal, Greece's relationship with the rest of Europe has been complicated by a variety of factors.[4] However, whereas Portugal's ambivalent position towards Europe was a function of Portuguese preoccupation with its overseas mission in Africa, the Greek position towards Europe was a product of Greece's direct experiences with Europe itself. In Greece there has been an ambivalence between European sensibilities, and historical connections to ancient Byzantium, Christian Eastern Orthodoxy, Slavic traditions, and Ottoman political heritage (Smith, 1991, pp.29-30). Furthermore, in the post-Ottoman period in Greece, 'Europeanization' not only became equated with modernization, but with entanglement in the social, political, and economic upheavals of late nineteenth and early twentieth century Europe. These entanglements pointed up the dependence of Greece on outside influences, and highlighted at once Greece's peripheral status in European affairs and its centrality and vulnerability to animosities in Southeastern Europe often played out among Western European states.

Over the past century and a half, Greek ambivalence over its place in Europe was highlighted by a series of wrenching experiences including independence from the Ottoman Empire and the consequent creation of a Greek diaspora, Nazi occupation during World War II, the Greek Civil War, and the Colonels's Regime of the late 1960s and early 1970s (Couloumbis, Petropulos, and Psomiades, 1976; McNeill, 1978; Coufoundakis, 1987). Greece's internal politics often have been a function of foreign intervention or invasion. In addition, geographic and historical peculiarities are reflected in the way that the norms of European integration are internalized in Greece to a lesser extent than in most other EU states. When Spain and Portugal joined the European Community in 1986, many Europeans celebrated this as proof of the triumph of democracy on the Iberian Peninsula. Greek EC membership in 1981 also was seen as confirmation of the victory of democracy over authoritarianism. Yet the accelerated nature of membership negotiations was also a reminder that the EC had suspended Greece's association agreement with the Community because of the imposition of a military regime in Greece between 1967 and 1974. Indeed, not all Europeans have been pleased with Greece's performance in the EU, and some European leaders have whispered that Greek membership was a mistake.

The formation of Greece's European policy in the first decade of the post-junta era was characterized by two distinct phases. In the first phase, the democratic government elected after the Colonels' Regime went about reestablishing ties with European institutions and reinstating Greece's application for EC membership which was suspended during the military regime. The New Democracy government, which was in power between the restoration of democracy in 1974 and 1981, was led by the pro-European statesman Constantine Karamanlis. Karamanlis negotiated EC membership and was guided by the conviction that membership in the European Community would reinforce Greek democratic consolidation. Karamanlis began his political career in the 1950s and represented a generation of politicians that favored close ties with the West. Regarding the European Community, for example, membership 'was seen by Karamanlis as a kind of insurance against such internal anomalies as the coup of 1967 and perhaps Turkish demands on Greek sovereignty' (Veremis, 1982, p.31). The Karamanlis administration attempted to replace the dominant influence of the United States with more formal ties to Western Europe (Papacosma, 1985, 208-209).

Karamanlis was replaced as prime minister in 1981 by Andreas Papandreou, the mercurial leader of the Greek Socialist Party (PASOK). Papandreou undertook the second trend in Greece's immediate post-junta European policy. The new prime minister styled himself as a maverick and became somewhat of an outcast in Europe at the same time that he was revered by his followers at home. Papandreou, who was educated in part in the United States and for a time was a professor of economics at the University of California-Berkeley, had a different world view from his predecessor. He espoused a variant of dependency theory in which social welfarism in the metropolis is not easily (or even eagerly) transferred to the periphery because it is not possible to create the sort of worker solidarity there as it is in the core (Stavrou, 1988, pp.14-16). His PASOK government in the early 1980s did not make great strides in harmonizing the Greek economy with EU norms. In addition, he mistrusted the United States and was suspicious of the economic goals of European integration.

Even more stark was Papandreou's avocation to pursue a unique direction to Greece's foreign policy, one which dallied with non-alignment, and friendship with such pariah regimes as Muammar Qadaffi's Libya.[5] Whereas Spanish and Portuguese leaders quickly repudiated the radical 'Third World' rhetoric that prevailed during the heady early days of democracy, Papandreou maintained an oppositional stance towards Europe for a longer period. Papandreou advocated an independent foreign policy and open confrontation with the West. Even more than Felipe González's early heated anti-Western rhetoric in Spain,

> Greek foreign policy since Papandreou's ascendancy... dismayed the European community and its NATO allies. Greece [became] a maverick among them. Athens took an international posture which seemed, on the surface, to favor the Soviet Union and the Warsaw Pact, and which contrasted with the oft-repeated statement of Karamanlis that 'Greece belongs to the West' (Brown, 1991, p.32).

Although Papandreou softened this stand by 1986, we can see that despite Papandreou's extensive personal ties to Western European leaders, he did not always share their vision for a united Europe (Feld, 1978; Featherstone 1988; Veremis, 1993). If anything, Papandreou preferred to assert the independence of Greek foreign policy while remaining part of the Western bloc. In addition, he emphasized Greek sovereignty by resisting the domination of larger European states while maintaining membership in European institutions. Even though Papandreou maintained a seemingly consistent anti-Western rhetoric, uncertainty still shaped his foreign policy (Borowiec, 1983, p.69). This uncertainty did not insure that leaders will look to the West, but it did establish the conditions in which they will be willing to consider new ways of looking at problems.

In addition, the highly personalistic and clientelistic nature of Greek politics often has meant that foreign policy doctrine will be closely identified with individual leaders and their ideational influences (Diamandouros, 1984; Lyrntzis, 1984). By the mid-1980s, Papandreou began to soften his positions towards Europe. He dropped a considerable amount of his anti-American rhetoric and began to abide by the norms of European integration (Lyrintzis, 1993; Couloumbis, 1993). Since we are concerned here only with the formation of European policy in new democracies, a complete review of Greek relations with the rest of Europe is not in order. However, we can note that from the mid-1980s forward the volatility in Greek positions towards Europe gave way to more regularized interactions, and debates among Greek leaders over the merit of European integration took on a less heated tone (Verney, 1987, 1993, 1996). In this way, Greece's early problems with the EC have given way to more regularized relations in Greek-European Union affairs (Kazakos and Ioakimidis, 1994). Finally, with Papandreou's death in 1996 it is not unreasonable to expect that pro-European leaders will be the norm in Greece. There is a sizable portion of the Greek political establishment that views Europeanization along the same line as modernizers in Spain and Portugal, and when they have been in power Greece has responded towards the rest of Europe in a fashion similar to the Iberian states.

Berta Álvarez-Miranda has observed that a combination of ideational and structural characteristics characterize the different responses of the new Southern European democracies to European integration. Spanish leaders have been almost unanimous in their support of Europe, while Portuguese leaders needed more time to sort out their foreign policy options. In Greece, divisions among the political class over the value of Europe to Greek politics are ongoing (Álvarez-Miranda, 1995). In addition, the Southern European democracies' positions towards Europe reflect international linkages. The nature of knowledge transmitted to the new Southern European democracies often is a function of the sources of that knowledge. The different ways that Spanish and Portuguese leaders think about European economic and security integration, for example, have had their origins in channels historically chosen to establish European linkages. The Spanish Socialists drew on their experiences with, and affinities to, fraternal socialist parties in Europe. This was clear during the EC membership negotiations process when Spain's status was predicated on the maintenance of positive relations with France. By the same token, in economic matters, Portuguese leaders have looked to Germany for guidance.[6] However, Portugal's 600 year-old alliance with Great Britain and close defense-related ties with the United States, together with its fear of being dwarfed by Spain, has meant that its leaders' construction of security-related reality has tended to be more 'Atlanticist' than the Europeanist bent pursued by Spain (Eisfeld, 1990, p.95). Greek Prime Minister Andreas Papandreou's links with the French Socialist Party may have influenced his affinity for France's style of loose alliance with the Western military apparatus (Brown, 1991, p.34), while Papandreou's successors draw on a larger variety of influences. Thus, post-Papandreou Greek foreign policy has tended to be more predictably European.

In short, the three Southern European democracies respond to European integration in a largely similar fashion, yet with distinctions that reflect ideational factors unique to each state. Varying historical situations account for certain differences in the way that Spanish, Portuguese, and Greek leaders think about European affairs. However, these differences can be accounted for by a theoretical framework that highlights the role of ideas, interests, and international political knowledge. Since all three countries occupy similar positions in the European system, examination of ideas and the transmission of knowledge provide the best account of country-by-country variance.

In the Central and Eastern European Countries (CEEC), the post-Cold War process of foreign policy formation is characterized by the same sort of uncertainty that existed in the new Southern European democracies in the 1970s and 1980s. Under the old system, the communist leaders' interests were shaped by their relationship with the Soviet Union. In the economic realm, this meant special trade and commercial relationships coordinated through Moscow with the USSR and the other CEEC. In the security realm, interests were shaped by Cold War bipolar blocs and rivalry with the West. In the absence of these arrangements, the new leaders of the formerly communist states must arrive at new conceptions of economic and defense interests.

As we saw in the Spanish case, leaders are receptive to new knowledge when they experience uncertainty with regards to existing ideas, interests, and knowledge based claims. For the CEEC, this uncertainty began to emerge as far back as the 1970 and 1980s as leaders saw that communist principles were inadequate in achieving economic prosperity (Feffer, 1992, p.125; Stokes, 1993, p.169). This provided an opening for greater accommodation with the West. As Valerie Bunce and Maria Csanadi observe:

> Uncertainty generates a particular type of situation, wherein people lack roles, rules, institutions and, therefore, interests...For [elites] there is also an absence or roles, rules and institutions, and interests, as a consequence, are hard to define. Thus, most feel vulnerable, harried and confused (Csanadi and Bunce, 1991 p.18).

Uncertainty in the CEEC is evident in the questions post-communist leaders have about their relationship with Western Europe. As Melvin Croan points out, even the 'Eurocentric' critics of the old communist regimes at first did not fully define a new direction:

> Those critical spirits who espouse a Central European identity differ among themselves on a whole range of quite basic issues, including such crucial matters as the precise delineation (territorial or other) of their novel allegiance, the definition of its essential contents, its origins, and strategies best tailored to guarantee that it has a future (Croan, 1989, p.183).

Thus, while there is a general perception that the CEECs' future lies with the West, there is the feeling, for example, that economic interests may not necessarily be advanced by a wholesale acceptance of brute Western capitalism (Bowers, 1991). With regards to the European Union in specific, leaders in Central and Eastern Europe wonder if the EU is willing to ease the transition towards membership for the new formerly Communist members if it means jeopardizing the economic health of the Union. Because 'the members of the [EU] tend to view the benefits and costs of accelerating the integration of East and West from differing national perspectives'(Brada, 1991, p.31), the way this uncertainty is resolved will revolve around which current EU states are able to dictate the nature of the debate and the procedures by which concessions on both sides of the East-West divide are made. For the time being, this is an open question. Contributing to all of these elements of uncertainty is that, as of this writing, even democracy and stability in the CEEC are by no means guaranteed.

The instability and uncertainty created by the demise of the Soviet bloc system also has created myriad foreign policy options in Central and Eastern Europe. In the military realm, the CEEC exist in a security environment in which the prevailing indecisiveness is a source of anxiety and has produced multiple visions of how best to create regional stability. For example, the government of Poland has 'consistently argued that Europe as a whole should develop a uniform security system for all countries in the area' (de Weydenthal, 1991b, p.23). Hungary apparently shares Poland's views on this matter. Hungarian security needs invariably will continue to be shaped by the large number of ethnic Hungarians living outside the country's current borders.[7] Yet, the problem of ethnic minorities is not an issue with which Western European leaders have been comfortable dealing in the past, nor seem especially eager to tackle at present. In marked contrast to the Polish, Czech, and Hungarian desire to extend NATO's influence east, the government of 'Romania has...expressed an interest in establishing a separate security system for all of Eastern Europe, which officials believe would contribute to greater stability and cooperation in the region' (Carp, 1991, p.28). Given these competing claims, the prevailing indecision in the CEEC means that leaders have to rely on generalized beliefs they have about what is in their countries' best interests.

Under these conditions of uncertainty, the 'idea of Europe' exerts a strong influence in one way or another in all of the CEEC much as it did under similar circumstances in Southern Europe in the 1970s and 1980s. This is the so-called 'return to Europe', an idea which can mean a variety of things. Judy Batt defines it as 'the task [of] internally reconstruct[ing] politics on the basis of open, democratic principles and the rule of law, and... reconstruct[ing] the economy on the basis of the market and the predominance of private property (Batt, 1994, p.35). For A. Herrberg and E. Moxon-Browne the return to Europe resonates on the mass level:

> European citizenship, if extended to Eastern and Central Europe, provides an antidote to authoritarian party politics, reactionary religious influence in legislation, and an emollient against upsurges of racist and ethnic tensions in countries where hitherto quiescent minorities may suddenly erupt into violence (Herrberg and Moxon-Browne, 1995, p.16).

In some cases, the 'return to Europe' actually is a return to the West broadly conceived:

> Western ideas and models offer Central Europe stimulation and guidance for transformation in the fields of civil society, culture, law, and human rights. Central Europe is not adapting Western models uncritically, but seems rather to be synthesizing American and West European experience with its own (Ners, et.al., 1992, p.32).

In other words, for many citizens of the CEEC, 'Europe' and things European initially were little more than abstractions. John Feffer observes: 'Denied a close-up view of the reality of today's capitalism, Eastern Europeans tend to see the market as just…an abstraction. In their eyes, the market has truly assumed utopian dimensions, as communism, fascism, and nationalism had in the past' (Feffer, 1992, p.127). The strength of the idea of Europe is especially true as regards the European Union (Brada, 1991; Van Brabant, 1994). However, it is not so much organizational membership that drives homogenization between Western norms and policy in the CEEC as the desire to emerge from the stagnation caused by a half-century of isolation from the West. To some degree this proved useful in the initial stages of post-communist transformation when leaders and the public alike were more receptive to emotional appeals than to 'rational', interest-based arguments (Batt, 1991, p.50).

Yet even the most malleable ideas must have some substance to them. The 'idea of Europe' in the CEEC is conditioned by the pace of democratic reform in Central and Eastern Europe, much as it was in Southern Europe.[8] This is especially true with respect to foreign policy in the uncertain post-Cold War period. Although the formerly communist states initially turned to the West at the advent of democracy, their future responses will have less to do with democracy *per se*, but with the needs of securing democracy, as defined by domestic actors with distinct historical memories. The Spanish case is notable in that with few exceptions, post-Franco Spanish elites were unified in their enthusiasm for increased economic links to Europe (however, initially there was not unanimity in Spain over defense ties to NATO). This was not true in Greece where Constantine Karamanlis and Andreas Papandreou differed sharply on membership in the EC and NATO. Furthermore, just as different paths to democracy lead to different types of domestic change, the distinctive paths by which new elites rise to power reveal differing degrees of receptivity to Western-oriented change (Szelenyi and Szelenyi, 1992, pp.23-26).

The ambiguous nature of the European idea and uncertainty over how this idea translates into policy can be demonstrated by the way it conflicts with Central and Eastern European leaders' perceptions of national interest. Here we find a rather startling comparison with the Spanish case in the area of security policy. We recall that the demise of dictatorship in Spain, Spanish democrats favored

Western institutions, but mistrusted the American presence in NATO despite the fact that other European leaders saw the United States as a stabilizing force in Europe. Petr Lunak argues that in the case of the formerly communist countries, the penchant for Western institutions is tempered by a mistrust of purely *European* influence. This is true especially for NATO:

> [Between 1992 and 1994], the governments of central and eastern Europe have developed almost an obsession with the idea of joining the Atlantic Alliance. Their interest in NATO membership, however, is not based on a thoughtful consideration of whether the alliance can in fact counter the threats facing central Europe, but rather on [an] emotional urge to ensure an American presence in the region (Lunak, 1994, p.128).

Just as anti-American Spanish leaders were guided by historical memory, leaders in the CEEC draw on past experiences as they view Europe and the West:

> The east Europeans have become prisoners of their historical memory. Looking to the past for insights into their traumatized present, they have tended to draw wholesale and inappropriate historical parallels. They fear that Europe without America might become what it had been before the United States anchored itself there - a scene of bickering and bloodshed (ibid., p.128).

As Central and Eastern European elites attempt to work out their notions of what it means to be European and reconcile these ideas with concrete foreign policy interests they likely will be receptive to knowledge of European political realities that helps them make sense of their position in the world. Each of the former Communist countries also will be guided by features peculiar to their situation, and their pasts will shape their ideas about various aspects of European integration.

With regards to regional variations on 'the return to Europe', the idea of 'Mitteleuropa' in Central Europe provides a basis by which to distinguish it from a more restrictive notion of post-Cold War 'Eastern Europe'. The Mitteleuropa idea, like the 'idea of Europe' itself, is a malleable concept that conjures up a variety of historic and symbolic memories (Glenny, 1990; Beller, 1991; Herrberg and Moxon-Browne, 1995). From a policy standpoint it can comprise, among other things, the creation of a Central European buffer zone between the EU West and a new nationalist Russia, or bridge for Western values to be transmitted to the 'Russian East' (Croan, 1989). However, the Mitteleuropa idea has not caught on with much enthusiasm. Jeffrey Goldfarb explains that in the early 1980s the interest in 'Mitteleuropa' or 'Central Europe' 'involved an act of symbolic secession from the Empire of the East,' but in the post-Cold War era 'such dreams confront hard and complex realities' (Goldfarb, 1992, pp.119-120).

Specifically, while the idea of Mitteleuropa may be necessary to defeat nationalist conflict among Central European states, the historic concept of Mitteleuropa - based as it was on the German language and the Jewish intelligentsia - is an impossibility given the obvious aftermath of World War II (ibid, pp.120-121). Instead, to the extent that their is a Central European identity, it exists within the wider context of European integration. Thus, most Central European leaders reject the notion of creating regional cooperative institutions and insist that their ultimate goal is membership in the European Union (Bugajski, 1993, p.185).[9]

Finally, the emergence of a European identity is by no means certain, and variations among the CEEC are a reflection of past historical experiences. The primary competing idea to the 'idea of Europe' in Central and Eastern Europe is the idea of ethnic nationalism (Ekiert, 1990). Anthony Smith points out that national identity emerged in two distinct patterns in Western and Eastern Europe. In Western Europe, monarchs first united certain areas of land under their power and this, in turn, created a sense of nation. In Eastern Europe, feelings of ethnic community came first - in response to resentment over living under Russian, Austrian, or Ottoman imperial rule - and political nations were created in response to those feelings. Thus, the Eastern notion actually comes closer to the concept of 'organic' nationalism than the West (Smith, 1992, pp.60-61). Furthermore, Smith argues that national identities have an advantage over European identity in that they are more grounded in history, symbol, custom, myth, etc. (ibid., p.62). As Herrberg and Moxon-Browne argue:

> In the Western part of Europe [self identification] is less concerned with the community identity of the *natio* than with *civitas* and *demos*. In the former Communist States of the East, however, it appears that the identification of oneself is based more on the *natio* and thereby experiences a return to the ethnic or religious movement, to *ethnos* (Herrberg and Moxon-Browne, 1995, p.8; see also Garcia, 1993).

As the Marxist idea of class identity loses its appeal in the CEEC, the fear is that these ethnic identities will resurface in the form of ethnic rivalries (Croan, 1989).

Above all, we should recall that shared ideas provide the glue that binds international societies together. The CEEC are re-thinking their place in Europe at the same time that Western European counties also are reconceptualizing what Europe means in the post-Cold War era. To some degree this is a wholly philosophical affair. However, their are policy implications as well. In a discussion of possible scenarios for European security, Barry Buzan et.al. describe four different geographic configurations for a future European security space. Each of these military scenarios - Europe as the region comprising the European Union, Europe 'from Portugal to Poland', Europe 'from the Atlantic to the Urals', and Europe 'from Vancouver to Vladivostok' - correspond to four different conceptions of what it means to be European or, in the case of the fourth, to be Western in identity and practice (Buzan, et.al., 1990, pp.45-63).

Uncertainty and pre-existing ideas provide a receptive environment for the socialization of knowledge based claims to Central and Eastern Europe. The third element of the equation is the nature of linkages between East and West that permit this international transmission of political knowledge. Knowledge based understandings of European political realities gradually have altered the rather abstract vision CEEC leaders have had of the 'return to Europe'.[10] The importance of chosen channels with the West is important with regard to the CEEC because leaders' wholesale rejection of communism has left a void that elites have tried to fill. In some cases, leaders of these states have relied on economists and intellectuals who are influenced by their neo-liberal counterparts in the West, and are guided by institutions like the International Monetary Fund and the World Bank. These linkages may even have been established before the demise of the old regime. During the Soviet Andropov and Chernenko period, for example, 'Kremlin policy began to change and Soviet clients were increasingly encouraged to cultivate contacts with the Western community...' (Bowers, 1991, p.136). Furthermore, it is not surprising that those European states most actively pursuing ties with the West are those with historical memories of intellectual linkages with the West and membership in pre-communist era European institutions (Hill and Zielonka, 1990; Liska, 1991; Michta and Prizel, 1992). With regards to the Soviet satellite states we can detect what has been called an 'anticipatory adaptation', in which 'a set of norms associated with a multilateral institution [are adopted] by a government before it has acquired full membership in that institution or even received guarantees of entry' (Weitz, 1993, p.377). This has occurred for the CEEC even with regards to Western security institutions such as NATO despite the fact that membership likely remains far off.

Space limitations do not permit a full review of all of the CEEC and their relationship to the rest of Europe. Rather, I will highlight some of the noticeable trends in the former communist bloc. Among the most eager to undertake the return to Europe after the fall of communism has been Hungary. During the Cold War Hungary already had become more Westernized in practice in part to historical memory (Hungary, after all, comprised one half of the Austro-Hungarian Empire) and in part to an economic opening that occurred in the 1960s.[11] In addition, the Hungarian Communist party was the most reform oriented party in Eastern Europe, perhaps because its ranks had not been cleansed by the Stalinist purges of the 1930s (Stokes, 1993, p.79). Hungary became a member of the International Monetary Fund and the World Bank in 1982 (ibid., p.80), and signed a cooperative agreement with the European Community in September 1988, a year before communism began its collapse in Eastern Europe (Bugajski, 1993, p.211).[12]

The experiences of the leaders of the Czechoslovak successor states also are illuminating for what they tell about the roles of idea and knowledge.

Immediately following the 'Velvet Revolution', Czechoslovakia showed itself to be firmly committed to the West. The Czechoslovak participation in the 1990-91 Persian Gulf War included:

A moral aspect based on Czechoslovakia's historical experience. President Vaclav Havel repeatedly said that giving in to aggressors was morally and politically wrong and would set a dangerous precedent. He made it clear that 'the policy of appeasement cannot be successful in the long run; on the contrary, it is malignant' (Obrman, 1991, p.10).

However, the dissolution of Czechoslovakia into the Czech and Slovak republics has revealed distinct differences between these two states and their attitudes towards the West. Vaclav Havel, the first Prime Minister of post-communist Czechoslovakia and current President of the reconstituted Czech Republic, was a dissident under the Communist regime and rode a wave of resentment during the 1989 revolution. Havel, a playwright, also has ties to Western intelligentsia. His orientation, therefore, has been towards the West, as has Civic Forum, whose election slogan in 1991 was 'With Us to Europe' (Feffer, 1992, p.179). By contrast, Vladimir Meciar, the Prime Minister of Slovakia, was a member of the wing of the Communist Party that favored 'Socialism with a Human Face' during the Prague Spring reform movement in 1968. Unlike Havel, Meciar does not favor a wholesale turn to the West nor total acceptance of capitalism. His rise to power was motivated by nationalist, inward-looking concerns and such that his policies do not reflect a concern with linkages with the rest of Europe.[13]

However, the responsibility for reaching out to formerly isolated countries also rests with the core European states. Poland, Hungary, and the Czech and Slovak successor states have benefitted from contacts initiated by the West (Bigler, 1992, p.440). Many of the formerly Communist states have looked towards Germany as a source of support (Stapanovsky, 1991). In Poland, however, historic suspicion of Germany has led Polish leaders to welcome current German tutelage with some skepticism, while still establishing economic ties in the hopes of speeding economic modernization (Davis, 1992; Kowalik-James, 1992). Great Britain and France have also taken a leading role in relations with the CEEC. The Hungarian case shows that informal linkages established before democratization (through tourism and migrant workers) laid the groundwork for increased institutional links during the post-communist period that are more extensive than formal organizational arrangements (Okolicsanyi, 1991; Böröcz, 1992; Feffer, 1992). Of course, the possibility always exists that leaders in Central and Eastern Europe will be influenced by purely domestic forces, by the United States and/or Japan, or by contacts with other countries in the region.

In contrast to Poland, Hungary, and the Czech Republic, Romania and Bulgaria have been left more to their own devices by the West.[14] One commentator noted:

A striking disparity will likely remain between Europe's northern and southern tiers as most Western officials simply dismiss the possibility for Bulgaria and especially Romania to make a fully democratic transition....The cultural/religious affinity and geopolitical self-interest which bonds Western Europe to the three northern-most countries could, if aid disparities persist, make stagnation and alienation in the Balkans a self-fulfilling prophesy (Laux, 1991, p.10).

Romania has taken fewer steps towards full-fledged democracy and has been less eager to appease the West than perhaps all of the other CEEC. Romania's government is run by new elites who were not directly involved with the Ceausescu regime. Nonetheless, the country 'has experienced something of a "half-way" or "aborted" revolution' in which 'state power was reconstituted by dissident (and not so dissident) members of the Romanian Communist Party and national army grouped into the so-called National Salvation Front' (Goodwin and Bunce, 1992, n.p.). Given the unfinished nature of regime change in Romania, the country's new leaders are preoccupied with consolidating domestic power. As with Spanish leaders during the provisional governments' period of the democratic transition (1975-77), this focus on domestic matters has directed the attention of Romania's re-constituted elite towards internal sources of influence. Partly as a result, they have pursued an independent foreign policy at variance with the rest of Europe (Ionescu, 1991). Romania's leaders would like to believe that their problems with the West are purely symptomatic of an image problem; 'however, realistic diplomats have pointed out that this image is largely dictated by Romania's internal situation' (Ionescu, 1991, p.31). In recent years, the Romanian government has increased its efforts to reach accommodation with the West and has sought better ties with European economic and security institutions (Bugajski, 1993, p.220). Romanian leaders have stressed the importance of the association agreement they signed with the EC in 1991 as a major turning point in Romanian foreign policy. However, European officials remain wary of Romania given its spotty human rights record, and skeptics within Romania see the government's efforts as an attempt to shore up their democratic reputation which remains questionable (Ionescu, 1993).

Given the new realities in Europe and the variety of conditions and responses in the CEEC, it has become almost common wisdom to assert that from the perspective of the existing members of the European Union, the membership aspirations of the Central and Eastern European countries present a problem (Gibb and Michalak, 1993; Kramer, 1993; Van Brabant, 1994, pp.186-189). On the one hand, EU states recognize that extending membership to some or all of the CEEC will help consolidate democracy much as it did in Southern Europe. On the other hand, the EU must attend to its own internal concerns and needs to complete the process of achieving complete economic integration. This is known as the problem of 'deepening versus widening'. As Vincent Cable writes: 'In a wider Europe there will be considerable, and quite unavoidable, tension between "deepening" and "widening". There is no simple choice between the two' (Cable, 1994, p.109). Yet, we have reason to believe that deepening and widening need not be contradictory agendas. As we saw in the Spanish case, the southern enlargement of the European Community in the 1980s was undertaken parallel to the EC's effort to reconcile long-standing inefficiencies as Community members negotiated the Single European Act (SEA). The norm that resulted from this process was that long term gains for the EC as a whole (which would only be possible if the EC's overall economic health was maintained) would occur if member states sacrificed short term interests. The current debate over deepening versus widening - embedded as it is in the process of completing the provisions of the Maastricht Treaty - provides a similar set of circumstances to compare with the Iberian enlargement in the 1980s when negotiations over the SEA were in progress (Reinicke, 1992, p.82; Batt, 1994, pp.42-46). Thus, we can hypothesize that if this idea continues to be supported by shared understandings about the nature of European integration, the countries of Central and Eastern Europe can be socialized into this system and adjust their expectations accordingly. Robin Niblett indicates that this indeed is the case, arguing that the high premium the EU places on internal cohesion will present a constrained institutional environment as Central European states are considered for membership (Niblett, 1995, pp.8-9).[15]

As in the Spanish case, we have evidence that in Central and Eastern Europe the transmission of knowledge based claims about European political realities occurs through a process of socialization in which material power discrepancies are not ready indicators of the influence of the West. Alexander Wendt and Daniel Friedheim argue that even in the case of East Germany - a country presumably wholly controlled by Moscow during the Cold War and then subsumed *en masse* into West Germany - unidirectional influence cannot be assumed. Rather, since East Germany's relationship to the USSR was one in which 'informal empire was constituted through both material and ideational factors, even as it remains materially weaker than the West, the collapse of the Soviet empire allows for new socially constructed identities to be created' (Wendt and Friedheim, 1995). It is reasonable to assume that for all of the CEEC, their relationship to the West will be one in which ideas and interests are redefined throughout the transition from the Cold War order.

Indeed, immediately following the collapse of the Soviet bloc, the CEEC have sought to be regular members of Europe, rather than weak supplicant states. 'Prior to 1989 the concept of *Europe* had a clear mythical aspect attached, representing freedom, wealth and progress. It is now when the East and Central European states see themselves as *part* of Europe, and they do so in a pragmatic sense' (Herrberg and Moxon-Browne, 1995, p.17). In addition, leaders in many of the CEEC sought to enmesh their countries in a variety of international institutions so as to minimize the influence of any single or set of dominant states.

The Conference on Security and Cooperation in Europe (CSCE) provided a congenial institutional setting given that the formerly communist countries were familiar with it from the process of detente and the United States could circumscribe the influence of Western European countries on the East (Weitz, 1993, pp.364-347). Herrberg and Moxon-Browne point out that the European Commission in 1990 issued the desirata of the European Agreements in which shared values and shared European identity were highlighted so as to reassure the East that Western Europe was not out to colonize it (Herrberg and Moxon-Browne, 1995, p.23).

In sum, much as in Southern Europe, the new democracies of Central and Eastern Europe are formulating foreign policies according to emergent ideas, interests, and knowledge based claims reflective of historical circumstances. The reintegration of the CEEC into the European mainstream occurs in an institutional context where political realities are created and shared. While certain ideas may compete with the 'idea of Europe', the European idea exerts a considerable influence such that uncertainty is reconciled and interests defined along the lines of European norms. Country-by-country variations are to be expected, yet ideational factors provide a framework for understanding the broad based trends among the Central and Eastern European states.

Counterfactuals: the cases of Turkey and Yugoslavia

The socialization of new European democracies into the European system does not necessarily occur in all cases. As we saw in the case of Romania, the process by which countries accept European political realities can be a long one. More importantly, both Europe and potential members of European society must be predisposed towards sharing common perceptions. In this section I shall discuss two cases where this accommodation ether has not taken place or occurs only with great difficulty. In the case of Turkey, Turkish leaders have made a concerted effort to 'join Europe', however European leaders largely have kept Turkey at arm's length. In the case of Yugoslavia, European leaders attempted to socialize the Balkan country to accept European norms, yet most Yugoslav leaders had a different, nationalist, agenda.

Turkey's political elite have long favored increased ties with Europe and the West. Yet the ongoing unwillingness of European states to include Turkey in the construction of a new economic and security space has forced Turkey's leaders to re-think their foreign policy ideas and options. This has shaped both the external and internal strategies of Turkey's leaders. Considered a sometime European democracy, Turkey frequently has been isolated from the rest of Europe. Its long-standing, though perennially postponed, application for membership in the EU, for example, has been continually and actively snubbed by Union states (Kramer, 1984). European Union members have made it clear that Turkish participation in European and international institutions is more than a simple reward for a return to democracy as in Spain, Greece, and Portugal.[16] Rather, Turkey must first get its own economic house in order, discontinue its human rights abuses, cease its military occupation of Cyprus, and halt its undeclared war on its Kurdish population if it ever wishes to join the EU. In addition, the coalition government formed in 1996 in Turkey is headed by Prime Minister Necmettin Erbakan's Welfare Party which favors conservative Islamic ideas. This orientation scares EU leaders who fear that Turkey is not so European after all.

Turkish leaders are aware of the European Union's continuing and long-standing desire to stall serious membership negotiations (Ertürk, 1984). However, the country has a long tradition of Westernization, pioneered by Kemal Atatürk. 'The modern Turkish nation-state was established with a western orientation. Turkish reformist leaders and intellectuals over the last century and a half have stressed the necessity of catching up with "contemporary civilization" which refers to material aspects of European advancement' (Evin, 1990, p.25). This orientation has favored persistent attempts at winning membership in the European Union (Cremasco, 1990). Nonetheless, the EU's response has been to actively discourage Ankara. One observer bluntly put it:

> [The European Community] has feigned to be enthusiastic for strengthening…relations whenever it has felt necessary to demonstrate that it is an 'open community', and whenever the conditions of member countries' economies have made it urgent to import cheap foreign labor. Apart from these instances, the Community, especially after the number of its member countries increased and when economic crisis spread around Europe, has tended to approach Turkey's membership with a negative attitude, thus causing the conflict to grow (Ilkin, 1990, pp.45-46).

This active discouragement reduces the likelihood that Turkey can be an active participant in the construction of European economic reality, with the result that Turkey may revert to isolationism and/or Islamic fundamentalism. Indeed, as long as priority is given to applications of more industrialized European countries to join the EU, Turkish leaders will continue to stress the country's domestic economic agenda, as they did throughout the 1980s when Community membership was not forthcoming.

Ironically, the end of the Cold War has done little to foster closer ties between Turkey and the rest of Europe.[17] Turkey's politics of security may be defined not so much by the existence of new international tensions left in the wake of the demise of the Soviet superpower, as by the lack of any unified European policy for dealing with them. More importantly, efforts in the rest of Europe have pointedly excluded Turkey from the construction of a post-Cold War new European security order and the shared knowledge this entails. As Ian Lesser points out: 'To the extent that Europe moves toward a common foreign and security policy, EC members will be increasingly unwilling to accept the immediate and additional exposure in the Middle East which Turkey's full participation in the WEU (or other European security arrangements) would imply' (Lesser, 1992, p.41). Lesser concludes from this that 'in the meantime, and in the absence of closer ties with Europe, Turkey's political and economic elite are looking to new areas of opportunity outside Europe or on the European periphery' (ibid.). For the Turks, these new areas of opportunity include the Balkan region and Central Asia, where Turkey is seen as both a Muslim superpower and a bridge to the West: 'Pointing to its "cultural, historic, linguistic, and religious ties" to the Turkic peoples of Central Asia and the Islamic minorities in the Balkans, Turkey has been increasingly emphasizing its big-brother role' (van Gent, 1992, p.13). Whereas the leaders of Turkey and the former communist states both see Turkey as a possible *entrée* to Europe, much will depend on whether or not the construction of a new European identity by the leaders of Western European institutions does, in fact, include them.[18]

Of course, Turkey has not yet left the Western orbit. Therefore, one could argue that what matters in predicting change in Europe are the overwhelming international systemic changes which characterize the end of the Cold War. The countries of East-Central Europe and Turkey alike are making steps towards becoming members of the European society of states. However, when we look at the universe of cases in post-Cold War Europe we see that the dissolution of the bipolar system has led to divergent outcomes in terms of the expected centripetal force of European integration. On the one hand, the end of the Cold War has allowed the formerly communist countries to draw closer to European institutions. On the other hand, the absence of the East-West rivalry has left a vacuum in which other countries have broken apart and have spun away from the rest of Europe. The case of Yugoslavia is the most obvious example of a state that has fractured in the post-Cold War environment. However, the Turkish case is also an example of a country potentially spiralling out of the European orbit.

The leaders of post-Franco Spain, the former Communist countries, and Turkey all possess a desire to share in the construction of a common European vision (Ito, 1992). Unfortunately for the latter, European leaders are not eager to include Turkey in this vision. Therefore, ideas are important not only in new democracies, but also among the leaders of 'core' European states who are constructing claims about what comprises the new European economic and security space. If these ideas do not include the notion that Islamic Turkey is a part of this new Europe, then it will be excluded from the process of consensual knowledge creation.

The violent disintegration of Yugoslavia at once surprises European observers and at the same time confirms their worst fears of what can happen when countries are not firmly anchored within international institutions. However, it would be facile to argue that the Balkan conflict could have been avoided if Yugoslavia had been more closely integrated in European or international organizations. In the first place, domestic regional rivalries are not necessarily pacified if a country participates in international institutions. Elites in the republics of the former Yugoslavia are more concerned with establishing domestic authority and legitimacy in the wake of the break-up of Yugoslavia than with establishing international credibility. In the second place, membership in international organizations is no guarantee that countries will always share a sense of 'collective' identity. Yugoslavia, which was an associate member of the EC, was not prevented from degenerating into internal chaos by its ties to the Community. In the third place, formal organizations and informal regimes alike possess weak enforcement mechanisms to produce compliance with institutional norms. The ongoing Balkan crisis shows that even the most formalized organizations find it difficult to resolve issues that generate intense domestic political debate.

An explanation that takes into account ideas and knowledge offers a richer account of events. The leaders of the former Yugoslav republics faced a fundamental problem based on tensions among ideas about national identity, knowledge based claims about the nature of democracy, and the competing interests of winning international support while pacifying domestic groups. Their dilemma is summed up by Robert Hayden:

> On the one hand, since 'democracy' was the shibboleth for leaving 'Eastern Europe' and joining 'Europe',...all proclaimed their 'democratic' nature. At the same time, however, the various nationalist governments had based their electoral appeal primarily on chauvinist grounds,...Thus nationalism had to be so open as to be clear to the faithful, yet in some way masked to avoid alienating either 'the west' or the moderate public in each republic (Hayden, 1991, p.8).

Furthermore, the nationalist idea in Yugoslavia held a powerful grip on political emotions, despite the conflicting aspects of this idea:

> There were in Yugoslavia from the very beginning actually two quite different models of integration. There was the one that saw Yugoslavia as a community of countries and peoples enjoying equal rights, with the stress on the Croat model of modernization. And there was the other model, which saw it as a Serbia expanded with fresh territory and associated peoples. All the principal Serb-Croat conflicts and all the other Yugoslav conflicts during their joint history can be interpreted by reference to this fundamental misunderstanding about the idea of integration (Pusić, 1992, p.250).

Ultimately, the prominence of nationalist ideas privileged domestic majoritarian factions that expressed their interests according to widely accepted claims that

146

support these ideas.

During the communist era in Yugoslavia, three factors were responsible for sublimating historical ethnic conflict: 'Marxism, which provided an ideology of internationalism; [the communists' wartime] partisan experience, which bonded the leadership together with powerful feelings of purpose and commitment; and...Josip Broz Tito, whose authority was unquestioned during his lifetime' (Stokes, 1993, p.223). However, as Gale Stokes observes, this equation would not last forever.

> The linkage of 'Yugoslav' and 'socialist' contained a critical weakness that Tito and his colleagues could never have imagined. As long as the Communist movement remained strong, Yugoslavism was not in danger. If nationalism reared its head the party could and did push it back under the surface. If the League of Communists of Yugoslavia should disintegrate, however, then the Yugoslavism it championed would disintegrate too (ibid., p.223).

This is precisely what transpired. During the Cold War, Yugoslavia occupied a no-man's land between the two superpower blocs. With no permanent institutional attachments to either Europe or the Soviet East, post-Tito Yugoslavs fell back on ethnic nationalism as a set of guiding political ideas.[19]

In reconciling the tension between nationalism and democracy by emphasizing the ethnic nationalist aspect, not only were domestic dissenters in Yugoslavia marginalized, but foreign claimants to alternative claims also were ignored (Pusić, 1992, p.251). The result, as is manifestly obvious, is that leaders in the former Yugoslav republics were not guided by European colleagues (as were, for example, post-Franco Spanish democrats) and have pursued policies inimicable to international norms. Complicating matters is the fact that even those leaders who looked to Europe for solutions did not find a uniform response. Unlike the unity the EU has exhibited in trade matters, for example, the Union's varied responses to the Balkan conflict demonstrates not only EU disunity but also revealed traditional rivalries among the former Yugoslav republics. For example, Greece and Great Britain enjoyed historic ties to Serbia while Germany has been linked at various junctures to Croatia and Slovenia. This had detrimental affects on EU policy towards Yugoslavia as the Balkan state began to implode (Moore, 1991). Furthermore, 'not all republics... centered their attention just on Europe. Bosnia and Herzegovina, which has a 44% ethnic Muslim plurality, [had] its main economic links with Europe but has not neglected relations with the Muslim world' (ibid., p.34). Thus, in the absence of agreement among major European states on how to deal with the break-up of Yugoslavia, the leaders of the rival Yugoslav republics had no clear picture of what to expect of they continued to brawl among themselves. In other words, without a concerted and unified European response, Yugoslav leaders could not discern the consequences of their actions in the rest of Europe, even if their had been willing or predisposed (which they seemed not) to consider the European point of view.

What the leaders of post-Franco Spain and other new democracies seem to possess, that the rulers of post-Tito Yugoslavia lack, is a desire to share in the construction of a common European vision. The multiple foreign policy orientation of the former Yugoslav republics has made less likely the possibility that knowledge based claims shared in Western Europe might serve as a means to resolve armed conflict. The leaders of the successor Yugoslav republics seem more intent on settling historical ethnic disputes and pursuing fragmentation than accepting the European logic of reconciling domestic factionalism through supranational integration. Even the Slovenians, who consider themselves the most 'European', did not understand the cause-and-effect relationship between leaving the Yugoslav Federation and provoking a military response from Belgrade. The combination of division within Europe and an unwillingness by Yugoslav leaders to dispense with ethnic nationalism meant that no 'definitive' knowledge of what Yugoslav fragmentation would mean for Europe existed and could be clearly understood by leaders in the Balkan capitals.

In short, peripheral European states that assume with core European countries a shared knowledge about mutual expectations and a common sense of political and economic reality pursue and conform to the same set of norms. States such as the former Yugoslav republics that are more bound by domestically generated ideas and imperatives are more likely to pursue deviant policy paths. However, states that are actively being snubbed by Europe can also be expected to pursue extra-European orientations. Thus Turkey's leaders, despite their intense desires to pursue Europeanization, are toying with the idea of pursuing a greater role in the Middle East and are adjusting their domestic and international strategies accordingly. We must therefore understand the domestic strategies of Turkish and Balkan leaders, at least in part, as outcomes of the ideas and knowledge based claims they either share, or do not share, with the rest of Europe.

Summary

My purpose in this chapter has been to begin to assess how well other new democracies conform to the patterns I observe in, and the categories I draw from, the Spanish case. I do not attempt a full explanation of European policy in other new European democracies, but merely to suggest that the theoretical construct presented in this book presents a valid framework with which to begin an analysis of countries beyond Spain. An initial exploration of new European democracies shows that where uncertainty exists, ideas that favor European integration predispose leaders towards accepting European norms. The international transmission of knowledge provides the conduit for these norms to be regularized in the countries examined. A preliminary investigation also shows that neither structural features of the international system, nor national elites' purely strategic domestic considerations, are of much use unless they are situated within a research agenda that examines what leaders think and believe about foreign affairs.

A focus on political ideas and knowledge provides a necessary addition to obvious measures of material capabilities in constructing a typology of peripheral European states and their responses to European integration.[20] In other words it is misleading to identify the existence of systemic change or domestic political strategies without understanding how they arise and what they means for states creating new identities and new definitions of their place in the emergent international system. This is especially true for the countries I look at in this chapter. The 'core' European states (France, Germany, Italy, Great Britain, Denmark, and the Benclux countries) enjoy a history of dealing with the dilemmas of peace and economic security that they have faced since the close of the Second World War. The new European democracies and other 'peripheral' European states are faced with the more momentous task of fundamentally reassessing the ideas they have had regarding their place in the European system. It is the feedback process between ideas and interests, with intersubjectively created knowledge of how the world works as the medium of interaction between system and state, that offers an approach to explain the policy patterns observed in this chapter. Where knowledge is transmitted, harmonization of norms likely occurs. Where it is not transmitted, the likelihood of normative homologization with the rest of Europe is reduced, and possibly eliminated completely.

Notes

1   With the end of the Cold War and the demise of the system of bipolar blocs, it is no longer geographically accurate to refer to the former Soviet satellite states as 'Eastern' Europe. For the sake of brevity, I will use the abbreviation 'CEEC' to refer to these formerly communist states, or Central and Eastern European Countries.

2   These European norms, enumerated at the 1990 meeting of the Conference on Security and Cooperation in Europe, include 'democratic institutions and economic freedom, economic reform relying on market forces, freedom of individual enterprise, private property, multiparty democracy based on free elections, the rule of law, the rights of workers to join trade unions, and market economies based on supply and demand' (Laux, 1991, pp.19-20; see also Mihalyi, 1990).

3   Portugal's long-ruling dictator Antonio Salazar was incapacitated by a stroke in 1967 and later died in 1970. He was succeeded by Marcelo Caetano who continued to govern with the constitution drawn up during

the Salazar regime.

4   Much of the material on Greece presented here was formulated in consultation with Susannah Verney with whom I have collaborated on another project. Many of the insights about Greece's relationship with the rest of Europe were developed by her in a series of memos, correspondences, and published and unpublished articles. I am indebted to her for her contributions. See selected works by Verney, 1987, 1990, 1993, 1994a, 1994b, 1996.

5   Papandreou failed to condemn the Soviet invasion of Afghanistan, the imposition of martial law in Poland, and the Soviet downing of Korean Airlines flight 007, and referred to Qadaffi's Libya as a 'direct democracy' (Kuniholm, 1986, p.139; see also Larrabee, 1981-82; Loulis, 1984-85; Dimitras, 1985; McCaskill, 1988; Lefeber, 1989-90).

6   The Portuguese Socialist Party (PS) was founded in Bonn with help of the German SPD. The PS's founder, Mario Soares, developed ideological affinities with SPD leader Willy Brandt. Whether or not this affinity had any bearing on EC negotiations with a CDU-led German government is an empirical question requiring additional research.

7   The ethnic Hungarian population living in the Romanian province of Transylvania numbers 2,000,000; in Slovakia the Magyar minority numbers 600,000; 160,000 ethnic Hungarians live in Ukraine; 450,000 ethnic Hungarians reside in the former Yugoslav republics, some of whom have been drafted into the Serbian army, raising the fear that Magyar soldiers have been involved in Serbian raids on Hungarian villages in eastern Croatia (Reisch, 1991, pp.18-19).

8   As David Stark argues, 'it is the relationship between *different types of democracy* and *different types of capitalism*, rather than the abstractions of Democracy and Capitalism, that holds the clue to explaining differences in contemporary Eastern Europe' (Stark, 1991, p.42, emphasis in the original).

9   Although leaders in the CEEC have membership in the European Union as their ultimate aim, the Central European countries (Poland, the Czech Republic, Slovakia, and Hungary) have modified their aims and realize that Central European cooperation can and should provide an interim solution to pressing economic and security concerns (Shumaker, 1993).

10   George Kolankiewicz observes: '[The] idea of Europe has...been confronted not just with the realities of EC association but also, more prosaically, with the consequences of trade liberalization, the mass influx of western media, tourism, alternative lifestyles, secularism and other influences, all of which have had their resonances at the grass roots. The adjustment and rationalization of the idea of Europe following on more direct experience of its nature will give rise to a constellation of competing economic and political interests in eastern Europe over the region's own future geopolitical and economic alignments, just as the process of ratifying the Maastricht Treaty has among the Twelve [sic]' (Kolankiewicz, 1994, p.479).

11   'Identification as a Western society and aspiration to democratic values and standards, patriotism and promotion of the welfare of the Hungarian minorities outside the boundaries of the state, and the ability to endure and even tolerate foreign rule, have been considered cornerstones of Hungarian political culture' (Bigler, 1992, p.438).

12   By 1991, only two years after the fall of communism, as much as 30 per cent of the Hungarian economy was in the private sector (Pinder 1991, p.54).

13   'In his [1993] New Year's Day address, [Meciar] pointedly rejected the twin pillars of politics in the Czech Republic: free markets and a ban on former Communists from top Government positions....Although Slovak officials stress the Western roots of their nation's cultural history, they have great hopes for developing markets in Ukraine, Russia and other countries that once made up the Eastern bloc' (*The New York Times*, 22 January 1993, p.A3).

14   The Socialist Party government that emerged victorious in Bulgaria after the first democratic election and the Bulgarian military both sought to preserve security ties with Moscow (Bugajski, 1993, p.197). Yet in recent years, Bulgarian leaders have made great strides to reject the communist past and adopt Western-style democracy.

15   Yang Zhong points out that during the Persian Gulf War, the CEEC were willing to support the allied war effort in hopes of reaping long term gains from cooperation with the West despite severe short term economic costs (Zhong, 1994, p.243).

16   The EU's founding principles restrict membership to democratic states. Clearly, however, the mere presence of elections does not qualify by a strict definition of democracy, and the Union will not seriously consider

the Turkish application as long as human rights abuses exist as a regular feature of political life (Barchard, 1985).

17   The 1990-91 Persian Gulf War raised the issue of Kurdish independence to a level that was uncomfortable for Ankara which subsequently cracked down. This further alienated the West, despite Turkey's participation in the war against Iraq.

18   Turkey's predicament resembles that of the North African states that seek closer ties to Europe: 'The fact that they are Islamic countries is inconvenient and worrisome: to absorb a larger Islamic population within the EC's borders would not be easy; to contemplate rising fundamentalism in North Africa or Turkey would be deeply disturbing' (H. Wallace, 1992, p.31).

19   There were exceptions to this rule. As Gale Stokes points out, the Slovenes in particular had a much stronger European identity than the other Yugoslav republics and thus mounted their secession from Yugoslavia on the basis of Western democratic, as opposed to ethnic nationalist, ideals (Stokes, 1993, p.236).

20   Several observers have noted that the CEEC can be divided into two groups, with the Central European states more European-oriented and the Eastern European countries focused more inwardly (Zhong, 1994). As Peter Katzenstein explains, a combination of historical memory and identity factors suggests a grouping of states that respond similarly to the institutions of integration despite very different structural characteristics. Thus, Sweden, Spain, and the Czech Republic can be seen to constitute one group of countries with a strong European orientation, while Norway, Greece, and Slovakia comprise a second, less *Euroenthusiastic* set of states (Katzenstein, forthcoming).

8 Conclusion

Throughout this book, Spain's European foreign policy has been discussed in a theoretical context focusing ideas, interests, and knowledge. To conclude this study it is useful to reexamine the analytical propositions that inform the project and evaluate their validity for analysis beyond the Spanish case. The story of Spain's policy towards the rest of Europe is not only one of a single state interacting with a set of international institutions. In an environment in which these institutions constitute a web of interlocking relationships, it is impossible to hold the European institutional environment constant. Rather, we must recognize that the institutions of European integration are constantly evolving as member state interact with one another. In this chapter I shall reprise the theoretical analysis developed in Chapter Three in order to reflect on the nature of European international relations in an institutional context. By doing so I hope to come to some conclusions about the nature of international organization that takes us beyond the single empirical case that has informed the book thus far.

European international relations evaluated

Analysis of European international relations must take account of certain historical trends. Throughout the post-World War II era in Western Europe the barriers between the realm of 'high politics' dealing with security matters and 'low politics' relating to economic interactions increasingly were blurred over time. American military leadership allowed traditional military rivals to coexist peacefully and institutionalize confidence building measures. This eventually rendered historical animosities virtually obsolete. By the same token, European economic integration gradually led to the establishment of political links with implications in the security realm. The end of the Cold War and the signing of the Maastricht Treaty on European Union solidified these trends such that it is possible to theorize about European international relations at the economic and security levels simultaneously. Therefore, it is fair to consider the validity of existing theories about European affairs as they pertain to the totality of relations among European states.

Skeptics of European integration contest this assertion. They argue that as long as nation-states remain the sole legitimate sovereign entities capable of existing in a system of international anarchy it is impossible to conceptualize anything other than the traditional interplay among European states. In this conception, power politics continue to shape European affairs with economic factors serving as constituent elements of power at best, but more likely merely as a function of the distribution of military power. In one of the most stark statements of this 'realist' thesis, John Mearsheimer predicts that the end of Cold War bipolarity actually increases the chances of war in Europe, economic integration within the EU notwithstanding (Mearsheimer, 1990). Mearsheimer's thesis depends on the assumption of international anarchy as a barrier to the creation of institutional arrangements which foster cooperation among states. Even those theorists who postulate increasing European cooperation over select policy areas in the post-Cold War era are not able to account for the range of cooperative solutions available. This is true as long as theorists believe that these solutions depend on conditions which ameliorate the 'fact' of international anarchy (Kupchan and Kupchan, 1991).

European economic integration within the institutions of the European Union provides convincing evidence that assumptions of international anarchy, 'hard-shelled' state sovereignty, and enduring and exogenously arising national interests no longer hold up empirically or theoretically. While the member states of the EU have not yet surrendered formal sovereignty to form a single federal state, they have transferred considerable legal authority to the Union and now formulate uniform policy in substantive and substantial policy areas ranging from agriculture to regional planning to treaty making with third party states. Even in those areas in which integration has not required a transfer of sovereignty, EU states act in a coordinated manner where cooperation is anticipated and institutionalized. The evolution of the European Union's Common Foreign and Security Policy (CFSP) is a good example of emergent patterns of integration in the EU. Infused with elements of 'high politics', the CFSP nonetheless demonstrates that member states of the European Union increasingly act in a cooperative fashion to protect common interests (Tiersky, 1991).

While the evolution of the European Union offers convincing evidence that European international relations contain a binding normative element, the debate over the dynamics of European economic integration remains contested. The analytical discourse has been dominated by an argument between theorists who maintain that traditional states ultimately retain sovereignty even as they agree to abide by certain norms and rules, and others who claim that European integration represents a gradual process by which traditional state sovereignty is rendered obsolete. This debate between 'intergovernmentalists' (Hoffmann, 1982; W.

154

Wallace, 1982; Moravcsik, 1991; Garrett, 1992) on the one hand and 'supranationalists' (E. Haas, 1958, 1964; Lindberg, 1963; Peters, 1992; Burley and Mattli, 1993) on the other is well-documented and need not be repeated here. However, despite their dispute over the question of sovereignty transfer, both sides of the debate have two things in common. First, they assume that states' interests arise largely in an exogenous fashion as European countries approach the integration process. Second, they assume that fixed power relationships play some role in determining the outcome of EU bargaining. As I shall discuss below, both of these assumptions are questioned by the Spanish case.

Researchers attempting to move beyond the intergovernmental versus supranational debate have turned to what is now commonly known as the 'constructivist' approach to international relations. The constructivist approach, which is also known as the 'interpretivist' or 'structurationist' approach, is based on the British sociological school of international relations (Bull and Watson, 1984; Onuf, 1989; Wendt, 1991, 1992, 1994). Quite simply, sociological constructivism holds that 'people and society [are] "co-constituted"' (Wendt, 1991, p.386). That is, individuals do not enter into society as fully developed beings with interests that are inherent from birth, nor does society spring to life spontaneously as if an act of nature. To put it another way, constructivism does not 'bracket' either society or individuals but considers them mutually constituting.

Constructivism has been offered as a solution to what has become known as the 'agent-structure' problem in international relations (Wendt, 1987). The agent-structure problem revolves around the riddle of how the structure and constituent elements of the international system can be co-constituted. Walter Carlsnaes puts it this way:

> What is referred to...as the structural dimension can no longer be conceived as a parametric given in the form of constraints on action. Whatever specific solution is proposed for the agency-structure problem, it must at a minimum include the notion that agents produce and reproduce, while *pari passu* being determined by, international and domestic structures. This constitutes, broadly speaking, the 'codetermination' aspect of the issue (Carlsnaes, 1992, p.260).

So if the international system and sovereign states are mutually constituted, then researchers are left to ponder how this mutual constitution takes place.[1] Alexander Wendt, who has pioneered theorizing in this field, suggests a solution to this problem: 'The core of this agenda is the use of structural analysis to theorize the conditions of existence of state agents, and the use of historical analysis to explain the genesis and reproduction of social structures' (Wendt, 1987, p.365). However, Wendt's attempt at a solution relies on a static explanation of agents and structures at a single point in time. Since mutual

155

constitution is a dynamic, ongoing process, one still has to find a temporal break in the circle of mutual constitution between agents and structures to avoid merely re-stating the nature of the agent-structure problem. In other words, unless one is satisfied with a static model, a catalytic role must be imputed to an some *independent* factor in order to explain the construction of international states and systems *over time*. To do this, Wendt suggests three types of mechanisms by which change takes place: 'structural contexts', 'systemic processes', and 'strategic practice' (Wendt, 1994). Of these, the most important are systemic process, or 'dynamics in the external context of state action' (ibid, p.389). These processes, interrupt the constructivist loop by altering the intersubjective meanings produced by collective action. With regards to an international system based on cooperation, these processes involve two trends: Rising interdependence, and the transnational convergence of domestic values (ibid).

Based on his outline of the constructivist approach, Wendt describes European integration as follows:

> A strong liberal or constructivist analysis...would suggest that four decades of cooperation may have transformed a positive interdependence of outcomes into a collective 'European identity' in terms of which states increasingly define their 'self'-interests. Even if egoistic reasons were its starting point, the process of cooperating tends to redefine those reasons by reconstituting identities and interests in terms of new intersubjective understandings and commitments (Wendt, 1992, p.417).

Working along the same lines, Wayne Sandholtz argues: 'EC institutions and policies directly affected national interest calculations.... Preferences are endogenous, dependent on actors' perceptions and objectives and on domestic politics' (Sandholtz, 1993, p.4). Wendt and Sandholtz present credible arguments, ones which I accept in principle. However, they are limited in their scope. First, as I show in Chapter Seven, interests of European Union countries are formed not only in relation to other EU member states, but also with regards to third-party countries that are attempting to obtain membership. In the process of seeking entry, these countries in North, Central, and Eastern Europe are forcing a re-examination of EC direction, much as Spain, Greece, and Portugal did in the early 1980s. Second, European integration operates in an institutional context much larger than the European Union *qua* formal organization.[2] European countries are embedded in a web of interlocking international organizational and institutional arrangements. The situation in post-Cold War Europe - where the formerly communist, neutral, and Western European countries, alike, are looking for new roles - is a factor in shaping the new face of Europe and is not confined solely to EU affairs (Hames, 1992; Moens, 1992). Thus, the end of the Cold War has unleashed a process of redefinition of European political realities in not only economic, but also security affairs and political matters in general.[3]

In fact, the end of the Cold War has created a sense of uncertainty that has called most, if not all, European institutional arrangements into question (Wæver, 1989; Buzan, et.al. 1990). Therefore, resolving this uncertainty will require a creative process by which a new European identity is established and interests are re-defined. My purpose in raising this point is not to predict how Europe will look in the future, but simply to point out that European political reality is intersubjectively created by political elites and not subject to an amorphous process of rising interdependence. I make this observation in order to highlight the theoretical framework I adopt in this book, and to show how it applies beyond the case of Spanish European integration in the 1980s. In Chapter Six we moved beyond 1986 to see that Spain is not now, nor was it in the early 1980s, a passive recipient of knowledge about what the rest of Western Europe expected of it.[4] Nor is European political reality something 'out there' having an impact on European structures and agents. Knowledge of European political realities is something actively shared and created among members of a political community over time (Sandholtz and Zysman, 1989, p.107, fn# 24).

Empirical tests on European integration reveal the shortcomings of constructivism discussed above. Wendt's formulation cannot solve the agent-structure problem as it pertains to cooperative international relations since interdependence and the transnational convergence of domestic values are themselves the product of state agency. The solution of the agent-structure problem that posits mutually constituted states and international systems underspecify the content and sequencing of international socialization. Instead, as I elaborate in Chapter Three of this book, *we must disaggregate the specific and sequential steps by which actors constitute and re-constitute the international structure and their position in it.* It is only by taking apart the mutual constitution of agents and structure and specifying the sequential relationship among these constituent elements that a picture emerges of how international relations change over time.

In Chapter Three of this book I suggest a formulation that disaggregates this process. First, with regards to *content*, each country's foreign policy can be understood by examining three factors: 1) Ideas, which comprise the abstract beliefs that guide the general contours of states' actions; 2) Material capabilities, which are expressed as states' tangible interests; and 3) Knowledge, which serves as the specific understanding of cause-and-effect relationships that govern political reality. When applied to a group of states interacting systematically over time, I propose that these elements represent the three constituent elements of international society.[5] Ideas supply a sense of communal belonging and shared moral vision, material capabilities define the range of interests in light of the distribution of power, and knowledge provides a shared conception of political reality.[6] By disaggregating international society in this way we can begin to open the closed circle of mutually constituted states and agents that characterizes the constructivist approach.

The second task is to disaggregate the *temporal* steps by which international socialization occurs. During periods of stasis, knowledge about political realities provides a set of commonly accepted expectations about the causes and effects of states' actions. States understand the parameters and limits of interests and power given these mutually accepted understandings. They also believe in shared common abstract ideas about the moral and normative nature of international society.[7] How then does change take place over time? As I discuss at length in Chapter Three, the comfortable relationship among ideas, interests, and knowledge for a single state can be shattered under a variety of circumstances including internal or external shocks that challenge accepted beliefs, gradual recognition of inconsistencies among ideas or between ideas and knowledge, learning inherent to a particular idea base, the need to reconcile past and present circumstances, conflicts between ideas and the implementation of current policies, and generalized uncertainty brought about by generational change. These same circumstances can be assumed to exist among states interacting in an international society. Therefore, knowledge about the political realities of international relations is the currency of the agent-structure dynamic. It is transmitted among states, changes leaders' ideas and interests, and influences foreign policy decisions, the outcomes of which subsequently change political realities anew.

In the case of European integration, where states are comparatively self-conscious about the changing nature of the integration process, they recognize that the ideological nature, material interests, and political realities of interstate relations are not fixed. One look no further than the relationship between France and Germany. There is no pre-determined form these relations must take now that the 'objective' structures that governed Europe during the Cold War have disappeared. Instead, the leaders of France and Germany are engaged in a dialog to actively shape post-Cold War relations between the two countries and within Europe in general. In a larger sense, Georg Sørensen writes of how change in the agent-structure dynamic in the European Union is manifested in a qualitative transformation of the states and system that comprise the European political condition. Sørensen calls what has transpired a shift from a 'modern' to a 'post-modern' state system in Europe:

> The EU does not fit well into conventional schemes of cooperation between states. It is a hybrid, qualitatively changing some aspects of sovereign statehood, while retaining the single member state as the key player, albeit within an increasingly strong transnational policy network (Sørensen, 1995, p.17).

Furthermore, it is wrong to assume that any aspect of European integration will remain static over time. For example, just because the common foreign and security policy may stall over issues like the Bosnian crisis does not mean that integrative progress in this area will not take place, just as it would have been wrong 25 years earlier to argue that the free movement of capital in the EU would never come to fr ition. European integration is a dynamic process that reflects the way that international socialization is continuous over time.

Does this mean that national interests, as apart from European interests, eventually disappear as European integration goes forward? Shlomo Weber and Hans Wiesmeth posit that even as the European Union achieves greater levels of cooperation, negotiations within the EU nonetheless represent the *prior* interests of member states. Thus, even when member states establish a 'community of interests' with 'a sense of common identity and objectives', it is a result of bargaining that assumes states' interests as primitive and mediated, but not transmuted, by interactions within the EU (Weber and Wiesmeth, 1991, pp.258-260). However, it is possible to accept that states retain a sense of self-interest at the same time that they develop a wider set of European interests. Furthermore, as Andrés Ortega argues, what constitutes national state interests in the context of European integration has mutated from a narrow conception of self-interest to each EU member states' understanding of its particular role in the process of European integration (Ortega, 1994, 153). Jonathan Mercer offers a novel interpretation, postulating that while egoistic self-interest is inherent in anarchic international relations, it is conceivable that European unification will result in a European self-interest shared by all EU member states as the Union competes with other countries around the world (Mercer, 1995, pp.249-251).

As I have demonstrated, the evolution of the European system today is a product of foreign policy interaction and knowledge construction among the leaders of European states. This is especially true regarding the expansion of the economic functions of the European Union to encompass broader political and defense related undertakings. This expansion is not due to some amorphous 'spillover effect' (Haas, 1958), nor to underspecified 'construction' of the European international system, but to the agency of European leaders actively working to create a new European political space. In 1993 John Ruggie described the process of European economic integration as a constitutive process where agency plays a role:

> Within this framework, European leaders may be thought of as entrepreneurs of alternative political identities - EC Commission President [Jacques] Delors, for example, is at this very moment exploiting the tension between community widening and community deepening so as to catalyze the further re-imagining of European collective existence (Ruggie, 1993, p.72).

We see that ongoing developments in European integration represent a process of communal learning and the construction of a new knowledge base about the realities of the post-Cold War order.

Furthermore, because shared knowledge needs ideas to hold it together, we need to see European international relations not only based on common understandings, but also on the cultural, symbolic, and identity-related forms which make up the substance of the new European idea. Therefore, it is fair to talk about an 'idea of Europe' that is more than the invocation of historical memory based on periods when Europe was unified in some distant past (Gruender and Moutsopoulos 1992; Heater, 1992; Keane, 1992). When Spain and Portugal were negotiating membership in the EC in the mid-1980s, the resolution of internal Community problems and the EC's ability to rise above the 'Eurosclerosis' of the 1970s were *products* of the efforts of EC states to connect the rejuvenated integration process to the southern expansion.[8] This process has continued through the creation of the SEA and beyond. As former European Commission President Jacques Delors declared: 'Europe needs a political identity to bring its ambitions - if indeed it has these ambitions - to fruition. Europe must want to be European' (Delors, 1991).

But what does this new European identity look like? Here is where the Spanish contribution is illustrative. The leaders of post-Franco Spain believed that they could insure democracy at home by tying the fate of Spain to Europe. This would entail some foregoing of short term gains in favor of the long term benefits all European states enjoy as a function of the integration project. Knowledge about the realties of how these long term gains can be secured reconciles any fears European states have about ceding sovereignty to larger international institutions. We witnessed how this worked for Spain in both the security and economic realms. Regarding the former, Spanish leaders learned that Spain's security interests would be better protected in a cohesive Europe in which Spain was a fully institutionalized member. Regarding the latter, the Spanish government has come to understand that economic gains can be secured only when the European Union as a whole experiences long-term economic growth. The idea of Europe in which all states' interests are bound to each other provides the ideational glue that hold these realities together. Speaking at the College of Europe in Bruges, Belgium in 1985, former Spanish Prime Minister Felipe González promoted this new idea of Europe:

> Without a doubt, today's nation-state has become too small for certain functions and too large for others, with the symptoms of a double crisis of both supra-nationalism and 'intra-nationalism'. The solution is not to revive sentimental and fanatical nationalism; if we want to advance we must do so with the clear understanding that the EC - and even more the European union of the future - requires a common exercise of our national sovereignties. Full integration will only be possible when all Europeans embrace the idea that true national interests are identical with EC interests; at this stage, isolated solutions are already impractical (*Europe*, January-February 1986, p.48).

Therefore, one must address the larger picture of European affairs as new relationships are forged in political, economic, and security issues - not only within the EU, but within these overlapping institutional spheres. As knowledge about long term benefits overcomes states' fears about short term costs, the idea of Europe becomes fully compatible with evolving state interests.

In the previous two chapters of this book, by extending the analysis of Spain and Europe both temporally (beyond the year of Spanish accession to the EC and the NATO referendum) and spatially (to include additional country cases), I have endeavored to show that, even as regards so-called 'weaker' states in the European system, the forging of Europe's future is a process that involves the construction of shared consensual knowledge by all states, and is not something imposed by seemingly more 'powerful' states whose interests are somehow independently derived. New knowledge about European political realities is thus constructed and transmitted *throughout* the system, and not just *from* 'strong' or 'core' European states *to* 'weak' or 'peripheral' ones. Knowledge of the realities of the present European system is one of purposeful and normative relationships created *among* states. Furthermore, as this knowledge is shared, states' interests are changed, and therefore the shaping of these interests must be understood as endogenous to the integration process.[9] Finally, common ideas about the moral nature of European integration bind states together in a shared belief system. By extending the Spanish case to the entirety of relations among states interacting in European institutions, as implied by the concept of mutually constituting agents and structures, we are able to conceptualize European international relations as a whole.

Summary

In its most basic form, this book represents an effort to develop a framework for studying the effects of ideas and knowledge in international relations. The approach I adopt makes more systematic use of these concepts than has been done in the past. As I have elaborated, traditional state-centered theories of international relations assume that power politics allow larger and wealthier states to dictate the terms of the integration process. Constructivist theories offer a better explanation for foreign policy change in general, and European integration in specific, than traditional approaches in international relations because they challenge the assumptions of power and interests inherent in the traditional models. However, they fail to fully disaggregate the concepts of international society and socially constructed norms. They also fail to specify the steps by which states enter into an international community. The model I have presented here, based on my research on Spain and other European states, offers a way out of this problem. International relations can be envisioned as a multi-stage process in which state leaders have ideas about the world, knowledge based claims on what makes the world work, and interests based on these conceptions. Interaction with other countries alters these conceptions.

As I have stressed, if one treats generalized ideas and specific knowledge as the same thing, then one loses the opportunity to trace the evolution from abstract beliefs to policy with internationally transmitted knowledge acting as the catalyst for change. In times of fundamental change, the knowledge based claims that underpin political ideas are forced to the surface and leaders reexamine the ideas and truth claims that guide their political decisions. As they do so, they often discover inconsistencies between the ideas they have about politics and their perceptions of political, economic, and security interests. During these periods of uncertainty, leaders are most receptive to new knowledge based claims - that is, new conceptions of political reality - especially those transmitted within international circles of elites. This political knowledge reconstitutes ideas and perceptions of interests. As politics re-enter a period of stasis, knowledge based claims are re-submerged for the sake of day-to-day politics, and leaders once again rely on generalized political ideas and the interests they perceive from these ideas. The framework I have presented here, then, accounts not only for Spain's European relations, but for European international relations in general, with implications for international relations in their totality.

Notes

1   Georg Sørensen defines an international system as 'composed of structure as well as of interacting units. Any separation of system-level (or international) and unit level (or domestic) forces can only be analytic' (Sørensen, 1995, p.1).

2   Sandholtz is aware of this limitation (1993, p.3 fn#6).

3   The emerging European Union (EU) is to have three pillars: 'The first, the Community pillar, is rooted in the Treaties of Paris and Rome....The second pillar consists of the common foreign and security activities of the EU....Justice and home affairs are to constitute the third pillar,...' (Michalski and Wallace, 1992, p.18).

4   Although no side could claim complete satisfaction from its agreements, the treaty by which Spain entered the EC 'represented that common denominator which all the parties involved could at least find acceptable' (Mujal-Leon, 1986, p.211).

5   Headly Bull and Adam Watson define an international society as 'a group of states which not merely form a system, in the sense that the behaviour of each is a necessary factor in the calculations of the others,

but also have established by dialog and consent common rules and institutions for the conduct of their relations, and recognize their common interests in maintaining these arrangements' (Bull and Watson, 1984, p.1).

6   In domestic society we might recognize these elements as ideology, wealth, and law. Ideology serves as the moral glue that binds society together, wealth shapes material relationships and defines the parameters of interested action, and law structures societal interactions within the confines of commonly accepted boundaries of action.

7   Note that the norms that underpin international society can be either cooperative or competitive in nature. International society can be conflictual just as easily as it can be harmonious. See Wendt, 1992.

8   A former economics advisor to Felipe González related in an interview for this project that the passage of the Single European Act (SEA) was a key event in EC history because EC leaders realized the only option left for the EC was to move forward. Having gotten past the SEA, the plan of the EC changed radically from 'Europessimism' to 'Euro-optimism'. This was reinforced by the entry process of Spain and Portugal into the Community. With the Iberian expansion of the EC people started to see that Europe was a 'valid idea'.

9   A good example of this process in which Spain played an important role is the EU's cohesion policy. As Georg Sørensen observes: 'Poorer members' support for the Single European Act creating the single market was...compensated in the form of economic development project in those member countries. Instead of national economies, there is an increasingly integrated economic space with a measure of redistribution' (Sørensen, 1995, p.22). This is a qualitative change in European economic brought about by new shared understandings, motivated by so-called 'weaker' members of the EU.

163

Bibliography

Abel, Christopher and Torrents, Nissa (eds.) (1984), *Spain: Conditional Democracy*, Croom Helm: London.

Actividades, Textos y Documentos de la Política Exterior Española (various dates), Ministerio de Asuntos Exteriores, Oficina de Información Diplomática: Madrid.

Adler, Emanuel (1987), *The Power of Ideology*, University of California Press: Berkeley.

Aggarwal, Vinod K. (1985), *Liberal Protectionism*, University of California Press: Berkeley.

Aguirre, Mariano (1983), 'El Gobierno Socialista y el Orden Militar Internacional', *Leviatán*, No. 12, Summer, pp. 33-44.

Aguirre, Mariano (1986), 'España: Seguridad, Defensa y la OTAN', *Revista de Estudios Internacionales*, Vol. 7, No. 1, January-March, pp. 47-56.

Alan, Ray (1977), 'The New Spain: A Survey', *The Economist*, 2 April.

Albuquerque, Francisco and Gomáriz, Enrique (1984), 'OTAN: Costes y Beneficios - Conversación con Angel Viñas', *Tiempo de Paz*, No. 4, pp. 6-28.

Aldecoa Luzárraga, Francisco (1983), 'Significado y Efectos de la Adhesión de España a la Alianza Atlántica en Su Proceso de Participación Activa en las Relaciones Internacionales', *Revista de Estudios Internacionales*, Vol. 4, No. 1, pp. 39-70.

Aldecoa Luzárraga, Francisco (1984), 'La Política Exterior de España en Perspectiva Histórica, 1945-1984', *Sistema*, Vol. 63, November 1984, pp. 111-131.

Aliboni, Roberto (ed.) (1992), *Southern European Security in the 1990s*, Pinter: London.

Almarcha Barbado, Amparo (ed.) (1993), *Spain and EC Membership Evaluated*, Pinter Publishers: London.

Alonso, Antonio (1985), *España en el Mercado Común*, Espasa-Calpe: Madrid.

Alonso Baquer, Miguel (1985), *Las Preferencias Estratégicas del Militar Española*, Estado Mayor del Ejército: Madrid.

Alonso Baquer, Miguel (1988), *Estrategia Para la Defensa*, Instituto de Estudios Económicos: Madrid.

Alonso de los Ríos, César and Elordi, Carlos (1982), *El Desafío Socialista*, Editorial Laia: Barcelona.

Alonso Zaldívar, Carlos (1983), '"Euromísiles", ¿Impedir o Ganar la Guerra Nuclear?', *Zona Abierta*, No. 27, January-March, pp. 93-133.

Alonso Zaldívar, Carlos; Herrero Rodríguez de Miñón, Miguel and Aguirre, Mariano (1987), *Política Española de Paz y Seguridad*, (Cuadernos y Debates #4), Centro de Estudios Constitucionales: Madrid.

Álvarez-Miranda, Berta (1995), *A Las Puertas de la Comunidad: Consenso y Disenso en el Sur de Europa*, (Working Paper, 1995/74), Centro de Estudios Avanzados en Ciencias Sociales (Instituto Juan March de Estudios e Investigaciones): Madrid.

Alvira Martín, Francisco, et.al. (1978), *Partidos Políticos e Ideologías*, Centro de Investigaciones Sociológicas: Madrid.

Anderson, Jeffery J. (1995), 'Structural Funds and the Social Dimension of EU Policy: Springboard or Stumbling Block', in Leibfried, Stephan and Pierson, Paul (eds.), *European Social Policy: Between Fragmentation and Integration*, The Brookings Institution: Washington, DC.

Del Arenal, Celestino and Aldecoa, Francisco (eds.) (1986), *España y la OTAN: Textos y Documentos*, Tecnos: Madrid.

Argyris, Chris and Schon, Donald (1978), *Organizational Learning*, Addison-Wesley: Reading, MA.

Armario, Diego (1981), *El Triángulo: El PSOE Durante la Transición*, Fernando Torres: Valencia.

Armero, José Mario (1989), *Política Exterior de España en Democracia*, Espasa-Calpe: Madrid.

Arrojo, Pedro, et.al. (1984), 'Debate OTAN', *Tiempo de Paz*. No. 3, Summer, pp. 46-71.

Ashley, Richard K. (1986), 'The Poverty of Neorealism', in Keohane, Robert O. (ed.), *Neorealism and Its Critics*, Columbia University Press: New York.

Axelrod, Robert (ed.) (1976), *Structure of Decision*, Princeton University Press: Princeton, NJ.

Axelrod, Robert (1984), *The Evolution of Cooperation*, Basic Books: New York.

Azcarate, Manuel (1984), 'La Crisis de la OTAN y la Europa Política', *Tiempo de Paz*, No. 2, Spring, pp. 12-21.

Badini, Antonio (1995), 'Efforts at Mediterranean Cooperation', in Holmes, John W. (ed.), *Maelstrom: The United States, Southern Europe, and the Challenges of the Mediterranean*, The World Peace Foundation: Cambridge, MA.

Baeza Betancort, Felipe (1983), *España y la OTAN: Un Ensayo de Política de Defensa*, Escuela de Guerra Naval: Madrid.

Baklanoff, Eric N. (ed.) (1976), *Mediterranean Europe and the Common Market*, University of Alabama Press: University, AL.

Baklanoff, Eric N. (1978), *The Economic Transformation of Spain and Portugal*, Praeger: New York.

Ballarín, Alberto (1979), 'Defensa Nacional', in *Perspectivas de Una España Democrática y Constitucionalizada*, Vol. 3., Unión Editorial: Madrid.

Barbé, Esther (1993), 'La Política Española de Seguridad en la Nueva Europa: Dimensión Mediterránea e Instrumentos Europeos', *Afers Internacionales*, No. 26.

Barbé, Esther (1995), 'European Political Cooperation: The Upgrading of Spanish Foreign Policy', in Gillespie, Richard; Rodrigo, Fernando and Story, Jonathan (eds.), *Democratic Spain: Reshaping Relations in a Changing World*, Routledge: London.

Barchard, David (1985), *Turkey and the West*, (Chatham House Paper #27), The Royal Institute of International Affairs: London.

Barnett, Michael N. (1993), 'Institutions, Roles, and Disorder: The Case of the Arab States System', *International Studies Quarterly*, Vol. 37, No. 3, September.

Barnett, Michael N. (1995), 'Sovereignty, Nationalism, and Regional Order in the Arab States System', *International Organization*, Vol. 49, No. 3, Summer.

Batt, Judy (1991), *East Central Europe From Reform to Transformation*, The Royal Institute of International Affairs: London.

Batt, Judy (1994), 'The Political Transformation of East Central Europe', in Miall, Hugh (ed.), *Redefining Europe: New Patterns of Conflict and Cooperation*, The Royal Institute of International Affairs: London.

Bell, David S. (ed.) (1983), *Democratic Politics in Spain*, Frances Pinter: London.

Beller, Steven (1991), *Reinventing Central Europe*, (Working Paper 92-5), Center for Austrian Studies: Minneapolis.

Benegas, José María (1985), 'Europa Como Proyecto Socialista', *Leviatán*, No. 21, Autumn, pp. 5-17.

Berling, Costa (1975), 'Bases USA en España', *Exprés Español*, No. 57, June.

Berman, Paul (1991), 'Still Sailing the Lemonade Se`', *The New York Times Magazine*, 27 October, pp. 32ff.

Bermeo, Nancy (1988), 'Regime Change and Its Impact on Foreign Policy: The Portuguese Case', *Journal of Modern Greek Studies*, Vol. 6, pp. 7-25.

Bermeo, Nancy and García-Durán, José (1992), 'The Political Economy of Structural Adjustment in New Democracies: The Case of Spain', unpublished manuscript.

Biehl, Dieter (1992), 'Structural Funds and Budgetary Transfers in the Community," in Hannequart, Achille (ed.), *Economic and Social Cohesion in Europe*, Routledge: London.

Bigler, Robert M. (1992), 'From Communism to Democracy: Hungary's Transition Thirty-Five Years After the Revolution', *East European Quarterly*, Vol. 25, No. 4, January, pp. 437-461.

Blum, Douglas W. (1993), 'The Soviet Foreign Policy Belief System: Beliefs, Politics, and Foreign Policy Outcomes', *International Studies Quarterly*, Vol. 37, No. 4, December.

Bonime-Blanc, Andrea (1987), *Spain's Transition to Democracy: The Politics of Constitution-Making*, Westview Press: Boulder, CO.

Borowiec, Andrew (1983), *The Mediterranean Feud*, Praeger: New York.

Botella, Francisco (1984), 'La Agricultura Española: Hacia un Fortalecimiento de la Europa Verde', speech devivered in Madrid, 15 September.

Boyd, Carolyn P. (1989), 'History in the Schools and the Problem of Spanish Identity', in Herr, Richard and Polt, John H.R. (eds.), *Iberian Identity: Essays on the Nature of Identity in Portugal and Spain*, Institute of International Studies: Berkeley, CA.

Borja, Jordi (1983), 'La Izquierda en la España de Hoy', *Zona Abierta*, No. 29, July-December, pp. 95-136.

Böröcz, József (1992), *Hungary Re-Linking: State Socialism and the Transformation of External Linkages*, (Program on Central and Eastern Europe Working Paper #18), Minda de Ginzburg Center for European Studies (Harvard University): Cambridge, MA.

Bowers, Stephen R. (1991), 'The East European Revolution', *East European Quarterly*, Vol. 25, No. 2, June, pp. 129-143.

Brada, Josef C. (1991), 'The European Community and Czechoslovakia, Hungary, and Poland', *Report on Eastern Europe*, Vol. 2, No. 49, 6 December, pp. 27-32.

Braga de Macedo, Jorge and Serfaty, Simon (eds.) (1981), *Portugal Since the Revolution*, Westview: Boulder, CO.

Breckinridge, Robert E. (1991), 'The Interaction of Regimes: The Influence of the European Community on Spanish Democracy', unpublished doctoral dissertation, Department of Political Science, University of Maryland: Collage Park.

Brenan, Gerald (1943), *The Spanish Labyrinth*, Cambridge University Press: Cambridge.

Brown, James (1991), *Delicately Poised Allies: Greece and Turkey*, Brassey's: London.

Bru, Carlos (1984), 'España Entre Dos Tratados', *Leviatán*, No. 17, Autumn, pp. 69-79.

Bruneau, Thomas C. (1977), 'Out of Africa and Into Europe: Towards an Analysis of Portuguese Foreign Policy', *International Journal*, Vol. 32, No. 2, Spring, pp. 288-314.

Bruner, Jerome (1986), *Actual Minds, Possible Worlds*, Harvard University Press: Cambridge, MA.

Brunner, Guido (1983), 'El Ingreso de España Desde el Punto de Vista de las Comunidades Europeas', *Jornadas Informativas Sobre Temas Internacionales - 1982*, Sociedad de Estudios Internacionales: Madrid, pp. 333-343.

Brunner, Guido (1985), 'La Integración de España en la Comunidad Económica Europea', *Jornadas Informativas Sobre Temas Internacionales - 1984*, Sociedad de Estudios Internacionales: Madrid, pp. 81-85.

Bruszt, László (1991), *Transformative Politics in East Central Europe*, (Cornell Project on Comparative Institutional Analysis Working Paper on Transitions from State Socialism #91-5), Cornell University Center for International Studies: Ithaca, NY.

Bueno y Vicente, José Miguel (1984), 'Política de Seguridad Española: La Orientación Europeísta', *Leviatán*, No. 17, Autumn, pp. 35-46.

Bueno y Vicente, José Miguel (1985), 'España y Sus Posibilidades de Neutralidad', *Jornadas Informativas Sobre Temas Internacionales- 1984*, Sociedad de Estudios Internacionales: Madrid, pp. 209-221.

Buesa, Mikel and Molero, José (1988), *Estructura Industrial de España*, Fondo de Cultura Económica: Madrid.

Buesa, Mikel and Molero, José (1989), *Inovación Industrial y Dependencia Tecnológica de España*, Eudema: Madrid.

Bugajski, Janusz (1993), *Nations in Turmoil: Conflict and Cooperation in Eastern Europe*, Westview Press: Boulder, CO.

Buhigas, José Luis (1984), 'Las Contradicciones de la Política Exterior del PSOE', *Nuestra Bandera*, No. 124, May-June, pp. 13- 17.

Bukovansky, Mlada (1992), 'Socialization in International Affairs', paper presented at the Annual Meeting of the American Political Science Association: Chicago, 3-6 September.

Bull, Hedley and Watson, Adam (eds.) (1984), *The Expansion of International Society*, Clarendon Press: Oxford.

Bulletin of the European Communities, (1983), Vol. 16, No. 6.

Burley, Anne-Marie and Mattli, Walter (1993), 'Europe Before the Court: A Political Theory of Legal Integration', *International Organization*, Vol. 47, No. 1, Winter, pp. 41-76.

Bustelo, Carlos (1986), *Economic Policy in Spain's Democracy*, (Center for European Studies, Working Paper 15), Harvard University: Cambridge. MA.

De Busturia, Daniel (1982), 'Aspectos Económicos de la Adhesión de España a la Comunidad Europea', in *Southern Europe and the Enlargement of the EEC*, Editorial Economía: Madrid.

Buzan, Barry, et.al. (1990), *The European Security Order Recast*, Pinter: London.

Cable, Vincent (1994), 'Key Trends in the European Economy and Future Scenarios', in Miall, Hugh (ed.), *Redefining Europe: New Patterns of Conflict and Cooperation*, The Royal Institute of International Affairs: London.

Caciagli, Mario (1984), 'Spain: Parties and the Party System', in Pridham, Geoffrey (ed.), *The New Mediterranean Democracies*, Frank Cass: London.

Calatrava Andrés, Ascensión and Melero Guillo, Ana María (1986), *Política y Economía en Los Países del Magreb: Sus Relaciones con España en el Marco de la CEE*, Instituto Hispano-Arabe de Cultura: Madrid.

Calvo Hernando, Pedro (1987), *Todos Me Dicen Felipe*, Plaza & Janés: Barcelona.

Cameron, David R. (1993), 'British Exit, German Voice, French Loyalty: Defection, Domination and Cooperation in the 1992-93 ERM Crisis', paper presented at the Workshop on International Political Economy, Columbia University: New York, March.

Cañada Martínez, Agustín (1986), 'Algunas Repercusiones de la Ampliación de la CEE Sobre el Desarrolo de los Países Ribereños del Mediterránco', *Información Comercial España*, No. 640, December, pp. 163-172.

Carlsnaes, Walter (1992), 'The Agency-Structure Problem in Foreign Policy Analysis', *International Studies Quarterly*, Vol. 36, No. 3, September, pp. 245-270.

Carp, Mihai (1991), 'Romania: New Foreign Policy Initiatives', *Report on Eastern Europe*, Vol. 2, No. 36, 6 September, pp. 26-31.

Carr, Raymond (1973), 'Spanish History from 1700', in Russell, P.E. (ed.), *Spain: A Companion to Spanish Studies*, Methuen & Co.: London.

Carr, Raymond and Fusi Aizpurua, Juan Pablo (1979), *Spain: Dictatorship to Democracy*, Allen & Unwin: London.

Carrascal, José María (1985), *La Revolución del PSOE*, Plaza & Janés: Barcelona.

Carreras Ares, Juan José (1981), 'El Marco Internacional de la II República', *Arbor*, Vol. 109, No. 426-427, June-July, pp. 37-50.

Casanova, José V (1983), 'The Opus Dei Ethic, the Technocrats and the Modernisation of Spain', *Social Science Information*, Vol. 22, No. 1, 1983, pp. 27-50.

Casanova Fernández, Luis Javier (1993), 'La Aportación de la UEO a la Seguridad Europea', *Segundas Jornadas de Defensa Nacional*, (Monografías del Centro Superior de Estudios de la Defensa Nacional, #8), Ministerio de Defensa: Madrid.

Central and Eastern Europe in Transition (1991), (Arbeitspapiere Zur Internationalen Politik, No. 64), Forschungsinstitutder Deutschen Gesellschaft für Auswärtige Politik: Bonn.

Chazarra, Antonio and García Yruela, Jesús (1985), 'Una Reflexión Sobre el Socialismo Español Hoy', *Leviatán*, No. 19, Spring, pp. 61-72.

Checkel, Jeff (1993), 'Ideas, Institutions, and the Gorbachev Foreign Policy Revolution', *World Politics*, Vol. 45, No. 2, January.

Chipman, John (ed.) (1988), *NATO's Southern Allies*, Routledge: London.

Clark, Michael T. and Serfaty, Simon (eds.) (1991), *New Thinking and Old Realities: America, Europe, and Russia*, Seven Locks Press: Washington, DC.

Clark, Robert P. and Haltzel, Michael P. (eds.) (1987), *Spain in the 1980s*, Ballinger: Cambridge, MA.

Clarke, Douglas L. (1991), 'European Multinational Organizations: A Primer', *Report on Eastern Europe*, Vol. 2, No. 32, 9 August.

Clarke, Michael (1991), 'Evaluating the New Western European Union: The Implications for Spain', in Maxwell, Kenneth (ed.), *Spanish Foreign and Defense Policy*, Westview Press: Boulder, CO.

Claudín, Fernando (1979), 'Entrevista Con Felipe González', *Zona Abierta*, No. 20, May-August, pp. 5-21.

Clogg, Richard (1987), *Parties and Elections in Greece*, Duke University Press: Durham, NC.

Coats, A.W. (1989), 'Economic Ideas and Economists in Government', in Colander, David C. and Coats, A.W. (eds.), *The Spread of Economic Ideas*, Cambridge University Press: Cambridge.

Colander, David C. and Coats, A.W. (eds.) (1989), *The Spread of Economic Ideas*, Cambridge University Press: Cambridge.

Collado Curiel, Juan Carlos and Fernández Marugán, Francisco (1989), 'Situación, Interpretaciones y Opciones de la Economía Española', *Sistema*, No. 19, March, pp. 3-13.

Comitè Per la Coordinació dels Moviments Anti-OTAN (1981), 'Per la Pau, Contra L'OTAN', *Mientras Tanto*, No. 9, pp. 122-123.

Congressional Research Service (1992), *An Overview of U.S. Assistance in Eastern Europe and the Former Soviet Union*, (Parliamentary Development No. 2), 3 March, Library of Congress: Washington, DC.

Consecuencias Para la Economía Española de la Inteₔración de España en la CEE (1986), Gabinete de Estudios de ESIC: Madrid.

Constas, Dimitri (1995), 'Southern European Countries in the European Community', Holmes, John W. (ed.), *Maelstrom: The United States, Southern Europe, and the Challenges of the Mediterranean*, The World Peace Foundation: Cambridge, MA.

Conte Barrera, Jesús (1977), *Los Partidos Políticos al Desnudo*, Gassó Hermanos: Barcelona.

Cortada, James W. (ed.) (1980), *Spain in the Twentieth-Century World*, Greenwood Press: Westport, CT.

Costa Morata, Pedro (1983), *Una Política Mediterránea Para España*, Fundación IESA: Madrid.

Coufoundakis, Van (1987), 'Greek Foreign Policy, 1945-1985: Seeking Independence in an Interdependent World - Problems and Prospects', in Featherstone, Kevin and Katsoudas, Dimitrios K. (eds.), *Political Change in Greece Before and After the Colonels*, Croom Helm: London.

Couloumbis, Theodore A. (1993), 'PASOK's Foreign Policies, 1981-89: Continuity or Change?', in Clogg, Richard (ed.), *Greece, 1981-89: The Populist Decade*, St. Martin's Press: New York.

Couloumbis, Theodore A.; Petropulos, John A. and Psomiades, Harry J. (1976), *Foreign Interference in Greek Politics*, Pella Publishing: New York.

Coverdale, John F. (1977), 'Spain from Dictatorship to Democracy', *International Affairs*, Vol. 53, No. 4, October, pp. 615-630.

Cox, Robert W. (1981), 'Social Forces, States, and World Orders', *Millennium*, Vol. 10, Summer, pp. 126-155.

Cravinho, João (1983), 'Characteristics and Motives for Entry', in Sampedro, José Luis and Payno, Juan Antonio (eds.), *The Enlargement of the European Community*, The Macmillan Press: London.

Cremasco, Maurizio (1990), 'The Strategic Importance of Relations Between Turkey and the European Community', in Evin, Ahmet O. and Denton, Geoffrey (eds.), *Turkey and the European Community*, Leske & Budrich: Opladen, Germany.

Croan, Melvin (1989), 'Lands In-Between: The Politics of Cultural Identity in Contemporary Eastern Europe', *Eastern European Politics and Societies*, Vol. 3, No. 2, Spring, pp. 176-197.

Csanadi, Maria and Bunce, Valerie (1991), 'A Systemic Analysis of a Non-System: Post-Communism in Eastern Europe', paper presented at the Hungarian-American Political Science Roundtable: Budapest, 17-18 December.

Cubells, Luis Alonso (1981), 'Diversas Formas de Participar en la OTAN', *Revista de Aeronáutica y Astronáutica*, No. 490, October, pp. 1135-1139.

Davies, D.R. and Parasuraman, R. (1981), *The Psychology of Vigilance*, Academic Press: London.

Davis, Patricia (1992), 'Economic Statecraft in Past and Future German Policies Toward Poland', paper presented at the Workshop on Economic Statecraft, American Institute for Contemporary German Studies (Johns Hopkins University): Washington, DC, 21 July.

De la Dehesa, Guillermo (1986), 'Spanish Economy Will Get Boost From E.C. Entry', *Europe*, No. 253, January-February.

De la Dehesa, Guillermo (1988a), 'Los Límites de la Política Económica Española', *Leviatán*, No. 32, Summer, pp. 27-37.

De la Dehesa, Guillermo (1988b), 'La Integración de la Peseta en el Sistema Monetario Europeo: El Gran Dilema de la Política Económica Española', *Revista de Economía*, No. 657, May, pp. 141-148.

171

Delors, Jacques (1980), 'Por un Enfoque Socialista de los Problemas Económicas de Europa', *Zona Abierta*, No. 25, May-June, pp. 96-100.

Delors, Jacques (1991), 'European Integration and Security', Alastair Buchan Memorial Lecture, IISS: London, 7 March.

Deubner, Christian (1980), 'The Southern Enlargement of the European Community: Opportunities and Dilemmas from a West German Point of View', *Journal of Common Market Studies*, Vol. 18, No. 3, March, pp. 229-245.

Deutsch, Karl W., et.al (1957), *Political Community and the North Atlantic Area*, Princeton University Press: Princeton, NJ.

Diamandouros, P. Nikiforos (1984), 'Transition to, and Consolidation of, Democratic Politics in Greece, 1974-1983: A Tentative Assessment', in Pridham, Geoffrey (ed.), *The New Mediterranean Democracies: Regime Transition in Spain, Greece, and Portugal*, Frank Cass: London.

Diamandouros, P. Nikiforos (1986), 'The Southern European NICs', *International Organization*, Vol. 40, No. 2, Spring, pp. 371-380.

Diario de Sesiones del Congreso de los Diputados (various dates), Cortes Generales: Madrid.

Díaz, Elías (1982), *Socialismo en España: El Partido y el Estado*, Editorial Mezquita: Madrid.

Diez Años de Política Económica Española (1987), Círculo de Empresarios: Madrid.

Díez Nicolás, Juan (1986), 'La Transición Política y la Opinión Pública Española Ante los Problemas de la Defensa y Hacia las Fuerzas Armadas', *Revista Española de Investigaciones Sociológicas*, No. 36, October-December, pp. 13-24.

Diggins, John Patrick (1986), *The Lost Soul of American Politics*, University of Chicago Press: Chicago.

Dillingam, Alan J. (1996), 'The Costs of Convergence: The Case of France', *ECSA Review*, Vol. 9, No. 2, Spring/Summer, pp. 9-13.

Dimitras, Panayote E. (1985), 'Greece: A New Danger', *Foreign Policy*, No. 58, Spring, pp. 134-150.

'Las Directrices Cierran el "Decálogo"' (1988), *Revista Española de Defensa*, No. 10, December, pp. 8-9.

Discursos y Declaraciones del Ministro de Asuntos Exteriores, D. José Pedro Pérez-Llorca, (1980-1982) (1982), Ministerio de Asuntos Exteriores, Oficina de Información Diplomática: Madrid.

Discursos y Declaraciones del Ministro de Asuntos Exteriores, D. Fernando Morán, (1982-83) (1984), Ministerio de Asuntos Exteriores, Oficina de Información Diplomática: Madrid.

Discursos y Declaraciones del Ministro de Asuntos Exteriores, D. Fernando Morán, (1984) (1985), Ministerio de Asuntos Exteriores, Oficina de Información Diplomática: Madrid.

Dobratz, Betty A. (1988), 'Foreign Policy and Economic Orientations Influencing Party Preferences in the Socialist Nation of Greece', *East European Quarterly*, Vol. 21, No. 4, January, pp. 413-430.

Donges, Juergen B., et.al. (1982), *The Second Enlargement of the European Community*, J.C.B. Mohr: Tubingen, Germany.

Douglas, Mary (1986), *How Institutions Think*, Syracuse University Press: Syracuse, NY.

Downs, Anthony (1957), *An Economic Theory of Democracy*, Harper & Brothers: New York.

Duchene, François (1979), 'Actitudes de la Comunidad', paper presented at the Second Conference on Integration and Unequal Development: The Implications of the Second Enlargement of the EEC: Madrid, 15-19 October.

Eckstein, Harry (1975), 'Case Study and Theory in Political Science', in Greenstein, Fred I. and Polsby, Nelson W. (eds.), *Handbook of Political Science*, (Volume 7, *Strategies of Inquiry*), Addison-Wesley: Reading, MA.

Eisfeld, Rainer (1990), 'The Ambiguity of Portugal's Foreign Policy in the World', in Maxwell, Kenneth and Haltzel, Michael H. (eds.), *Portugal: Ancient Country, Young Democracy*, Woodrow Wilson Center Press: Washington, DC.

Ekiert, Grzegorz (1990), 'Transitions from State-Socialism in East Central Europe', *States and Social Structures Newsletter* (Social Science Research Council), No. 12, Winter, pp. 1-7.

Ekiert, Grzegorz (1992), 'Peculiarities of PostCommunist Politics: The Case of Poland', paper presented at the Second U.S.-Polish Roundtable: Warsaw, 5-7 June.

II Encuentro Hispano-Magrebi Sobre Cooperación en el Sector Agroalimentario (Primer Informe #13) (1988), Instituto Hispano-Arabe de Cultura: Madrid.

Entrevistas Con el Presidente del Gobierno, D. Felipe González (1990), Ministerio del Poratvoz del Gobierno: Madrid.

Ertürk, Ismail (1984), 'Turkey and the European Community', *International Relations*, Vol. 8, No. 2, November, pp. 137-156.

Equipo Jaime Vera (1977), *La Alternativa Socialista del PSOE*, Editorial Cuadernos Para el Diálogo: Madrid.

España Ante el Reto de Europa (1985), PSOE: Madrid.

España, Compromiso de Solidaridad: Resoluciones Socialistas Para los Años 80 (1985), PSOE: Madrid.

España y Francia Ante la Ampliación de la Comunidad Europea (1981), Consejo Federal Español del Movimiento Europeo: Madrid.

España y el Tratado de la Unión Euopea (1994), Editorial Colex: Madrid.

Estrategia Económica del PSOE (1980), Editorial Pablo Iglesias: Madrid.

Evan, William M. (ed.) (1981), *Knowledge and Power in a Global Society*, Sage Publications: Beverly Hills, CA.

Evin, Ahmet O. (1990), 'Communitarian Structures, Values and Cultural Behaviour in Turkey', in Evin, Ahmet O. and Denton, Geoffrey (eds.), *Turkey and the European Community*, Leske & Budrich: Opladen, Germany.

Evin, Ahmet O. and Denton, Geoffrey (eds.) (1990), *Turkey and the European Community*, Leske & Budrich: Opladen, Germany.

'La Evolución del Voto, 1979-1982', (1984), *Revista Española de Investigaciones Sociológicas*, No. 28, October-December, pp. 305-343.

'La Evolución de la Intención de Voto y Otros Indicadores Políticos: 1983-1986' (1986), *Revista Española de Investigaciones Sociológicas*, No. 35, July-September, pp. 269-340.

Fearon, James D. (1991), 'Counterfactuals and Hypothesis Testing in Political Science', *World Politics*, Vol. 43, No. 2, January, pp.1 69-195.

Featherstone, Kevin (1988), *Socialist Parties and European Integration*, Manchester University Press: Manchester.

Featherstone, Kevin (1989), 'Socialist Parties in Southern Europe and the Enlarged European Community', in Gallagher, Tom and Williams, Allan M. (eds.), *Southern European Socialism*, Manchester University Press: Manchester.

Featherstone, Kevin and Katsoudas, Dimitrios (eds.) (1987), *Political Change in Greece*, St. Martin's Press: New York.

Feffer, John (1992), *Shock Waves: Eastern Europe After the Revolutions*, South End Press: Boston.

Feld, Werner J. (ed.) (1978), *The Foreign Policies of West European Socialist Parties*, Praeger: New York.

Feldmann, Josef (1981), 'Política de Seguridad y Concepción de la Defensa de España', (translated by González Pascual, Marino), *CESEDEN: Boletín de Información*, No. 142-VIII, February, reprinted from *Revue Militaire Suisse*, No. 10, (October 1980).

Ferguson, Yale H. and Mansbach, Richard W. (1991), 'Between Celebration and Despair: Constructive Suggestions for Future International Theory', *International Studies Quarterly*, Vol. 35, No. 4, December, pp. 363-386.

Fernández Buey, Paco (1981), 'La Oposición a la OTAN', *Mientras Tanto*, No. 10, pp. 35-51.

Fernández Espeso, Carlos (1984), '¿Qué es la OTAN?', *Ideas Para la Democracia*, No.1, pp. 263-277.

Fernández Espeso, Carlos (1985), 'Defensa Nacional y Seguridad Nacional', *Jornadas Informativas Sobre Temas Internacionales - 1984*, Sociedad de Estudios Internacionales: Madrid, pp.95-105.

Fernández Marugán, Francisco Miguel (1989), 'Las Políticas Europeas de Concertación Social y de Democracia Industrial', *Sistema*, No. 91, July, pp. 17-28.

Fernández Marugán, Francisco Miguel (1990), 'La Construcción de Una Sociedad del Bienestar en el Contexto de la Economía Española', *Sistema*, No. 94-95, January, pp.51-66.

Fernández Marugán, Francisco Miguel and Collado, Juan Carlos (1990), 'Recuperación Económica y Políticas de Redistribución en España, 1986-1989', *Sistema*, No. 97, July, pp. 11-27.

Fernández Ordóñez, Miguel Angel (1986), 'La Política Económica del Gobierno Socialista', *Leviatán*, No. 23-24, Spring-Summer, pp. 41-51.

50 Preguntas Sobre la OTAN (1981), PSOE: Madrid.

Finnemore, Martha (1993), 'International Organizations as Teachers of Norms: The United Nations Educational, Scientific, and Cultural Organization and Science Policy', *International Organization*, Vol. 47, No. 4, Autumn.

Fishman, Robert M. (1990), 'Rethinking State and Regime: Southern Europe's Transition to Democracy', *World Politics*, Vol. 42, No. 3, April, pp. 422-440.

Fiske, Susan T. and Taylor, Shelly E. (1984), *Social Cognition*, Addison-Wesley: Reading, MA.

Foweraker, Joe (1987), 'Corporatist Strategies and the Transition to Democracy in Spain', *Comparative Politics*, Vol. 20, No. 1, October, pp. 57-72.

Fraga Iribarne, Manuel and Cerami, Charles A. (1977), 'Evolution in Spain: The Meaning for Europe', *The Atlantic Community Quarterly*, Vol. 15, No. 1, Spring, pp.85-96.

Frey, Peter (1988), *Spanien Und Europa: Die Spanischen Intellektuellen Und Die Europäische Integration*, Europa Union Verlag: Bonn.

Galinos, Alexis (1994), 'Central Europe and the EU: Prospects for Closer Integration', *RFE/RL Research Report*, Vol. 3, No. 29, 22 July, pp.19-25.

Gallagher, Tom and Williams, Allan M. (eds.) (1989), *Southern European Socialism*, Manchester University Press: Manchester.

Gama, Jaime (1990), 'Foreign Policy', in Maxwell, Kenneth and Haltzel, Michael H. (eds.), *Portugal: Ancient Country, Young Democracy*, The Woodrow Wilson Center Press: Washington, DC.

Garcia, S. (1993), 'Europe's Fragmented Identities and the Frontiers of Citizenship', in Garcia, S. (ed.), *European Identity and the Search for Legitimacy*, Royal Institute of International Affairs: London.

García Delgado, José Luis (ed.) (1988), *España Economía*, Volume 2, Espasa-Calpe: Madrid.

García Delgado, José Luis (ed.) (1990), *Economía Española de la Transición y la Democracia*, Centro de Investigaciones Sociológicas: Madrid.

García Santesmases, Antonio (1985), 'Evolución Ideológica del Socialismo en la España Actual', *Sistema*, Vol. 68-69, pp. 61-78.

García Santesmases, Antonio (1988), 'Cesión y Claudicación: La Transición Política Española', *Pensamiento Iberoamericano*, No. 14, July-December, pp. 273-283.

175

Garrett, Geoffrey (1992), 'International Cooperation and Institutional Choice: The European Community's Internal Market', *International Organization*, Vol. 46, No. 2, Spring, pp. 533-560.

Garrett, Geoffrey (1993), 'The Politics of Structural Change: Swedish Social Democracy and Thatcherism in Comparative Perspective', *Comparative Political Studies*, Vol. 25, No. 4, January, pp. 521-547.

Garrett, Geoffrey and Weingast, Barry R. (1991), *Ideas, Interests and Institutions: Constructing the EC's Internal Market*, (Working Paper 1.2), Center for German and European Studies (University of California): Berkeley.

Garrigues y Díaz-Cañabate, Antonio (ed.) (1986), *España Dentro de la Alianza Atlántica*, Instituto de Cuestiones Internacionales: Madrid.

Gédeon, Peter (1992), 'Hungary', paper presented at the Workshop on Unified Germany in an Integrating Europe, Cornell University: Ithaca, NY, 12-13 May.

Geertz, Clifford (1973), *The Interpretation of Cultures*, Basic Books: New York.

George, Alexander L. (1979), 'The Causal Nexus Between Cognitive Beliefs and Decision-Making Behavior', in Falkowski, Lawrence S. (ed.), *Psychological Models in International Politics*, Westview Press: Boulder, CO.

George, Bruce and Stenhouse, Mark (1991), 'Western Perspectives of Spain', in Maxwell, Kenneth (ed.), *Spanish Foreign and Defense Policy*, Westview Press: Boulder, CO.

Gibb, Richard and Michalak, Wieslaw (1993), 'The European Community and Central Europe: Prospects for Integration', *Geography*, Vol. 78, January, pp. 16-30.

Gil, Federico G. and Tulchin, Joseph S. (eds.) (1988), *Spain's Entry Into NATO*, Lynne Rienner: Boulder, CO.

Gillespie, Richard (1989), *The Spanish Socialist Party*, Clarendon Press: Oxford.

Gillespie, Richard (1990), 'The Break-Up of the "Socialist Family": Party-Union Relations in Spain, 1982-89', *West European Politics*, Vol. 13, No. 1, January, pp. 47-62.

Gillsepie, Richard (1995a), 'Spain and the Maghreb: Towards a Regional Policy?', in Gillespie, Richard; Rodrigo, Fernando and Story, Jonathan (eds.), *Democratic Spain: Reshaping External Relations in a Changing World*, Routledge: London.

Gillespie, Richard (1995b), 'Perspectives on the Reshaping of External Relations', in Gillespie, Richard; Rodrigo, Fernando and Story, Jonathan (eds.), *Democratic Spain: Reshaping External Relations in a Changing World*, Routledge: London.

Gillespie, Richard (1996), 'The Spanish Socialists', in Gaffney, John (ed.), *Political Parties and the European Union*, Routledge: London.

Gilpin, Robert and Wright, Christopher (eds.) (1964), *Scientists and National Policy Making*, Columbia University Press: New York.

176

Glenny, Misha (1984), *The Rebirth of History: Eastern Europe in the Age of Democracy*, Penguin: London.

El Gobierno Ante la Crisis Económica (1984), PSOE: Madrid.

Goldfarb, Jeffrey C. (1992), *After the Fall: The Pursuit of Democracy in Central Europe*, Basic Books: New York.

Goldstein, Judith (1989), 'The Impact of Ideas on Trade Policy', *International Organization*, Vol. 43, No. 1, Winter, pp. 31-71.

Goldstein, Judith and Keohane, Robert O. (eds.) (1993), *Ideas and Foreign Policy: Beliefs, Institutions and Political Change*, Cornell University Press: Ithaca, NY.

Gómez Llorente, Luis (1979), 'En Torno a la Ideología y la Política del PSOE', *Zona Abierta*, No. 20, May-August, pp. 23-36.

González, Felipe (1987), 'La Europa Que Queremos', *Leviatán*, No. 29/30, Autumn/Winter, pp. 5-14.

González, Felipe (1988), Speech at Harvard University: Cambridge, MA, 29 April.

González, Felipe (1990), 'Reflexiones Sobre el Proyecto Socialista', *Leviatán*, No. 41, Autumn, pp. 5-13.

González, Felipe and Guerra, Alfonso (1977), *Partido Socialista Obrero Español*, Ediciones Albia: Bilbao.

González Sánchez, Enrique (1980), 'La Política de Pesca de la Comunidad Económica Europea', *Documentación Administrativa*, No. 185, January-March.

González Sánchez, Enrique (1983), 'España-CEE: Las Negociaciones de Adhesión a Lo Largo de 1982', *Revista de Instituciones Europeas*, Vol. 10, No. 1, January-April, pp. 95-114.

González Sánchez, Enrique (1984), 'Las Negociaciones de Adhesión de España a las Comunidades Europeas: Enero 1983-Marzo 1984', *Revista de Instituciones Europeas*, Vol. 11, No. 2, May-August, pp. 477-497.

González Sánchez, Enrique (1985), 'Las Negociaciones de Adhesión de España a las Comunidades Europeas Desde Abril de 1984 Hasta Su Conclusión', *Revista de Instituciones Europeas*, Vol. 12, No. 2, May-August, pp. 439-464.

Gooch, Anthony (1986), 'A Surrealistic Referendum: Spain and NATO', *Government and Opposition*, Vol. 21, No. 3, Summer, pp. 300-316.

Goodwin, C.D.W. and Holley, I.B., Jr. (1968), *The Transfer of Ideas*, Duke University Press: Durham, NC.

Goodwin, Jeff and Bunce, Valerie (1992), 'Eastern Europe's "Refolutions" in Comparative and Theoretical Perspective' unpublished manuscript.

Gravalos González, Luis (1985), 'Consecuencias de la Salida de España de la OTAN', *CESEDEN: Boletín de Información*, No. 183-VIII, May.

Gruender, C. David and Moutsopoulos, Evanghelos (eds.) (1992), *The Idea of Europe: Its Common Heritage and Future*, Professors World Peace Academy: New York.

Guerra, Alfonso (ed.) (1978), *XXVII Congreso del Partido Socialista Obrero Español*, Avance: Barcelona.

Guerra, Alfonso (1984), *Felipe González: De Suresnes a la Moncloa*, Novatex: Madrid.

Guerra, Alfonso (1985), 'Europa en el Mundo', *Leviatán*, No. 19, Spring, pp. 7-14.

Gunther, Richard (1986), 'The Spanish Socialist Party', in Payne, Stanley G. (ed.), *The Politics of Democratic Spain*, Chicago Council on Foreign Relations: Chicago.

Gunther, Richard (1987), 'Democratization and Party Building: The Role of Party Elites in the Spanish Transition', in Clark, Robert P. and Haltzel, Michael H. (eds.), *Spain in the 1980s*, Ballinger Publishing: Cambridge, MA.

Gunther, Richard (1988), *Politics and Culture in Spain*, CPS, University of Michigan: Ann Arbor.

Gunther, Richard; Sani, Giacomo and Shabad, Goldie (1986), *Spain After Franco*, University of California Press: Berkeley.

Gutierrez, José Luis and De Miguel, Amando (1989), *La Ambición del César*, Ediciones Temas de Hoy: Madrid.

Haas, Ernst B. (1958), *The Uniting of Europe*, Stanford University Press: Stanford, CA.

Haas, Ernst B. (1964), *Beyond the Nation-State*, Stanford University Press: Stanford, CA.

Haas, Ernst B. (1975), 'Is There a Hole in the Whole? Knowledge, Technology, Interdependence, and the Construction of International Regimes', *International Organization*, Vol. 29, No. 3, Summer, pp. 827-876.

Haas, Ernst B. (1976), 'Turbulent Fields and the Theory of Regional Integration', *International Organization*, Vol. 30, No. 2, Spring, pp. 173-212.

Haas, Ernst B. (1980), 'Why Collaborate? Issue-Linkage and International Regimes', *World Politics*, Vol. 32, No. 3, April, pp. 357-405.

Haas, Ernst B. (1990), *When Knowledge is Power*, University of California Press: Berkeley.

Haas, Peter M. (1989), 'Do Regimes Matter? Epistemic Communities and Mediterranean Pollution Control', *International Organization*, Vol. 43, No. 3, Summer, pp. 377-404.

Haas, Peter M. (1990), *Saving the Mediterranean: The Politics of International Environmental Protection*, Columbia University Press: New York.

Haas, Peter M. (1992), 'Epistemic Communities and International Policy Coordination', *International Organization*, Vol. 46, No. 1, Winter, pp. 1-35.

Hacia el Cambio: 100 Días de Gobierno (1983), PSOE: Madrid.

Haggard, Stephen and Simmons, Beth A. (1987), 'Theories of International Regimes', *International Organization*, Vol. 41, No. 3, Summer, pp. 491-517.

Hall, John A. (1993), 'Ideas and the Social Sciences', in Goldstein, Judith and Keohane, Robert O. (eds.), *Ideas and Foreign Policy: Beliefs, Institutions and Political Change*, Cornell University Press: Ithaca, NY.

Hall, Peter (1986), *Governing the Economy*, Oxford University Press: New York.

Hall, Peter (ed.) (1989), *The Political Power of Economic Ideas*, Princeton University Press: Princeton, NJ.

Hall, Peter (1990), *Policy Paradigms, Social Learning and the State*, (Working Paper 1990/4), Instituto Juan March de Estudios e Investigaciones: Madrid.

Hall, Peter A. and Pérez-Díaz, Victor (eds.) (1990), 'Public Policy-Making in Spain', special issue of the *International Journal of Political Economy*, Vol. 20, No. 2, Summer.

Hamdani, Smail (1986), 'La Política Exterior de Argelia en Relación a España', *Jornadas Informativas Sobre Temas Internacionales - 1985*, Sociedad de Estudios Internacionales: Madrid, pp. 145-149.

Hames, Tim (1992), 'Two Debates in Search of a Dialogue: U.S.-European Community Tensions in the Post-Cold War Era', paper presented at the Annual Meeting of the American Political Science Association: Chicago, 3-6 September.

Harrison, Joseph (1985), *The Spanish Economy in the Twentieth Century*, St. Martin's Press: New York.

Hayden, Robert M. (1991), *Constitutional Nationalism in Yugoslavia, 1990-91*, (Working Paper on Transitions from State Socialism), Mario Einaudi Center for International Studies (Cornell University): Ithaca, NY.

Heater, Derek (1992), *The Idea of European Unity*, St. Martin's Press: New York.

Hechter, Michael (1992), 'Rational Choice Theory and Historical Sociology', *International Social Science Journal*, No. 133, pp. 367-373.

Heiberg, William L. (1983), *The Sixteenth Nation: Spain's Role in NATO*, (National Security Affairs Monograph Series 83-1), National Defense University Press: Washington, DC.

Heisler, Martin O. and Breckinridge, Robert E. (1989), 'What Would the Neighbors Think? Influences of International Regimes on Domestic Regimes - The Case of Spain in Theoretical Perspective', paper presented at the Joint Annual Meeting of the British and U.S. International Studies Associations: London, 28 March - 1 April.

Herr, Richard (1971), *Spain*, Prentice-Hall: Englewood Cliffs, NJ.

Herr, Richard and Polt, John H. R. (eds.) (1989), *Iberian Identity: Essays on the Nature of Identity in Portugal and Spain*, Institute of International Studies: Berkeley, CA.

Herrberg, A. and Moxon-Browne, E. (1995), 'Eastern and Western Europe: Forging a New European Identity?', paper presented at the 4th Biennial Meeting of the European Community Studies Association: Charleston, SC, 11-14 May.

Herrmann, Richard K. (1985), *Perceptions and Behavior in Soviet Foreign Policy*, University of Pittsburgh Press: Pittsburgh.

Hershberg, Eric (1989), 'Transitions from Authoritarianism and Eclipse of the Left: Toward a Reinterpretation of Political Change in Spain', unpublished doctoral dissertation, Department of Political Science, University of Wisconsin: Madison.

Hershberg, Eric (1991), 'Changing Interpretations of Democracy and Socialism: The Transformation of Socialist Thought in Spain and Chile', paper presented at the Annual Meeting of the Latin American Studies Association: Washington, DC, 4-6 April.

Higley, John and Gunther, Richard (eds.) (1992), *Elites and Democratic Consolidation in Latin America and Southern Europe*, Cambridge University Press: Cambridge.

Hill, B.J.W. (1969), *Background to Spain*, Longmans, Green and Co.: London.

Hill, Ronald J. and Zielonka, Jan (eds.) (1990), *Restructuring Eastern Europe*, Edward Elgar: Hants, UK.

Hills, George (1970), *Spain*, Praeger: New York.

Hoffmann, Stanley (1982), 'Reflections on the Nation-State in Western Europe Today', *Journal of Common Market Studies*, Vol. 21, Nos. 1-2, September-December, pp.21-37.

Holman, Otto (1987-88), 'Semiperipheral Fordism in Southern Europe', *International Journal of Political Economy*, Vol. 17, No. 4, Winter, pp.11-55.

Holman, Otto (1989), 'In Search of Hegemony: Socialist Government and the Internationalization of Domestic Politics in Spain', *International Journal of Political Economy*, Vol. 19, No. 3, Fall, pp. 76-101.

Holman, Otto (1996), *Integrating Southern Europe: EC Expansion and the Transnationalization of Spain*, Routledge: London.

Holsti, Ole (1976), 'Foreign Policy Formation Viewed Cognitively', in Axelrod, Robert (ed.), *Structure of Decision*, Princeton University Press: Princeton, NJ.

Howard, Michael (1989), 'Ideology and International Relations', *Review of International Studies*, Vol. 15, pp. 1-10.

Howe, Paul (1995), 'A Community of Europeans: The Requisite Underpinnings', *Journal of Common Market Studies*, Vol. 33, No. 1, March.

Hudson, Mark and Rudcenko, Stan (1988), *Spain to 1992: Joining Europe's Mainstream*, (Special Report #1138), The Economist Intelligence Unit: London.

Hunt, Michael H. (1987), *Ideology and U.S. Foreign Policy*, Yale University Press: New Haven, CT.

Hurwitz, Jon; Peffley, Mark and Seligson, Mitchell A. (1993), 'Foreign Policy Belief Systems in Comparative Perspective: The United States and Costa Rica', *International Studies Quarterly*, Vol. 37, No. 3, September.

Ilkin, Selim (1990), 'A History of Turkey's Association With the European Community', in Evin, Ahmet O. and Denton, Geoffrey (eds.), *Turkey and the European Community*, Leske & Budrich: Opladen, Germany.

Ikenberry, G. John and Kupchan, Charles A. (1990), 'Socialization and Hegemonic Power', *International Organization*, Vol. 44, No. 3, Summer, pp.283-315.

Instituto Español de Estudios Estratégicos (1982), *Intereses Estratégicos Nacionales*, CESEDEN: Madrid.

Instituto Español de Estudios Estratégicos (1983), *Costes Posibles a España en el Caso de Ingreso en la OTAN*, CESEDEN: Madrid.

Instituto Español de Estudios Estratégicos (1988), *Estado Actual y Evaluación del Triángulo España-Portugal-Marruecos*, CESEDEN: Madrid.

Instituto Español de Estudios Estratégicos (1988), *Estrategia Regional en el Mediterraneo Occidental*, CESEDEN: Madrid.

Ionescu, Dan (1991), 'Romania: Striving for a Better Image', *Report on Eastern Europe*, Vol. 2, No. 51-52, 20 December.

Ionescu, Dan (1993), 'Romania Signs Association Accord with the EC', *RFE/RL Research Report*, Vol. 2, No. 10, 5 March, pp. 33-37.

Ito, Takayuki (1992), 'Eastern Europe: Achieving Legitimacy', in Rozman, Gilbert (ed.), *Dismantling Communism: Common Causes and Regional Variations*, Woodrow Wilson Center Press: Washington, DC.

La Izquierda y Europa (1987), Editorial Pablo Iglesias: Madrid.

Jacobsen, John Kurt (1995), 'Much Ado about Ideas: The Cognitive Factor in Economic Policy', *World Politics*, Vol. 47, No. 2, January.

Jaen, Rafael (1989), 'La Aplicación en España de la Política Común para las Estructuras Pesqueras', *Revista de Estudios Agro-Sociales*, No. 148, April-June.

Jauregui, Fernando (1982), 'El "Complejo de los Montes Pirineos"', *Movimiento Europeo*, No. 3, March, p. 27.

Johnson, Harry G. (1981), 'Networks of Economists: Their Role in International Monetary Reforms', in Evan, William M. (ed.), *Knowledge and Power in a Global Society*, Sage Publications: Beverly Hills, CA.

Johnson, James (1992), 'Symbol and Strategy: Cultural Bases of Political Possibility', unpublished manuscript.

Johnson, James (1993), 'Is Talk Really Cheap? Prompting Conversation Between Critical Theory and Rational Choice', *American Political Science Review*, Vol. 87, March.

Johnson, Peter A. (1991), "Unpopular Measures: Transplanting Monetarism Into Monetary Policy in the Federal Republic of Germany and the United States', unpublished doctoral dissertation, Department of Government, Cornell University: Ithaca, NY.

Jordan, David C. (1979), *Spain, the Monarchy and the Atlantic Community*, Institute for Foreign Policy Analysis: Cambridge, MA.

Jornadas de Estudio 'OTAN y Seguridad Nacional' (1981), CESEDEN: Madrid.

Juliá, Santos (1983), 'Los Socialistas en la Crisis de los Años Treinta', *Zona Abierta*, No. 27, January-March, pp. 63-77.

Juliá, Santos (1988), *Historia Económica y Social Moderna y Contemporánea de España*, Volume 2, Universidad Nacional de Educación a Distancia: Madrid.

Juliá, Santos (1990), 'The Ideological Conversion of the Leaders of the PSOE, 1976-1979', (translated by Ellwood, Sheelagh), in Lannon, Frances and Preston, Paul (eds.), *Elites and Power in Twentieth Century Spain*, Clarendon Press: Oxford.

Kàdàr, Béla (1992), 'The Spirit of Visegrád', *1992 Annual Meeting Report of the Trilateral Commission*, The Trilateral Commission: Lisbon.

Kadiri, Abdelhafid (1986), 'La Política Exterior de Marruecos en Relación a España', *Jornadas Informativas Sobre Temas Internacionales - 1985*, Sociedad de Estudios Internacionales: Madrid, pp. 121-133.

Kaplan, Lawrence S., et.al., (eds.) (1985), *NATO and The Mediterranean*, Scholarly Resources: Wilmington, DE.

Kazakos, Panos and Ioakimidis, P.C. (eds.) (1994), *Greece and EC Membership Evaluated*, Pinter: London.

Katzenstein, Peter J. (ed.), (forthcoming), *Tamed Power: Germany in Europe*, Cornell University Press, Ithaca, NY.

Katzenstein, Peter J. and Tsujinaka, Yutaka (1991), *Defending the Japanese State*, Cornell East Asia Program: Ithaca, NY.

Keane, John (1992), 'Questions for Europe', in Nelson, Brian; Roberts, David and Veit, Walter (eds.), *The Idea of Europe: Problems of National and Transnational Identity*, Berg Publishers: New York.

Keefe, Eugene K., et.al. (1976), *Area Handbook for Spain*, U.S. Government Printing Office: Washington, DC.

Keohane, Robert O. (1984), *After Hegemony*, Princeton University Press: Princeton, NJ.

Keohane, Robert O. (ed.) (1986), *Neorealism and Its Critics*, Columbia University Press: New York.

Keohane, Robert O. (1988), 'International Institutions: Two Approaches', *International Studies Quarterly*, Vol. 32, No. 4, December, pp. 379-396.

Keohane, Robert O. and Hoffmann, Stanley (eds.) (1991), *The New European Community*, Westview Press: Boulder, CO.

King, Anthony (1973a), 'Ideas, Institutions and the Policies of Governments: A Comparative Analysis: Parts I and II', *British Journal of Political Science*, Vol. 3, No. 3, July, pp. 291-313.

King, Anthony (1973b), 'Ideas, Institutions and the Policies of Governments: A Comparative Analysis: Part III', *British Journal of Political Science*, Vol. 3, No. 4, October, pp. 409-423.

Kingdon, John W. (199^), 'Memo on Ideas and Politics', paper presented at the Conference on Ideas and Politics, Stanford University: Stanford, CA, 18-20 January.

Klotz, Audie (1995), 'Norms Reconstituting Interests: Global Racial Equality and U.S. Sanctions Against South Africa', *International Organization*, Vol. 49, No. 3, Summer.

Kohl, Helmut (1983), 'Pensar en las Consecuencias: El Político y la Realidad', in Veen, Hans-Joachim (ed.), *Argumentos Para la Paz y la Libertad*, Konrad Adenauer Stiftung: Bonn.

Kohler, Beate (1982), *Political Forces in Spain, Greece and Portugal*, European Centre for Political Studies: London.

Kolankiewicz, George (1994), 'Consensus and Competition in the Eastern Enlargement of the European Union', *International Affairs*, Vol. 70, No. 3, July, pp. 477-495.

Kophamel, Wolfgang (1987), 'Der Spanische NATO-Beitritt Als Innen-Und Aussenpolitisches Problem: Die Sicherheitspolitik der PSOE, 1980-1986', unpublished doctoral dissertation, Free University of Berlin: Berlin.

Kornai, János (1990), *The Road to a Free Economy: Shifting From a Socialist System, The Example of Hungary*, Norton: New York.

Kourvetaris, George A. (1986), 'Europe Moves Towards Economic and Political Integration', *The Journal of Social, Political, and Economic Studies*, Vol. 11, No. 2, Summer, pp. 131-162.

Kowalik-James, Marzenna (1992), 'Sleeping With the Elephant: East European Responses to German Hegemony, Past and Present', paper presented at the Annual Meeting of the International Studies Association: Atlanta, 31 March - 4 April.

Kowert, Paul A. (1992), 'Presidents, Personality, and Foreign Policy Decision Making', unpublished doctoral dissertation, Department of Government, Cornell University: Ithaca, NY.

Kramer, Heinz (1983), 'The EC In the Process of Southern Enlargement', *Aussenpolitik*, Vol. 34, July, pp. 243-256.

Kramer, Heinz (1984), 'Turkey and EC's Southern Enlargement', *Aussenpolitik*, Vol. 35, No. 1, pp. 99-116.

Kramer, Heinz (1993), 'The European Community's Response to the "New Eastern Europe"', *Journal of Common Market Studies*, Vol. 31, No. 2, June, pp. 213- 244.

Krasner, Stephen D. (ed.) (1983), *International Regimes*, Cornell University Press: Ithaca, NY.

Kratochwil, Friedrich (1982), 'On the Notion of "Interest" in International Relations', *International Organization*, Vol. 36, No. 1, Winter, pp. 1-30.

Kratochwil, Friedrich (1989), *Rules, Norms, and Decisions*, Cambridge University Press: Cambridge.

Kratochwil, Friedrich and Ruggie, John G. (1986), 'International Organization: A State of the Art on an Art of the State', *International Organization*, Vol. 40, No. 4, Autumn, pp. 753-775.

Kühn, Michael (1989), 'Widersprüche Spanischer Sicherheitspolitik Unter Besonderer Berücksichtigung des EG-Und NATO-Beitritts', unpublished masters thesis, Universität Hamburg: Hamburg.

Kuhn, Thomas S. (1962), *The Structure of Scientific Revolutions*, University of Chicago Press: Chicago.

Kuniholm, Bruce R. (1986), 'Rhetoric and Reality in the Aegean: U.S. Policy Options Toward Greece and Turkey', *SAIS Review*, Vol. 6, Winter/Spring.

Kupchan, Charles A. and Kupchan, Clifford A. (1991), 'Concerts, Collective Security, and the Future of Europe', *International Security*, Vol. 16, No. 1, Summer, pp.114-161.

Kurlansky, Mark J. (1983), 'Convalescent Spain', *The Progressive*, Vol. 47, No. 10, October, pp. 30-32.

Lancaster, Thomas D. (1989), *Policy Stability and Democratic Change: Energy in Spain's Transition*, Pennsylvania State University Press: University Park.

Lancaster, Thomas D. and Prevost, Gary (1985), 'A Coalitional Perspective on Politics and Change in Spain', in Lancaster, Thomas D. and Prevost, Gary (eds.), *Politics and Change in Spain*, Praeger: New York.

Lancaster, Thomas D. and Prevost, Gary (eds.) (1985), *Politics and Change in Spain*, Praeger: New York.

Lannon, Frances and Preston, Paul (eds.) (1990), *Elites and Power in Twentieth-Century Spain*, Clarendon Press: Oxford.

LaPalombara, Joseph and Weiner, Myron (eds.) (1966), *Political Parties and Political Development*, Princeton University Press: Princeton, NJ.

Larrabee, Stephen F. (1981-82), 'Dateline Athens: Greece for the Greeks', *Foreign Policy*, No. 45, Winter, pp. 158-174.

Larrabee, Stephen F. (1992), 'Democratization and Change in Eastern Europe', in Treverton, Gregory F. (ed.), *The Shape of the New Europe*, Council on Foreign Relations Press: New York.

Larroque, Luis (1984), 'Un Programa Económico Frente a la Crisis', *Leviatán*, No. 15, Spring.

Larson, Deborah Welch (1985), *Origins of Containment*, Princeton University Press: Princeton, NJ.

Laux, Jeanne Kirk (1991), *Reform, Reintegration and Regional Security: The Role of Western Assistance in Overcoming Insecurity in Central and Eastern Europe*, (Working Paper #37), Canadian Institute for International Peace and Security: Toronto.

Lecturas Sobre la Agricultura Española Ante la CEE (1985), Ministerio de Agricultura: Madrid.

Lefeber, Louis (1989-90), 'The Socialist Experience in Greece', *International Journal of Political Economy*, Vol. 19, No. 4, Winter, pp. 32-55.

Leguina, Joaquín (1985), 'Viejas y Nuevas Ideas de la Izquierda', *Leviatán*, No. 19, Spring, pp. 39-50.

Leigh, Michael and Van Praag, Nicholas (1978), *The Mediterranean Challenge*, Sussex European Research Centre: Sussex.

Lesser, Ian O. (1992), *Bridge or Barrier? Turkey and the West After the Cold War*, Rand: Santa Monica, CA.

Levy, Jack S. (1992), 'Learning and Foreign Policy', paper presented at the Annual Meeting of the American Political Science Association: Chicago, 3-6 September.

Levy, Jack S. (1994), 'Learning and Foreign Policy: Sweeping a Conceptual Minefield', *International Organization*, Vol. 48, No. 2, Spring.

Levy, Marc (1991), 'East-West Environmental Politics After 1989: Transborder Air Pollution, International Institutions, and Domestic Reform', paper presented for the Center for International Affairs Project on Post-Cold War International Institutions: New York, 27 October.

Lewis, Paul H. (1972), 'The Spanish Ministerial Elite, 1938-1969', *Comparative Politics*, Vol. 5, No. 1, October, pp. 83-106.

Lieberman, Sima (1982), *The Contemporary Spanish Economy: A Historical Perspective*, Allen & Unwin: London.

Lijphart, Arend, et.al. (1988), 'A Mediterranean Model of Democracy? The Southern European Democracies in Comparative Perspective', *West European Politics*, Vol. 11, No. 1, January, pp. 7-25.

Lindberg, Leon N. (1963), *The Political Dynamics of European Economic Integration*, Stanford University Press: Stanford, CA.

Linz, Juan J. (1981), 'A Century of Politics and Interests in Spain', in Berger, Suzanne (ed.), *Organizing Interests in Western Europe*, Cambridge University Press: Cambridge.

Lipietz, Alain (1987), *Mirages and Miracles*, (translated by Macey, David), Verso: London.

Liska, George (1991), 'Between East and West: East-Central Europe's Future Past', in Clark, Michael T. and Serfaty, Simon (eds.), *New Thinking and Old Realities: America, Europe, and Russia*, Seven Locks Press: Washington, DC.

Lobo, Angel (1981), *OTAN y España: El Precio de una Alianza*, Sábado Gráfico: Madrid.

Lomana, Gloria (1987), *El Ciclón Socialista*, Plaza & Janés: Barcelona.

López Garcia, Bernabé and Nuñez Villaverde, Jesús A. (1994), 'Europe and the Maghreb: Towards a Common Space', in Ludlow, Peter (ed.), *Europe and the Mediterranean*, Brassey's: London.

López Pina, Antonio (ed.) (1977), *La España Democrática y Europa*, Editorial Cambio 16: Madrid.

Loulis, John C. (1984-85), 'Papandreou's Foreign Policy', *Foreign Affairs*, Vol. 63, No. 2, Winter, pp. 375-391.

Lovelace, Ricardo (1980), 'La Ideología de la Crisis (España 1979)', *Zona Abierta*, No. 25, May-June), pp. 61-73.

Ludlow, Peter (1992), 'Europe's Institutions: Europe's Politics', in Treverton, Gregory F. (ed.), *The Shape of the New Europe*, Council on Foreign Relations Press: New York.

Lukauskas, Arvid (1992), 'The Political Economy of Financial Market Liberalization: The Case of Spain', unpublished doctoral dissertation, Department of Political Science, University of Pennsylvania: Philadelphia.

Lunak, Petr (1994), 'Security for Eastern Europe: The European Option', *World Policy Journal*, Vol. 11, No. 3, Fall, pp. 128-131.

Lyrntzis, Christos (1984), 'Political Parties in Post-Junta Greece: A Case of "Bureaucratic Clientelism"?', in Pridham, Geoffrey (ed.), *The New Mediterranean Democracies: Regime Transition in Spain, Greece, and Portugal*, Frank Cass: London.

Lyrintzis, Christos (1993), 'PASOK in Power: From "Change" to Disenchantment', in Clogg, Richard (ed.), *Greece, 1981-89: The Populist Decade*. St. Martin's Press: New York.

MacDonald, Glen D. (1988), 'European Community Enlargement and the Evolution of French-Spanish Cooperation, 1977-1987', in Gil, Federico G. and Tulchin, Joseph S. (eds.), *Spain's Entry Into NATO*, Lynne Rienner: Boulder, CO.

Malefakis, Edward (1970), *Agrarian Reform and Peasant Revolution in Spain*, Yale University Press: New Haven, CT.

Manera Regueyra, Enrique (1977), 'Reflexiones Sobre la Integración de España en la Defensa de Europa', *Revista de Política Internacional*, No. 150, March-April, pp. 49-61.

Manuel, Paul Christopher (1996), 'Regime Change, Elite Players, and Foreign Policy in Portugal, 1960-1991', *Perspectives on Political Science*, Vol. 25, No. 2, Spring, pp. 69-73.

Maravall, Fernando (1987), *Economía y Política Industrial en España*, Ediciones Pirámide: Madrid.

Maravall, José María (1982), *The Transition to Democracy in Spain*, St. Martin's Press: New York.

Maravall, José María (1991), 'Economic Reforms in New Democracies: The Southern European Experience'. unpublished manuscript.

March, James G. and Olsen, Johan P. (1984), 'The New Institutionalism: Organizational Factors in Political Life', *The American Political Science Review*, Vol. 78, No. 3, September, pp. 734-749.

Marías, Julián (1990), *Understanding Spain*, (translated by López-Morillas, Frances M.), University of Michigan Press: Ann Arbor.

Marks, Gary (1996), 'Exploring Variation in Cohesion Policy', in Hooghe, Liesbet (ed.), *Cohesion Policy, the European Community and Subnational Government*, Oxford University Press: Oxford.

Marks, Michael P. (1995), 'Researching the Origins of Ideas in Foreign Policy: The Case of Spain', *International Studies Notes*, Vol. 20, No. 1, Winter, pp. 21-31.

Marks, Michael P. (forthcoming), 'Moving at Different Speeds: Spain and Greece in the European Union', in Katzenstein, Peter J. (ed.), *Tamed Power: Germany in Europe*, Cornell University Press: Ithaca, NY.

Márquez Reviriego, Víctor (1982), *Felipe González: Un Estilo Ético*, Editorial Argos Vergara: Barcelona.

Marquina Barrio, Antonio (1985), 'Spain and its North African Enclaves', in Lasky Shub, Joyce and Carr, Raymond (eds.), *Spain: Studies in Political Security*, Praeger: New York.

Marquina Barrio, Antonio (1986a), 'NATO, The EEC, Gibraltar, North Africa: Overlapping Issues for Spain', *The International Spectator*, Vol. 21, No. 1, January-March, pp. 43-46.

Marquina Barrio, Antonio (1986b), 'Consideraciones Geoestratégicas Sobre el Magreb', *Jornadas Informativas Sobre Temas Internacionales - 1985*, Sociedad de Estudios Internacionales: Madrid, pp. 211-226.

Marquina Barrio, Antonio (1991), 'Spanish Foreign and Defense Policy Since Democratization', in Maxwell, Kenneth (ed.), *Spanish Foreign and Defense Policy*, Westview Press: Boulder, CO.

Martin, Benjamin (1984), 'Spanish Socialists in Power', *Dissent*, Vol. 31, No. 1, Winter, pp. 116-120.

Martínez-Alier, J. and Roca, Jordi (1986), *Spain After Franco: From Corporatist Ideology to Corporatist Reality*, (Working Paper 15), Center for European Studies (Harvard University): Cambridge, MA.

Martínez de la Cruz, Félix (1984), 'Neutralidad, Otra Opción', *Nuestra Bandera*, No. 127, November-December, pp. 36-41.

Maurín, Joaquín (1966), *Revolución y Contrarevolución en España*, Ruedo Ibérico: Paris.

Maxwell, Kenneth, (1976), 'The Thorns of the Portuguese Revolution', *Foreign Affairs*, Vol. 54, No. 2, January.

Maxwell, Kenneth (ed.) (1991), *Spanish Foreign and Defense Policy*, Westview Press: Boulder, CO.

Maxwell, Kenneth and Haltzel, Michael H. (eds.) (1990), *Portugal: Ancient Country, Young Democracy*, The Woodrow Wilson Center Press: Washington, DC.

Maxwell, Kenneth and Spiegel, Steven (1994), *The New Spain: From Isolation to Influence*, Council on Foreign Relations Press: New York.

McCaskill, Charles W. (1988), 'PASOK's Third World/Nonaligned Relations', in Stavrou, Nikolaos A. (ed.), *Greece Under Socialism: A NATO Ally Adrift*, Orpheus Publishing: New Rochelle, NY.

McClellan, Grant S. (ed.) (1978), *Spain and Portugal: Democratic Beginnings*, H.W. Wilson Company: New York.

McDonough, Peter and López Pina, Antonio (1984), 'Continuity and Change in Spanish Politics', in Dalton, Russell J.; Flanagan, Scott C. and Beck, Paul (eds.), *Electoral Change in Advanced Industrial Economies*, Princeton University Press: Princeton, NJ.

McMillion, Charles W. (1981), 'International Integration and Intra-National Disintegration: The Case of Spain', *Comparative Politics*, Vol. 13, No. 3, April, pp. 291-312.

McNeill, William (1978), *The Metamorphosis of Greece Since World War II*, University of Chicago Press: Chicago.

Mearsheimer, John J. (1990), 'Back to the Future: Instability in Europe After the Cold War', *International Security*, Vol. 15, No. 1, Summer, pp. 5-56.

Medina, Manuel (1976), 'Spain in Europe', *Government and Opposition*, Vol. 11, No. 2, Spring, pp. 143-155.

Meisler, Stanley (1977), 'Spain's New Democracy', *Foreign Affairs*, Vol. 56, No. 1, October, pp. 190-208.

Menéndez Pidal, Ramón (1950), *The Spaniards in Their History*, (translated by Starkie, Walter), Hollis & Carter: London.

Mercer, Jonathan (1995), 'Anarchy and Identity', *International Organization*, Vol. 49, No. 2, Spring, pp. 229-252.

Merlini, Cesare (1983), 'El Nuevo Contexto de la Seguridad Europea y Perspectivas de la Cooperación en Materia de Defensa a Nivel Comunitario', *Jornadas Informativas Sobre Temas Internacionales-1982*, Sociedad de Estudios Internacionales: Madrid.

Mesa Garrido, Roberto (1982), 'La Política Exterior en la España Democrática', *Revista de Estudios Internacionales*, Vol. 3.

Mesa Garrido, Roberto and Aldecoa Luzárraga, Francisco (1982), 'Las Ofertas Electorales en Materia de Política Exterior y Relaciones Internacionales en los Programas de los Partidos Políticos en las Elecciones Legislativas de 28 de Octubre de 1982', *Revista de Estudios Internacionales*, Vol. 3, No. 4, October-December, pp. 1005-1026.

Meyer-Dohner, Kurt F. (1983), 'Sobre el Significado del Potencial Defensivo Español Para la OTAN', (translated by Belloch Marques, Vincent), *CESEDEN: Boletín de Información*, No. 161-IV, January, (reprinted from *Stiftung Wissenschaft un Politik*).

Michalski, Anna and Wallace, Helen (1992), *The European Community: The Challenge of Enlargement*, (European Programme Special Paper), The Royal Institute of International Affairs: London.

Michta, Andrew A. and Prizel, Ilya (eds.) (1992), *Postcommunist Eastern Europe*, St. Martin's Press: New York.

Miguel, Firmino (1981), 'Portugal, España y la OTAN', (translated by Moiño Carrillo, Ramón), *CESEDEN: Boletín de Información*, No. 142-IV, February, (reprinted from *Revista Militar*, No.11-12, November-December 1979).

Mihalyi, Peter (1990), 'Eastern European Investment and Prospective Inward Resource Flow', paper presented to the NATO Advanced Research Workshop, St. Anthony's College: Oxford, 16-19 December.

Milner, Helen (1992), 'International Theories of Cooperation Among Nations', *World Politics*, Vol. 44, No. 3, April, pp. 466-496.

Minet, G.; Siotis, J. and Tsakaloyannis, P. (1981), *The Mediterranean Challenge, VI: Spain, Greece and Community Politics*, Sussex European Research Centre: Sussex.

Modelski, George (1990), 'Is World Politics Evolutionary Learning?', *International Organization*, Vol. 44, No. 1, Winter, pp. 1-24.

Moens, Alexander (1992), 'Behind Complementarity and Transparency: The Politics of the European Security and Defence Identity', paper presented at the Annual Meeting of the American Political Science Association: Chicago, 3-6 September.

Moore, Patrick (1991), 'Yugoslavia: "The New Europe's Humpty Dumpty" on the International Stage', *Report on Eastern Europe*, Vol. 2, No. 51/52, 20 December, pp. 32-38.

Morales Lezcano, Víctor (1984), 'El Aislacionismo Español y la Opción Neutralista: 1815-1945', *Ideas Para la Democracia*, No. 1, pp. 251-261.

Morán, Fernando (1979), 'Principios de Una Política Exterior Socialista', in *Perspectivas de Una España Democrática y Constitucionalizada*, Volume 3, Unión: Madrid.

Morán, Fernando (1980a), *Una Política Exterior Para España: Una Alternativa Socialista*, Planeta: Barcelona.

Morán, Fernando (1980b), 'El Socialismo y el Nuevo Orden Mundial', *Zona Abierta*, No. 25, May-June, pp. 75-94.

Morán, Fernando (1980c), 'La OTAN y los Escenarios de Defensa Que Afectan a España', *Sistema*, No. 35, March, pp. 119-152.

Morán, Fernando (1982), 'El Europeísmo, Señal de Identidad de la Restauración Democrática Española', *Movimiento Europeo*, No. 3, March, pp. 18-19.

Morán, Fernando (1983), 'Spain and NATO', *NATO's Sixteen Nations*, Vol. 28, No. 6 (Special #2), pp. 16-20.

Morán, Fernando (1984a), 'Las Bazas de la Política Exterior Española', *Ideas Para la Democracia*, No.1, pp. 19-31.

Morán, Fernando (1984b), 'Principios de la Política Exterior Española', *Leviatán*, No. 16, Summer, pp. 7-19.

Morán, Fernando (1990), *España en Su Sitio*, Plaza & Janés: Barcelona.

Moravcsik, Andrew (1991), 'Negotiating the Single European Act: National Interests and Conventional Statecraft in the European Community', *International Organization*, Vol. 45, No. 1, Winter, pp. 19-56.

Morawitz, Rudolf (1979), 'The Impact of the Extension of the Community Southwards to The Mediterranean Basin', paper presented at the 33rd Roundtable of the Association Pour L'Etude des Problemes de L'Europe: Madrid, 9-10 November.

Morgenthau, Hans J. (1985), *Politics Among Nations*, Sixth Edition, Alfred Knopf: New York.

Moyser, George (1988), 'Non-Standardized Interviewing in Élite Research', *Studies in Qualitative Methodology*, Vol.1, pp. 109-136.

Mujal-Leon, Eusebio (1986), 'Foreign Policy of the Socialist Government', in Payne, Stanley G. (ed.), *The Politics of Democratic Spain*, Chicago Council on Foreign Relations: Chicago.

Múgica, Enrique (1980), 'La Defensa de España', *Sistema*, No. 38-39, October, pp. 145-158.

Munilla Gómez, Eduardo (1980), 'Esquema de la Política de Defensa de España', *CESEDEN: Boletín de Información*, No. 140-X, November-December.

Munilla Gómez, Eduardo (1983), *Introducción a la Estrategia Militar Española*, Estado Mayor del Ejército: Madrid.

Munilla Gómez, Eduardo (1985), 'La Seguridad Europea y las Fuerzas Armadas Españolas', *Jornadas Informativas Sobre Temas Internacionales - 1984*, Sociedad de Estudios Internacionales: Madrid, pp. 129-145.

Muñiz, Miguel (1980), 'La Estrategia Económica del PSOE', *Zona Abierta*, No. 23, January-February, pp.19-26.

Muñoz, Juan; Roldán, Santiago and Serrano, Angel (1979), 'The Growing Dependence of Spanish Industrialization on Foreign Investment', in Seers, Dudley; Schaffer, Bernard and Kiljunen, Marja-Liisa (eds.), *Underdeveloped Europe: Studies in Core-Periphery Relations*, Humanities Press: Atlantic Highlands, NJ.

Nadal, Jordi (1982), *El Fracaso de la Revolución Industrial en España, 1814-1913*, Ariel: Barcelona.

Naylon, John (1981), 'Spain, Portugal and the EEC', *Bank of London & South America Review*, Vol. 15, No. 3, August, pp. 122-130.

Las Negociaciones Para la Adhesión de España a las Comunidades Europeas (1985), Ministerio de Asuntos Exteriores; Consejo Superior de Cámaras de Comercio, Industria y Navegación de España: Madrid.

Nelson, Brian; Roberts, David and Veit, Walter (eds.) (1992), *The Idea of Europe: Problems of National and Transnational Identity*, Berg Publishers: New York.

Ners, Krzysztof, et.al. (1992), *Beyond Assistance: Report on the IEWS Task Force on Western Assistance to Transition in the Czech and Slovak Federal Republic, Hungary and Poland*, Institute for EastWest Studies: New York.

Neumann, Iver B. (1990), 'The European Free Trade Association: The Problems of an All-European Role', *Journal of Common Market Studies*, Vol. 28, No. 4, June.

Niblett, Robin (1995), 'EC-Central European Relations, 1989-92: A Study of the Union as an International Actor', paper presented at the 4th Biennial International Conference of the European Community Studies Association: Charleston, SC, 11-14 May.

Nogues, Francisco (1986), 'Repercusiones en el Sector Pesquero del Ingreso en la CEE', *Jornadas Informativas Sobre Temas Internacionales - 1985*, Sociedad de Estudios Internacionales: Madrid, pp. 99-109.

North, Douglass C. (1981), *Structure and Change in Economic History*, W.W. Norton: New York.

Noticias Sobre La Comunidad Económica Europea (various dates), Ministerio de Agricultura, Pesca y Alimentación: Madrid.

Nye, Joseph S. (1987), 'Nuclear Learning and U.S.-Soviet Security Regimes', *International Organization*, Vol. 41, No. 3, Summer.

Obrman, Jan (1991), 'Czechoslovakia: From Idealism To Realism', *Report on Eastern Europe*, Vol. 2, No. 51/52, 20 December, pp. 9-13.

Odell, John (1982), *U.S. International Monetary Policy: Markets, Power, and Ideas as Sources of Change*, Princeton University Press: Princeton, NJ.

Odell, John and Matzinger-Tchakerian, Margit (1992), *European Community Enlargement and the United States*, (Pew Case Studies in International Affaris #130), Institute for the Study of Diplomacy (Georgetown University): Washington, DC.

O'Donnell, Guillermo; Schmitter, Philippe C. and Whitehead, Laurence (eds.) (1986), *Transitions from Authoritarian Rule*, The Johns Hopkins University Press: Baltimore.

Okolicsanyi, Karoly (1991), 'Hungary: Relations With the European Community', *Report on Eastern Europe*, Vol. 2, No. 30, 26 July, pp. 33-35.

Oliver, Miguel (1985), 'La Política Pesquera', *Papeles de Economía Española*, No. 25.

Olmo, Julia (1991), 'La Reunión de Palma: La CSCE y el Mediterráneo', *Política Exterior*, Vol. 5, No. 19, Winter, pp. 180-187.

Onuf, Nicholas Greenwood (1989), *World of Our Making: Rules and Rule in Social Thoeory and International Relations*, University of South Carolina Press: Columbia.

'Opciones Españolas de Defensa' (1984), *Ideas Para la Democracia*, No. 1, pp. 111-164.

'La Opinión Pública Española Ante la Comunidad Económica Europea, 1968-1985' (1985), *Revista Española de Investigaciones Sociológicas*, No. 29, January-March, pp. 289-396.

'La Opinión Pública Española Ante la OTAN' (1983), *Revista Española de Investigaciones Sociológicas*, No. 22, April-June, pp. 187-262.

Ortega, Andrés (1994), *La Razón de Europa*, El País/Aguilar: Madrid.

Ortega, Andrés (1995), 'Relations with the Maghreb', in Holmes, John W. (ed.), *Maelstrom: The United States, Southern Europe, and the Challenges of the Mediterranean*, The World Peace Foundation: Cambridge, MA.

Ortega y Gasset, José (1950), *Obras Completas*, Volume 1, Second Edition, Revista de Occidente: Madrid.

'OTAN: Por un Debate Clarificador' (1984), *Tiempo de Paz*, No. 2, Spring, pp. 78-85.

Oye, Kenneth A. (ed.) (1986), *Cooperation Under Anarchy*, Princeton University Press: Princeton, NJ.

Pallá, Ernö (1988), 'España y el Sistema Monetario Europeo', *Revista de Economía*, No. 657, May, pp. 5-11.

Papa, Gian Paolo (1985), 'La Integración de España en la Comunidad Económica Europea', *Jornadas Informativas Sobre Temas Internacionales - 1984*, Sociedad de Estudios Internacionales: Madrid, pp. 63-67.

Papacosma, S. Victor (1985), 'Greece and NATO', in Kaplan, Lawrence S., et.al. (eds.), *NATO and the Mediterranean*, Scholarly Resources: Wilmington, DE.

Paramio, Ludolfo (1979), '¿Es Posible Una Política Socialista?', *Zona Abierta*, No. 20, May-August, pp. 77-88.

Paramio, Ludolfo (1985), 'La Gira Europea de Reagan y la Izquierda', *El Socialista*, No. 381, 15-31 May.

Payne, Stanley G. (1972), 'Political Ideology and Economic Modernization in Spain', *World Politics*, Vol. 25, No. 1, October, pp. 155-181.

Payne, Stanley G. (ed.) (1986), *The Politics of Democratic Spain*, Chicago Council on Foreign Relations: Chicago.

Payno, Juan Antonio (1983), 'Introduction: The Second Enlargement from the Perspective of the New Members', in Sampedro, José Luis and Payno, Juan Antonio (eds.), *The Enlargement of the European Community*, MacMillan: London.

Penniman, Howard R. and Mujal-León, Eusebio (eds.) (1985), *Spain at the Polls*, American Enterprise Institute: Durham, NC.

Pensamiento Político de Franco (1975), Ediciones del Movimiento: Madrid.

Pérez, Sofía A. (1994), 'Imported Credibility and the "Strong *Peseta*": Bundesbank Dominance and Spanish Economic Policy in the EMS', paper presented at the Council for European Studies - 9th International Conference of Europeanists: Chicago, 31 March - 2 April.

Pérez-Díaz, Victor (1990), *The Emergence of Democratic Spain and the 'Invention' of a Democratic Tradition*, Centro de Estudios Avanzados en Ciencias Sociales (Instituto Juan March): Madrid.

Pérez-Díaz, Victor (1991), *La Emergencia de la España Democrática: La 'Invención' de Una Tradición y la Dudosa Institucionalización de Una Democracia*, (Working paper 1991/18), Centro de Estudios Avanzados en Ciencias Sociales (Instituto Juan March): Madrid.

Pérez-Llorca, José Pedro (1984), 'De Cómo y Por Qué Entramos en la Alianza Atlántica', *Ideas Para la Democracia*, No. 1, pp. 311-319.

Perspectivas de Una España Democrática y Constitucionalizada (1979), Volume 3, Unión Editorial: Madrid.

Peters, B. Guy (1992), 'Politics and the Institutions of the EC', in Sbragia, Alberta M. (ed.), *Euro-Politics: Institutions and Policymaking in the 'New' Europe*, Brookings: Washington, DC.

Peterson, M.J. (1992), 'Whalers, Cetologists, Environmentalists, and the International Management of Whaling', *International Organization*, Vol. 46, No. 1, Winter, pp. 147-186.

Phares, E. Jerry (1976), *Locus of Control in Personality*, General Learning Press: Morristown, NJ.

Pinder, John (1991), *The European Community and Eastern Europe*, The Royal Institute of International Affairs: London.

De Pitta e Cunha, Paulo (1983), 'Portugal and the European Economic Community', in Graham, Lawrence S. and Wheeler, Douglas L. (eds.), *In Search of Modern Portugal*, University of Wisconsin Press: Madison.

Plamenatz, J. (1971), *Ideology*, Pall Mall Press: London.

Planas, Luis (1985), 'España y la Unión Europea', *Leviatán*, No. 20, Summer, pp. 31-37.

La Política Económica de los Socialistas: Balance de Un Ajuste Solidario (1986), PSOE: Madrid.

'Política Exterior, Política de Defensa' (1984), *Ideas Para la Democracia*, No. 1, pp. 165-199.

Una Política de Paz y Seguridad Para España (1985), PSOE: Madrid.

Pollack, Benny and Hunter, Graham (1987a), 'Spanish Democracy After Four General Elections', *Parliamentary Affairs*, Vol. 40, No. 3, July, pp. 357-373.

Pollack, Benny with Hunter, Graham (1987b), *The Paradox of Spanish Foreign Policy: Spain's International Relations from Franco to Democracy*, St. Martin's Press: New York.

Pollack, Benny and Hunter, Graham (1989), 'The Spanish Socialist Workers' Party's Foreign and Defence Policy: The External Dimension of Modernisation', in Gallagher, Tom and Williams, Allan M. (eds.), *Southern European Socialism*, Manchester University Press: Manchester.

Por El Cambio: Programa Electoral, PSOE (1982), PSOE: Madrid.

Preston, Paul (1983), *The Coming of the Spanish Civil War*, Methuen: London.

Preston, Paul (1984), *Revolution and War in Spain, 1931-1939*, Methuen: London.

Preston, Paul (1986a), *The Spanish Civil War, 1936-39*, Weidenfeld and Nicholson: London.

Preston, Paul (1986b), *The Triumph of Democracy in Spain*, Methuen: London.

Preston, Paul and Smyth, Denis (1984), *Spain, the EEC and NATO*, The Royal Institute of International Affairs: London.

Prevost, Gary (1985-86), 'Spain and NATO: The Socialists' Decision', *The Atlantic Community Quarterly*, Vol. 23, No. 4, Winter, pp. 349-355.

Pridham, Geoffrey (ed.) (1984), *The New Mediterranean Democracies: Regime Transition in Spain, Greece, and Portugal*, Frank Cass and Co.: London.

Pridham, Geoffrey (ed.) (1990), *Securing Democracy: Political Parties and Democratic Consolidation in Southern Europe*, Routledge: London.

'Problems of Enlargement: Taking Stock and Proposals' (1983), *Bulletin of the European Communities*, Supplement 8/82.

Programa 1986/1990: Para Seguir Avanzando Por Buen Camino (1986), PSOE: Madrid.

Prügl, Elisabeth (1996), 'Gender in International Organization and Global Governance: A Critical Review of the Literature', *International Studies Notes*, Vol. 21, No. 1, Winter.

El PSOE Ante la Situación Política (1981), PSOE: Madrid.

PSOE en Sus Documentos, 1879-1977 (1977), Ediciones HOAC: Madrid.

Pusić, Vesna (1992), 'A Country By Any Other Name: Transition and Stability in Croatia and Yugoslavia', *East European Politics and Societies*, Vol. 6, No. 3, Fall, pp. 242-259.

Racionero, Luis (1987), *España en Europa*, Planeta: Barcelona.

Ramos, Ramón (1987), *Actitudes y Opiniones de los Españoles Ante las Relaciones Internacionales*, (Estudios y Encuestas 7), Centro de Investigaciones Sociológicas: Madrid.

Reich, Robert B. (ed.) (1988), *The Power of Public Ideas*, Ballinger Publishing: Cambridge, MA.

Reich, Simon (1990), *The Fruits of Fascism: Postwar Prosperity in Historical Perspective*, Cornell University Press: Ithaca, NY.

Reinicke, Wolfgang H. (1992), *Building a New Europe*, The Brookings Institution: Washington, DC.

Reisch, Alfred A. (1991), 'Hungary: Foreign-Policy Reorientation a Success', *Report on Eastern Europe*, Vol. 2, No. 51/52, 20 December, pp. 14-21.

'Resoluciones del XXIX Congreso del Partido Socialista Obrero Español' (1982), *Revista de Estudios Internacionales*, Vol. 3, No. 1, January-March, pp. 411-428.

Risse-Kappen, Thomas (1994), 'Ideas Do Not Flow Freely: Transnational Coalitions, Domestic Structures, and the End of the Cold War', *International Organization*, Vol. 48, No. 2, Spring.

Robinson, R.A.H. (1979), *Contemporary Portugal*, George Allen & Unwin: London.

Robles Piquer, Carlos (1986-87), 'Spain in NATO: An Unusual Kind of Participation', *The Atlantic Community Quarterly*, Vol. 24, No. 4, Winter, pp. 325-330.

Rodrigo, Fernando (1992), 'The End of the Reluctant Partner: Spain and Western Security in the 1990s', in Aliboni, Roberto (ed.), *Southern European Security in the 1990s*, Pinter Publishers: London.

Rodrigo, Fernando (1995a), 'Western Alignment: Spain's Security Policy', in Gillespie, Richard; Rodrigo, Fernando and Story, Jonathan (eds.), *Democratic Spain: Reshaping External Relations in a Changing World*, Routledge: London.

Rodrigo, Fernando (1995b), 'Southern European Countries and European Defense', in Holmes, John W. (ed.), *Maelstrom: The United States, Southern Europe, and the Challenges of the Mediterranean*, The World Peace Foundation: Cambridge, MA.

Rodríguez, Emilio A. (1988), 'Atlanticism and Europeanism: NATO and Trends in Spanish Foreign Policy', in Gil, Federico G. and Tulchin, Joseph S. (eds.), *Spain's Entry Into NATO*, Lynne Rienner: Boulder, CO.

Rodríguez López, Julio (1988), 'La Ponencia Económica del 31° Congreso', *Leviatán*, No. 31, Spring, pp. 19-27.

Rodríguez Mojón, Marisa (1993), 'The Impact of EC Membership on Spanish Foreign Policy', in Almarcha Barbado, Amparo (ed.), *Spain and EC Membership Evaluated*, Pinter Publishers: London.

Rodríguez Saiz, Luis (1986), 'Aspectos Económicos del Espacio Estratégico Mediterraneo', *Jornadas Informativas Sobre Temas Internacionales - 1985*, Sociedad de Estudios Internacionales: Madrid, pp. 247-263.

Rogers, Everett M. (1983), *Diffusion of Innovations*, (Third Edition), The Free Press: New York.

Rohrlich, Paul Egon (1987), 'Economic Culture and Foreign Policy: The Cognitive Analysis of Economic Policy Making', *International Organization*, Vol. 41, No. 1, Winter, pp. 61-92.

Roitman, Marcos (1985), *La Política del PSOE en América Latina*, Editorial Revolución: Madrid.

Rosenberg, Robin L. (1992), *Spain and Central America: Democracy and Foreign Policy*, Greenwood Press: Westport, CT.

Rothstein, Robert L. (1984), 'Consensual Knowledge and International Collaboration: Some Lessons from the Commodity Negotiations', *International Organization*, Vol. 38, No. 4, Autumn, pp. 733-762.

Rozman, Gilbert (ed.) (1992), *Dismantling Communism*, Woodrow Wilson Center Press: Washington, DC.

Ruggie, John Gerard (1986), 'Continuity and Transformation in the World Polity', in Keohane, Robert O. (ed.), *Neorealism and Its Critics*, Columbia University Press: New York.

Ruggie, John Gerard (1993), 'Territoriality and Beyond: Problematizing Modernity in International Relations', *International Organization*, Vol. 47, No. 1, Winter, pp. 139-174.

Ruiz-Navarro Pinar, José Luis (1991), 'La Reforma de los Fondos Estructurales', *Boletín de Derecho de las Comunidades Europeas*, No. 34, July-August.

Russell, P.E. (ed.) (1973), *Spain: A Companion to Spanish Studies*, Methuen & Co.: London.

De Salas López, Fernando (1982), 'El Proceso de Integración de España en la OTAN', *Revista de Estudios Internacionales*, Vol. 3, No. 1, January-March, pp. 137-172.

De Salas López, Fernando (1984), *Nuevos Planteamientos de España Ante la OTAN*, Sociedad de Estudios Internacionales: Madrid.

De Salas López, Fernando (1986), 'Aspectos Estratégicos de los Países del Mediterraneo', *Jornadas Informativas Sobre Temas Internacionales - 1985*, Sociedad de Estudios Internacionales: Madrid, pp. 183-197.

Salgado Alba, Jesús (1986), 'España y el Mediterraneo', *Jornadas Informativas Sobre Temas Internacionales - 1985*, Sociedad de Estudios Internacionales: Madrid, pp. 199-209.

Salmon, Keith (1995), 'Spain in the World Economy', in Gillespie, Richard; Rodrigo, Fernando and Story, Jonathan (eds.), *Democratic Spain: Reshaping External Relations in a Changing World*, Routledge: London.

Salmon, Trevor C. (1989), *Unneutral Ireland: An Ambivalent and Unique Security Policy*, Clarendon Press: Oxford.

Sampedro, José Luis and Payno, Juan Antonio (eds.) (1983), *The Enlargement of the European Community: Case-Studies of Greece, Portugal and Spain*, Macmillan: London.

Sandholtz, Wayne (1993), 'Choosing Union: Monetary Politics and Maastricht', *International Organization*, Vol. 47, No. 1, Winter, pp. 1-39.

Sandholtz, Wayne and Zysman, John (1989), '1992: Recasting the European Bargain', *World Politics*, Vol. 42, No. 1, October, pp. 95-128.

Santesmases, Antonio (1979), 'Las Dos Opciones del PSOE', *Zona Abierta*, No. 20, May-August, pp. 37-48.

Santesmases, Antonio (1984), 'PSOE y OTAN', *Leviatán*, No. 17, Autumn, pp. 59-68.

Sartori, Giovanni (1969), 'Politics, Ideology, and Belief System', *American Political Science Review*, Vol. 63, pp. 398-411.

Sassoon Walker, Joseph (1980), 'El Crecimiento Industrial Español y Su Competitividad Internacional Ante la Ampliación de la Comunidad', (translated by Fernández Beceiro, Luis), *CESEDEN-Boletín de Información*, No. 138-VII, August-September, (reprinted from *Lo Spettatore Internazionale*, October-December 1979).

Sassot Cañadas, Manuel (1986), 'Aspectos Políticos de Países Mediterraneos: España y Sus Vecinos Norteafricanos', *Jornadas Informativas Sobre Temas Internacionales - 1985*, Sociedad de Estudios Internacionales: Madrid, pp. 159-182.

Scarbrough, Elinor (1990), 'Attitudes, Social Representations, and Ideology', in Fraser, Colin and Gaskell, George (eds.), *The Social Psychological Study of Widespread Beliefs*, Clarendon Press: Oxford.

Schneider, J.W. (ed.) (1980), *From Nine to Twelve: Europe's Destiny?*, Sijthoff & Noordhoff: Alphen aan den Rijn, Netherlands.

Schulman, Paul R. (1988), 'The Politics of "Ideational Policy"', *Journal of Politics*, Vol. 50, No. 2, May, pp. 263-291.

Sedgwick, Henry Dwight (1926), *Spain: A Short History of its Politics, Literature, and Art From Earliest Times to The Present*, Little, Brown and Co.: Boston.

Seers, Dudley and Vaitsos, Constantine (eds.) (1982), *The Second Enlargement of the EEC*, St. Martin's Press: New York.

Seers, Dudley; Schaffer, Bernard and Kiljunen, Marja-Liisa (eds) (1979), *Underdeveloped Europe: Studies in Core-Periphery Relations*, Humanities Press, Atlantic Highlands, NJ.

Semprún, Jorge (1987), 'España en Europa', *Sistema*, No. 76, January, pp. 3-32.

Sequeiros Tizón, Julio Gaspar (1987), *La Adhesión de España a la CEE: Un Análisis Sectorial-Regional*, (Serie Universitaria #239), Fundación Juan March: Madrid.

Serra, Narcís (1986), 'La Política Española de Defensa', *Revista Española de Investigaciones Sociológicas*, No. 36, October-December, pp. 173-188.

Sesión Informativa Sobre el Conflicto del Golfo Pérsico (September 11, 1990) (1990), Ministerio del Portavoz del Gobierno: Madrid.

Sesión Informativa Sobre el Conflicto del Golfo Pérsico (January 18, 1991) (1991), Ministerio del Portavoz del Gobierno: Madrid.

Share, Donald (1985), 'Two Transitions: Democratisation and the Evolution of the Spanish Socialist Left', *West European Politics*, Vol. 8, No. 1, January, pp. 82-103.

Share, Donald (1986), *The Making of Spanish Democracy*, Praeger: New York.

Share, Donald (1989), *Dilemmas of Social Democracy: The Spanish Socialist Workers Party in the 1980s*, Greenwood Press: Westport, CT.

Shub, Joyce Lasky and Carr, Raymond (eds.) (1985), *Spain: Studies in Political Security*, Praeger: New York.

Shumaker, David (1993), 'The Origins and Development of Central European Cooperation: 1989-1992', *East European Quarterly*, Vol. 27, No. 3, September, pp. 351-373.

Sikkink, Kathryn (1991), *Ideas and Institutions: Developmentalism in Brazil and Argentina*, Cornell University Press: Ithaca. NY.

Singer, Marshall R. (1972), *Weak States in a World of Powers*, The Free Press: New York.

'Síntesis del Acuerdo' (1985), *Comunidad Europea*, Vol. 20, No. 216-217, May-June, pp. 8-12.

Smith, Anthony D. (1991), *National Identity*, University of Nevada Press: Reno.

Smith, Anthony D. (1992), 'National Identity and the Idea of European Unity', *International Affairs*, Vol. 68, No. 1, January.

Solana Madariaga, Luis. (1985), 'Defensa Nacional y Seguridad en el Momento Actual', *Jornadas Informativas Sobre Temas Internacionales - 1984*, Sociedad de Estudios Internacionales: Madrid, pp. 147-159.

Solbes, Pedro (1979), 'Los Obstáculos de la Adhesión de España a las Comunidades Europeas', *Información Comercial Española*, No. 550-551, June-July, pp. 179-186.

Solbes, Pedro (1989-90), 'Efectos de la Integración de España en las CE', *Información Comercial Española*, December-January, pp. 119-129.

Solé Tura, Jordi (1988), 'Transición a la Democracia y Estabilidad: El Caso de España', *Pensamiento Iberoamericano*, No. 14, July-December, pp. 263-272.

Sørensen, Georg (1995), 'States are Not Like Units: Types of State and Forms of Anarchy in the Present International System', paper presented at the Annual Meeting of the American Political Science Association: Chicago, 31 August - 3 September.

Sotelo, Ignacio (1986), *Los Socialistas en el Poder*, Ediciones El País: Madrid.

'Spain' (1981), *NATO's Fifteen Nations*, Vol. 26, No. 3, June-July.

'Spain' (1983), *NATO's Sixteen Nations*, Vol. 28, Special Issue No. 2.

Spanger, Hans-Joachim (1991), 'Trapped in a Vicious Circle: Systemic Change and Economic Crisis in Eastern Europe and the Soviet Union', paper presented at the Joint Cornell Peace Studies-PRIF Conference on The New Europe, Cornell University: Ithaca, NY, 6-7 September.

Spengler, Joseph J. (1970), 'Notes on the International Transmission of Economic Ideas', *History of Political Economy*, Vol. 2, No. 1, Spring, pp. 133-151.

Staniland, Martin (1991), *American Intellectuals and African Nationalists, 1955-1970*, Yale University Press: New Haven, CT.

Stark, David (1991), *Privatization Strategies in East Central Europe*, (Working Paper on Transitions from State Socialism #91-6), Cornell Project on Comparative Institutional Analysis: Ithaca, NY.

Stavrou, Nikolaos A. (1988), 'Ideological Foundations σι the Panhellenic Socialist Movement', in Stavrou, Nikolaos A. (ed.), *Greece Under Socialism*, Orpheus Publishing: New Rochelle, NY.

Steinbruner, John D. (1974), *The Cybernetic Theory of Decision*, Princeton University Press: Princeton, NJ.

Stepanovsky, Jiri. 'Relations to the West and to Germany in Particular', *Central and Eastern Europe in Transition*, (Arbeitspapiere Zur Internationalen Politik No.64), Forschungsinsititutder Deutschen Gesellschaft für Auswärtige Politik: Bonn.

Stokes, Gale (1993), *The Walls Came Tumbling Down: The Collapse of Communism in Eastern Europe*, Oxford University Press: New York.

Story, Jonathan (1976), 'Portugal's Revolution of Carnations: Patterns of Change and Continuity', *International Affairs*, Vol. 52, No. 3, July, pp. 417-433.

Story, Jonathan (1995), 'Spain's External Relations Redefined: 1975-89', in Gillespie, Richard; Rodrigo, Fernando and Story, Jonathan (eds.), *Democratic Spain: Reshaping External Relations in a Changing World*, Routledge: London.

Stryker, Sheldon (1980), *Symbolic Interactionism: A Social Structural Version*, Benjamin/Cummings: Menlo Park, CA.

Stuart, Douglas T. (ed.) (1988), *Politics and Security in the Southern Region of the Atlantic Alliance*, Johns Hopkins University Press: Baltimore.

Szelenyi, Ivan (1990), 'Alternative Futures for Eastern Europe: The Case of Hungary', *East European Politics and Societies*, Vol. 4, No. 2, Spring, pp. 231-254.

Szelenyi, Ivan and Szelenyi, Balazs (1992), 'Why Socialism Failed? Towards a Theory of System Breakdown: Causes of Disintegration of East European State Socialism', paper presented at the Workshop on Explaining the Transition from State Socialism, Cornell University: Ithaca, NY, 2 May.

Tamames, Ramón (1986), *Guía del Mercado Común Europeo: España en la Europa de los Doce*, Alianza: Madrid.

Taylor, Charles (1979), 'Interpretations and the Sciences of Man', in Rabinow, Paul and Sullivan, William M. (eds.), *Interpretive Social Science: A Reader*, University of California Press: Berkeley.

Taylor, Robert (1980), 'Implications For the Southern Mediterranean Countries of the Second Enlargement of the European Community', *Europe Information*, Commission of the European Communities Spokesman's Group and Directorate General for Information: Brussels.

Tezanos, José Félix; Cotarelo, Ramón and De Blas, Andres (eds.) (1989), *La Transición Democrática Española*, Editorial Sistema: Madrid.

Thomas, Hugh (1961), *The Spanish Civil War*, Harper & Brothers: New York.

Thorn, Gaston (1984), *European Union or Decline: To Be or Not To Be*, Office for Official Publications of the European Communities: Luxembourg.

Tiersky, Ronald (1991), 'European Integration and European Security', paper presented at the Conference on The New Europe, Cornell University: Ithaca, NY, 6-7 September 6-7.

Tovias, Alfred (1984), 'The International Context of Democratic Transition', *West European Politics*, Vol. 7, No. 2, April, pp. 153-179.

Tovias, Alfred (1995), 'Spain in the European Community', in Gillespie, Richard; Rodrigo, Fernando and Story, Jonathan (eds.), *Democratic Spain: Reshaping External Relation in a Changing World*, Routledge: London.

Treverton, Gregory F. (1986), *Spain: Domestic Politics and Security Policy*, (Adelphi Paper 204), International Institute for Strategic Studies: London.

Treverton, Gregory F. (1988), 'Spain, the United States, and NATO: Strategic Facts and Political Realities', in Gil, Federico G. and Tulchin, Jospeh S. (eds.), *Spain's Entry into NATO*, Lynne Rienner: Boulder, CO.

Tusell, Javier (1988), 'The Transition to Democracy and Spain's Membership in NATO', in Gil, Federico G. and Tulchin, Joseph S. (eds.), *Spain's Entry Into NATO*, Lynne Rienner: Boulder, CO.

De Unamuno, Miguel (1968), *Obras Completas*, Volume 3, Escelicer: Madrid.

De Unamuno, Miguel (1983), *En Torno Al Casticismo*, 10th Edition, Colección Austral: Madrid.

Vaitsos, Constantine (1982), 'Transnational Corporate Behaviour and the Enlargement', in Seers, Dudley and Vaitsos, Constantine (eds.), *The Second Enlargement of the EEC: The Integration of Unequal Partners*, St. Martin's Press: New York.

Van Brabant, Jozef M. (1994), 'Trade, Integration and Transformation in Eastern Europe', *Journal of International Affairs*, Vol. 48, No. 1, Summer, pp. 165-192.

Van Gent, Amalia (1992), 'Turkey Extends a Helping Hand', *Neue Zürcher Zeitung*, reprinted in *World Press Review*, July 1992.

Vargas Quiroz, Carlos (ed.) (1993), *Africa, España y la Comunidad Europea: Flujos Migratorios y Cooperación al Desarrollo*, (Documentos y Estudios #78), Fundación Friedrich Ebert: Madrid.

Vasconcelos, Alvaro (1985), 'Portugal e a Espanha e as Transformacoes Estrategicas os Conflictos fora da Area', *Jornadas Informativas Sobre Temas Internacionales - 1984*, Sociedad de Estudios Internacionales: Madrid, pp. 117-128.

Veremis, Thanos (1982), *Greek Security: Issues and Politics*, (Adelphi Paper No. 179), The International Institute for Strategic Studies: London.

Veremis, Thanos (1993), 'Defence and Security Policies Under PASOK', in Clogg, Richard (ed.), *Greece, 1981-89: The Populist Decade*, St. Martin's Press: New York.

Verney, Susannah (1987), 'Greece and the European Community', in Featherstone, Kevin and Katsoudas, Dimitrios K. (eds.), *Political Change in Greece Before and After the Colonels*, Croom Helm: London.

Verney, Susannah (1990), 'To Be or Not To Be Within the European Community: The Party Debate and Democratic Consolidation in Greece', in Pridham, Geoffrey (ed.), *Securing Democracy: Political Parties and Democratic Consolidation in Southern Europe*, Routledge: London.

Verney, Susannah (1993), 'From the "Special Relationship" to Europeanism: PASOK and the European Community, 1981-89', in Clogg, Richard (ed.), *Greece, 1981-89: The Populist Decade*, St. Martin's Press: New York.

Verney, Susannah (1994a), 'Panacea or Plague: Greek Political Parties and Accession to the European Community, 1974-1979', unpublished doctoral dissertation, Department of Political Science, Kings College, University of London: London.

Verney, Susannah (1994b), 'Central State-Local Government Relations,' in Kazakos, Panos and Ioakimidis, P.C. (eds.), *Greece and EC Membership Evaluated*, Pinter: London.

Verney, Susannah (1996), 'The Greek Socialists', in Gaffney, John (ed.), *Political Parties and the European Union*, Routledge: London.

Viñas, Angel (1983), 'El Debate de la Seguridad en Europa', *Revista de Estudios Internacionales*, Vol. 4, No. 4, October-December, pp. 711-734.

Viñas, Angel (1984a), 'Coordenadas de la Política de Seguridad Española', *Leviatán*, No. 17, Autumn, pp. 7-33.

Viñas, Angel (1984b), 'Estrategia Nacional y Entorno Exterior: El Caso de España', *Revista de Estudios Internacionales*, Vol. 5, No. 1, January-March, pp. 73-101.

Viñas, Angel (1985), 'La Política Industrial Española de Defensa', *Leviatán*, No. 20, Summer, pp. 53-63.

Viñas, Angel (1986a), 'Apertura Exterior y Modernización Democrática', *Leviatán*, No. 26, Winter, pp. 57-68.

Viñas, Angel (1986b), 'The Evolution of Spanish Foreign and Defense Policy and the Question of Spanish Membership in the Atlantic Alliance', *The International Spectator*, Vol. 21, No. 1, January-March, pp. 36-42.

Wallace, Helen (1992), 'What Europe for Which Europeans?', in Treverton, Gregory F. (ed.), *The Shape of the New Europe*, Council on Foreign Relations Press: New York.

Wallace, William (1982), 'Europe as a Confederation: The Community and the Nation-State', *Journal of Common Market Studies*, Vol. 21, September/December.

Waltz, Kenneth A. (1979), *Theory of International Politics*, Addison-Wesley: Reading, MA.

Washio, Tomoharu (1991), *Market Economy Transformations: A Comparative Study of Hungary, Poland and Czechoslovakia*, (Policy Paper 48E), International Institute for Global Peace: Tokyo.

Wæver, Ole (1989), 'Conflicts of Vision - Visions of Conflict', in Wæver, Ole; Lemaitre, Pierre and Tromer, Elzbieta (eds.), *European Polyphony: Perspectives Beyond East-West Confrontations*, Macmillan: London.

Wæver, Ole; Lemaitre, Pierre and Tromer, Elzbieta (eds.) (1989), *European Polyphony: Perspectives Beyond East-West Confrontations*, Macmillan: London.

Weber, Shlomo and Wiesmeth, Hans (1991), 'Issue Linkage in the European Community', *Journal of Common Market Studies*, Vol. 29, No. 3, March, pp. 255-267.

Weir, Margaret and Skocpol, Theda (1985), 'State Structures and the Possibilities for Keynesian Responses to the Great Depression', in Evans, Peter, et.al. (eds.), *Bringing the State Back In*, Cambridge University Press: Cambridge.

Weitz, Richard (1993), 'Pursuing Military Security in Eastern Europe', in Keohane, Robert O.; Nye, Joseph S. and Hoffmann, Stanley (eds.), *After the Cold War*, Harvard University Press: Cambridge, MA.

Welfens, Paul J.J. (1991), 'Creating a European Central Bank After 1992', in Welfens, Paul J.J. (ed.), *European Monetary Integration*, Springer-Verlag: Berlin.

Wendt, Alexander (1987), 'The Agent-Structure Problem in International Relations Theory', *International Organization*, Vol. 41, No. 3, Summer, pp. 335-370.

Wendt, Alexander (1991), 'Bridging the Theory/Meta-Theory Gap in International Relations', *Review of International Studies*, Vol. 17, No. 4, October, pp. 383-392.

Wendt, Alexander (1992), 'Anarchy is What States Make Of It: The Social Construction of Power Politics', *International Organization*, Vol. 46, No. 2, Spring, pp. 391-425.

Wendt, Alexander (1994), 'Collective Identity Formation and the International State', *American Political Science Review*, Vol. 88, No. 2, June, pp. 384-396.

Wendt, Alexander and Friedheim, Daniel (1995), 'Hierarchy Under Anarchy: Informal Empire and the East German State', *International Organization*, Vol. 49, No. 4, Autumn, pp. 689-721.

Westendorp y Cabeza, Carlos (1985), 'La Tercera Ampliación de las Comunidades Europeas: El Caso Español', *Jornadas Informativas Sobre Temas Internacionales - 1984*, Sociedad de Estudios Internacionales: Madrid, pp. 69-80.

De Weydenthal, Jan B. (1991a), 'Poland: Policy Toward the Eastern Neighbors', *Report on Eastern Europe*, Vol. 2, No. 47, 22 November, pp. 18-20.

De Weydenthal, Jan B. (1991b), 'Poland: Rapprochement With the West Continues', *Report on Eastern Europe*, Vol. 2, No. 51/52, 20 December, pp. 22-26.

Wiarda, Howard J. (1981), *Does Europe Still Stop at the Pyrenees? or Does Latin America Begin There? Iberia, Latin America and the Second Enlargement of the European Community*, Center for Hemispheric Studies: Cambridge, MA.

Wiarda, Howard J. (ed.) (1986), *The Iberian-Latin American Connection*, Westview Press: Boulder, CO.

Wiarda, Howard J. (1989), *The Transition to Democracy in Spain and Portugal*, American Enterprise Institute: Washington, DC.

Williams, Allan (ed.) (1984), *Southern Europe Transformed*, Harper & Row: London.

Woods, Ngaire (1995), 'Economic Ideas and International Relations: Beyond Rational Neglect', *International Studies Quarterly*, Vol. 39, No. 2, June.

Yáñez, Luis (1984), 'El PSOE y la Seguridad Europea', *Ideas Para la Democracia*, No. 1, pp. 321-330.

Yee, Albert S. (1996), 'The Causal Effect of Ideas on Policies', *International Organization*, Vol. 50, No. 1, Winter.

Yergin, Angela Stent (1979), 'West Germany's Südpolitik: Social Democrats and Eurocommunism', *Orbis*, Vol. 23, No. 1, Spring, pp. 51-72.

Yesilada, Birol A (1995), 'The Challenge of Enlargement: The Mediterranean Perspective', paper presented at the Fourth Biennial International Conference of the European Community Studies Association: Charleston, SC, 11-14 May.

Young, Oran (1990), *International Cooperation*, Cornell University Press: Ithaca, NY.

Zhong, Yang (1994), 'The Fallen Wall and Its Aftermath: Impact of Regime Change Upon Foreign Policy Behavior in Six East European Countries', *East European Quarterly*, Vol. 28, No. 2, June, pp. 235-257.

Zoppo, Ciro Elliot (1980), 'The Left and European Security: France, Italy, and Spain', *Orbis*, Vol. 24, No. 2, Summer, pp. 289-310.